A STRIKING SUMMER

A STRIKING SUMMER

How cricket united
a divided nation

Stephen Brenkley

FAIRFIELD BOOKS

First published by Fairfield Books in October 2024

fairfield books

Fairfield Books
Bedser Stand
Kia Oval
London
SE11 5SS

This book is printed on paper certified
by the Forest Stewardship Council

Every effort has been made to trace copyright and any oversight
will be rectified in future editions at the earliest opportunity

A CIP catalogue record for this title is available from the British Library

Printed by CPI Group (UK) Ltd

Contents

to
Doff and **Evie**

INTRODUCTION

Almost a century on from the events described in this book, cricket has altered virtually beyond recognition. Formats are played now that would have driven to apoplexy the likes of Lord Harris, the elder statesman and, as he would like to see himself, protector of the game in 1926. Limited-overs cricket in all its manifestations – 50 overs, Twenty20, The Hundred, without yet touching on, say, the Indian Premier League – would probably have seen the old boy off. The four-day County Championship would also not have done much for his constitution.

But the major change in the game is something else that Lord Harris and his pals could not have countenanced. In a way that is hard to grasp now, cricket was part of the English, nay the British national psyche. It might have been run by toffs, many of them from the aristocracy, deference was mandatory, but it was a game for all, from top to bottom. It is not a myth that snotty-nosed kids played the game in the streets and that snooty-nosed ones played it on the playing fields of Eton and its like. And, somehow, they came together to play it.

People from all backgrounds watched the game, both county and Test. Club cricket was vibrant in communities everywhere, especially in the north where professionals could earn as much, sometimes more, than they could for representing a county.

When the Australians arrived in 1926, the country was in a mess. It had not recovered from a horrific war; its citizens wanted and deserved a better deal. The General Strike, the miners' lock-out and myriad other industrial disputes which lingered afterwards, left the country on the precipice of mass rebellion. Inequality was matched by righteous resentment which threatened to lead to all kinds of dark places. Yet for a few brief months in a wet summer the Ashes series between England and Australia, and the host country's desperate desire to win for the first time in 14 years, fostered a sense of community and a spirit of unity that was out of the reach of politicians and the ruling classes. The nation was hooked. There have been magnificent Ashes series since, many containing more gripping matches, but this was the only one where something beyond the game seemed to be at stake.

Somewhere along the way, the game lost its universal appeal in England. It did not entirely slip from the national consciousness, but it was no longer a natural part of its very soul. Perhaps the game was simply not entertaining enough and the players forgot that it was their duty to entertain. Every amendment and addition to cricket that has been made over the last 80-odd years when it became evident that 'something must be done' has been to try to reclaim that place. When The Hundred format was devised its mission was plain and simple, if oddly focused: to try to encourage young people who would not otherwise give a fig for cricket to take an interest. Such a step would have been laughable in 1926. People were simply entranced by the game and those who played it. Jack Hobbs, who features prominently in the story that follows, was a national hero but he was not alone in the England team that year. Many of the players who adorned both teams were among the greatest of all time.

Hobbs, like the others, is referred to as a batsman, rather than a batter, now the official term for those who score runs. The change was probably necessary and overdue but it still seemed out of place, even faintly heretical, in reporting the matches from so long ago, and I hope that nobody will find this disrespectful. Similarly, the book uses other terms that applied then and not those of more modern vintage, for the sake of context not perversity.

Wherever appropriate the text uses nicknames rather than proper names. For instance, Pelham Warner is usually referred to as Plum and without inverted commas because that is how he was known by the bulk of cricket followers. HDG Leveson Gower, similarly, is Shrimp because nobody who knew him called him Henry. This convention applies to others in the story too.

It was a troubling time for Britain and its place in the world and neither cricket nor society learned the lessons that they should have done. It is by no means certain that they have learned them now. But it is a wonderful story of determination and perseverance and cricket's place in the scheme of things.

1

THE BEGINNING OF THE END

I do not think that I am likely to forget Sunday, August 8, when the Selection Committee met for the last time. The prestige of English cricket seemed to depend on our decisions.
Pelham Warner

The pity is that at this grave emergency the great strength of the British character should be concentrated on secondary matters. If the whole nation were as keen on ending the coal stoppage as it is on winning the Test matches our troubles would be soon over.
G Ward Price

Throughout the tense, damp summer of 1926 England was in turmoil. Division and rancour disfigured a society in which inequality was rife. For nine days in May revolution was in the air, as a General Strike took place which merely reinforced the profound differences. Fears were widely propagated in many newspapers that the nation was under threat from a Communist takeover. When the strike ended, a bitter dispute between coal miners and colliery owners continued. Lock-out or strike, depending on where your political allegiances lay, it was a grievously damaging conflict affecting a million men and their families. Other industries were barely less afflicted with grave tales of mistreatment and discrimination against those who had withdrawn their labour.

Cricket provided a vital bandage of unity. If it could not heal the wounds, it was a comforting balm that disguised them and encouraged people to remember that life could be joyful. The Test series between England and Australia gripped the nation. Day after day it vied with the industrial bleakness to dominate the headlines in all newspapers, whichever class of people they were aimed at, high to low. The *Daily Herald*, owned by the Trades Union Congress, was as concerned about the destiny of the Ashes as the *Daily Telegraph*, owned by Viscount Burnham. Queues formed round the block to gain entry at every single ground from Trent Bridge, via Lord's and Headingley, to Old Trafford.

The Prime Minister, Stanley Baldwin, was as caught up with the cricket as anybody. He was trying to resolve the most serious peace-time crisis to affect the country but it did not distract from his passion for the game. For this, he was lampooned by the Press, but Baldwin was only reflecting the mood of the people he governed, and the papers, in turn, were following the lead of the people. He recognised the role that the series was playing and that it went beyond England recapturing the Ashes after 14 years.

Britain had never truly settled down after the end of the First World War. Some nine million men died in the conflict and victory had brought the promise that the survivors would return to a nation that would recognise their sacrifice and treasure their contribution. It never quite worked out like that. In the eight years since the Armistice, political upheaval had been regularly accompanied by industrial unrest. Society was still divided between us and them, them and us, and cricket, a game of all the people for all the people, perfectly embodied this. It needed the professionals, the workers, but it was run by the landed classes, often from the aristocracy. All county teams and the national team had to have an amateur, otherwise known as a gentleman, as captain, even if the other ten were all professionals, otherwise known as players.

Amidst the turbulence, the embryonic BBC was trying to rise above the noise. Newspapers ceased publication during the strike and the BBC – still the British Broadcasting Company – was trying to find its voice as an honest broker. It played a crucial, controversial part in the coverage of the General Strike when, in the absence of newsprint, wireless sets, battery-operated and crystal, swiftly became a staple part of many homes. And cricket, equally quickly, became a regular feature of the output.

That it rained too often, that the matches themselves, full of brilliant individual performances on both sides, ended in stalemate mattered not a jot. After years of subjugation to Australia in which England had won one Test match in 19, and that in a dead rubber, they were still in the contest. The impending Fifth Test, at The Oval, was described as the most talked about in the history of cricket and that was probably under-selling it. The game's allure was merely enhanced when it was confirmed that it would be played to a finish, something that had happened only once before in England where three-day Tests were the norm. In the circumstances it was a sensible decision, but it led to dire warnings and gentle satire about precisely how long it would last.

And then, starkly, the England Selection Panel added to the widespread sense of chaos. With the series level at 0-0 after four matches, and anticipation for the final, decisive tie at an unprecedented pitch the team was announced. Its unexpected composition and its leadership only brought into sharper focus the notion of social justice in Britain.

The atmosphere surrounding the game had been febrile since the end of the Fourth Test on July 27. Who would, who could, be picked for such a seminal moment? Some of the batsmen, but by no means all, had enjoyed a profitable series. All the bowlers had found it difficult from time to time, but most had put in punishingly long spells. The wicketkeeping had been fitful and there was a clamour, starting a trend that would never go out of fashion, for the place to go to someone who could also bat competently.

Were batsmen wanted who could bat for days, nay weeks on end without worrying too much about scoring runs? Did the situation require bowlers who could contain but be otherwise unthreatening, or those who might be expensive but produce the wicket-taking ball when least expected? Opinion among the newspaper-writing cohort, a mixture then as now of former cricketers and career journalists, was as divided as the country at large.

The six selectors met in London on Sunday, August 8, not at Lord's, the natural venue where the spotlight of press attention might have been inescapable, but at a suburban house in the south-west of the city out of the immediate sight of reporters. Their deliberations lasted four hours and when they emerged, they announced five changes in the team from that which had drawn at Old Trafford twelve days earlier. Even now almost a century later much of the list seems extraordinary.

Out went:

Arthur Carr (Nottinghamshire), the captain and a widely popular choice to lead the team earlier in the summer.

Roy Kilner (Yorkshire), a stylish all-rounder, forcing batsman and left-arm spinner who had played in the four matches so far.

Bert Strudwick (Surrey), veteran wicketkeeper who had won 27 Test caps starting 16 years earlier and had been in place all series.

Ernest Tyldesley (Lancashire), a batsman in the form of his life who made 81 in his only innings of the previous match.

Fred Root (Worcestershire), a leg-theory specialist, top of the series bowling averages, who had scared the Australians witless on one memorable day earlier in the season.

In came:

Percy Chapman (Kent), the new captain, a rumbustious 25-year-old amateur left-handed batsman with virtually no captaincy experience but who had played in the first three matches of the series before being dropped.

Wilfred Rhodes (Yorkshire), venerable 48-year-old all-rounder, himself one of the six selectors, who had last played a Test five years earlier; like Kilner, a left-arm spinner but 13 years older.

George Brown (Hampshire), the new wicketkeeper, who wore the gloves only occasionally for his county but was enjoying a successful season with the bat.

Harold Larwood (Nottinghamshire), the tyro fast bowler who had made his debut earlier in the series at Lord's and whose raw express pace was now considered essential.

George Geary (Leicestershire), dependable seamer, whose batting could be useful and had already proved handy in a crisis in the Third Test.

Retained were:

Jack Hobbs (Surrey), the greatest batsman in the world.

Herbert Sutcliffe (Yorkshire), Hobbs' opening partner who was barely less formidable.

Frank Woolley (Kent) who continued to personify left-handed elegance on the cricket field and was about to play in his 52nd consecutive Test match.

Patsy Hendren (Middlesex), a stocky, durable middle-order batsman and outstanding fielder who was always difficult to overlook.

Greville Stevens (Middlesex), a gifted if mercurial amateur who was being asked to fulfil a key dual role as number six batsman and leg-spinner.

Maurice Tate (Sussex), whose quiet series did not make him other than the most feared seam bowler around.

The team then entrusted to answer the prayers of a nation was, in probable batting order:

Hobbs, Sutcliffe, Woolley, Hendren, Chapman (capt),
Brown (wk), Stevens, Rhodes, Geary, Tate, Larwood.
Twelfth man: Tyldesley.

Ten of the chosen eleven had made first-class hundreds. It was effectively a team without a tail. The reaction was as stunned as the announcement was staggering. Although the coal dispute was at another critical juncture, as it marked its 100th day with the miners now at loggerheads with their leadership, the cricket story led the way. Confronted with this improbable dozen, cricket correspondents, like children at a fairground, hardly knew where to turn first. The outstanding figures were Carr, Chapman and Rhodes, with Brown a little way behind.

At first it seemed that the panel, despite the length of its deliberations, had reached amicable conclusions. The omission of Carr was hugely significant, of course, but he had been short of runs in the county matches (800 first-class runs in 30 innings to that point for an average of 26, when he had averaged above 50 in 1925). And he had missed the latter stages of the Fourth Test when he had fallen ill with what was reported to be tonsillitis. At Leeds in the third match he had put Australia in to bat after winning the toss, almost unheard of, then dropped a difficult slip catch which had huge consequences. His judgement generally had been called into question but that is the fate of all cricket captains – then, now and always.

The selection committee which made the shock decision comprised:

Pelham Warner, the chairman, Plum to his chums; **Arthur Gilligan** and **Percy Perrin**, the original trio of worthies appointed by the MCC Board of Control; **Jack Hobbs** and **Wilfred Rhodes**, who had been co-opted as the first professional cricketers to be selectors and men with unparalleled experience and wisdom; and finally, also with full voting rights, **Arthur Carr** who took his place as the sitting captain. 'A difficult meeting,' wrote Warner years later. It can be safely presumed that he was understating the case.

The statement issued by the Selection Committee could only have been written by Warner. It bore the qualities of emollience and a desire not to rock the boat, in public at least, for which he was renowned even then – and even when the boat was being buffeted up, down and sideways in stormy seas.

Billed as the official minute of the meeting it said: 'Mr AW Carr, the England cricket captain, who has not been in good health recently, generously offered to resign his place in the eleven, and after due consideration this unselfish action on the part of Mr Carr was accepted by the Selection Committee with the greatest possible regret.'

To a man, the press accepted this at face value. In fairness, the reporters had also to find space to write about Chapman, Rhodes and Brown. But their credulousness lasted only a day. On Monday morning Carr broke his silence. Far from having made a generous offer he was angry and aggrieved. Far from being a polite tea party the selection committee had been a dust-up.

The removal of Carr was by no means unanimous. Two of the selectors, Rhodes and Gilligan, supported his staying to finish the job. But they were outvoted. The same pair was more successful in arguing hard against the appointment of the only other amateur player in the team that played in Manchester, Stevens. If it was imperative that the side be led by an amateur – despite severe misgivings in many quarters – then he had his season as captain of Oxford University in 1922 to offer. Being one of the Varsity captains was still a big deal. Warner and Perrin argued in favour of Stevens; Warner wanted to omit Chapman altogether. The eventual eleven seems to have been a desperate compromise. Perhaps that is how all teams should be determined.

Carr spoke to a string of journalists to air his grievances, the interviews all variations on a theme. 'I am broken-hearted about having to relinquish the captaincy of the England Test team,' he said. 'I was asked at the meeting how I was feeling and if I was quite fit. I replied, "Yes, I feel all right but if it would be any benefit to England for me to stand down because I have been somewhat out of form, I am quite willing to do so." To my surprise and disappointment, they accepted the offer and left me out of the team. I felt the world trembling beneath me.'

The selectors, by and large, stayed tight-lipped. Part of the difficulty with this, a large part, was Plum Warner's day job: he was cricket correspondent of the establishment paper, the *Morning Post*. He was also editor and founder of *The Cricketer* magazine.

At this distance it seems a clear conflict of interest, but the MCC committee had waved it through. Not that it went entirely unnoticed. Soon after Warner's appointment had been confirmed in March *The People*, decidedly not an establishment paper, included an item in its gossip column.

'Cricketing folk are expecting a piquant situation concerning the make-up of the selection committee for the forthcoming Test matches. Rumblings of a stand-off have already been heard. It all centres round the position of Pelham Warner who as everyone knows has been appointed chairman of the selection committee. Now it so happens that Warner has in the past been acting as cricket reporter for a London morning newspaper, and it is understood is to act again this summer. Will that mean he will sit in judgement as a critic on the team he has selected and on their opponents? If he does, it will be a ridiculous position for the MCC, the other members of the selection committee, and himself, for as a critic he must criticise favourably or unfavourably his own work.'

Quite, it might be said. But Warner saw nothing odd in this. His assessment was that if anybody could pick the team and then sit in judgement the next day as a journalist it was him. In the days after the squad was chosen, he declined to comment. As did the rest of the panel, except for Perrin, the 50-year-old Essex amateur batsman, who was to the point, as you might expect of a publican's son from the East End of London. 'The dropping of Mr Carr was purely on account of cricket form. We want to play the team most likely to recover the Ashes.' No mention there of injury, illness or generous gestures.

There was more to come in the Arthur Carr saga both later in 1926, much of it involving Warner, and in the years ahead, but this was not the week to dwell for long on the former captain's misfortune. More particularly, it was the time to assess Chapman and celebrate the return of Rhodes.

Chapman was a genial left-handed biffer who liked to get on with it. After being omitted from the team on the morning of the Fourth Test he provided timely evidence of his worth by immediately afterwards going to the Canterbury Festival and making 136 and 81 not out in a thrilling County Championship match against Hampshire when he and Woolley cracked the last 135 runs needed to win in an hour.

At the very least he was in form (which he was never to better), but like many others he was non-plussed by his shock elevation. Indeed, he was blissfully unaware until he was rung at his home in Hythe on the Kent coast by a reporter who had to try to make him understand what had happened. Chapman thought his leg was being pulled – 'It isn't true' – so the reporter read out the team.

'Well, it's news to me, complete news,' Chapman said. 'I have heard nothing about it. Are you absolutely sure? Read out the team again ... Rhodes in, eh, I think it's perfectly splendid, and Brown too, he's a great cricketer.' At last convinced, he said: 'Why, I feel the proudest man in the world. It's unbelievable.'

These replies seemed to bespeak an easy-going nature, though it seemed a strange way for the selectors to be plotting Ashes glory – keeping in the dark the man they hoped would be its architect. Many had immediate doubts about his leadership skills since he had barely been given the chance to demonstrate that he possessed any. But there was another element. Why did England persist with the policy of having an amateur captain? Hobbs had led England in the Fourth Test when Carr was unable to take the field on the second and third days and acquitted himself admirably. He was England's greatest and most loved batsman, a man of natural grace and universally respected. But he was a professional, and professionals did not captain England at cricket.

Not unexpectedly, the *Herald* was distinctly sniffy. Asking why Hobbs had been overlooked, it concluded that the answer was 'snobbery which has so often handicapped England teams in the past.' Elsewhere, there was a feeling that Chapman would be captain in name only and that Rhodes, 'possessor of more cricket brains than anyone in England today will be the real skipper.'

Hobbs, characteristically, referred all inquiries to Mr Warner as the chairman. He was slightly more expansive in his column in the popular Sunday paper, the *Weekly Dispatch*. When Carr was indisposed at Old Trafford, Hobbs had been preferred as stand-in captain to Stevens, the only other amateur in the side. Having read that at least one journalist said that Stevens should have been anointed then, Hobbs temporarily dropped his unassuming persona to write that 'at least three professionals in the side were more qualified for the emergency' and that in home Tests 'I see no reason whatsoever why a paid player should be debarred from the captaincy of his country.' In the unlikely event that he made such an argument in the selection room, he lost it to Warner.

Without this story to occupy them, the newsmen might have beaten a path to Rhodes' door in Huddersfield. But they probably knew better. The old pro's taciturnity was legendary, a quality he shared with his fellow Yorkshireman, Herbert Smith, the president of the Miners' Federation. Smith's mantra in negotiations with the government was 'We've nowt to give', and Rhodes adopted a similar policy.

His recall, remarkable as it was, made eminent sense. A solid claim could be made for his still being the country's pre-eminent spinner and when the team was chosen he was a clear leader of the country's bowling averages with 95 wickets at 14.87 runs each, more than a run a wicket better than the next man. He was conceding fewer than two runs an over. Attempts had been made earlier in the series to persuade him to play but he had rebuffed them. 'Let the younger men have their chance,' he insisted.

Perhaps Rhodes' place on the selection panel made the matter more delicate. There was also the question of the particular younger man he would replace. Roy Kilner was his team-mate at Yorkshire, who by now usually batted higher in the order, bowled ahead of Rhodes and was 13 years his junior. At the start of the series Kilner was an undisputed choice as England's left-arm spinning all-rounder. But it had not gone well. While he was never collared by the batsmen, his 121 overs had yielded only seven wickets. It made him vulnerable. Nor was there a place for the Gloucestershire left-arm spinner, Charlie Parker, the country's leading wicket-taker who had been named in the squads for the previous two matches, controversially without making the eleven.

Rhodes attended the crucial selection meeting after making 60 in Yorkshire's first innings against Warwickshire at Sheffield on the previous afternoon (and more pertinently taking 7-116 in the top-of-the-table Roses meeting with Lancashire a week earlier). The discussion on his inclusion, not mentioned at the time, was eventually revealed by Warner.

It went like this –

Warner: 'We think, Wilfred, that you should play. You are still the best left-handed slow bowler in England and in a match which is to be played to the finish it is likely that we shall have rain at some time or other. You can still spin 'em, you know.'

Perrin: 'And your length is as good as ever.'

Rhodes: 'Well, I can keep 'em there or thereabouts.'

Gilligan: 'And you make runs for Yorkshire.'

Rhodes: 'I can get a few.'

Hobbs: 'And your fielding is all right.'

Rhodes: 'The further I run, the slower I get.'

And so the deal was done. To Rhodes was entrusted a primary role in making English cricket feel good about itself again, in making it feel young, if that were not a contradiction for a cricketer two months short of his 49th birthday.

At the other end of the scale was Larwood, the young prince from Nottinghamshire. He had been fairly impressive on his debut in the Second Test at Lord's and was then quietly dropped. Not fully formed yet was the general feeling. But as well as wily spin, England needed pace and Larwood had it. Only five days before the panel convened he had made a compelling case to be chosen. In a Championship match for Notts against Sussex at Hastings, the 21-year-old Larwood had match figures of 12-127, eight of his victims bowled. The opposition captain was the selector, Arthur Gilligan. Larwood had timed his run for a place to perfection.

The wicketkeeping position had been the subject of contention all summer long. Everyone liked old Struddy but he was 46, was no longer consistently sharp and had never made runs. He probably came close to being dropped after a poor match at Lord's when chances went begging and too many byes were allowed. Strudwick had pulled his socks up since then, but his complete lack of batting ability swayed Warner and the rest (even Hobbs, Struddy's best friend in the game) that a change had to be made.

George Brown was the preferred but not necessarily the ideal candidate. He was in splendid form with the bat, but he was hardly keeping wicket for Hampshire where Walter Livsey occupied the position. But Brown had taken over before from Strudwick in the England side. In 1921 when they were being mauled by Australia, he had been called up to bat in the top order and wear the gloves, doing so with some distinction. Brown seemed to have the talent to take over as wicketkeeper at a moment's notice and perform as if he spent his life in gauntlets. It was a risk but a calculated one.

Australia had their own worries. Injury and illness had dogged them since their arrival in England days before the General Strike. The chief conundrum for their selection panel was whether to bring back the tour captain, Herbie Collins, who had missed two Tests because of a debilitating attack of neuritis in the shoulder. It had gradually subsided but the condition, an inflammation of the nerve, was still causing Collins some discomfort. Since he was one of the trio picking the side it was probably a straightforward decision. But another of the three, Jack Ryder, was left out after playing the first four matches. That, too, was probably clear-cut given Ryder's lack of form: he had scored only 73 runs in four Tests.

The tourists had plenty of other batsmen in form, however. Like England, their deficiencies lay in bowling, though there was a suspicion that Jack Gregory, leader of the attack, was at last recovering some of his former spark after a disappointing tour. If that proved to be the case, England would have trouble.

Of Australia's 16-strong touring party, three suffered long-term illness or injury during the tour. They used 13 players in all during the series and eventually chose a team comprising seven players from New South Wales, two from Victoria and two from South Australia. In likely batting order this was:

Bill Woodfull (Vic), Warren Bardsley (NSW), Charlie Macartney (NSW), Bill Ponsford (Vic), Tommy Andrews (NSW), Herbie Collins (NSW, capt), Jack Gregory (NSW), Arthur Richardson (SA), Bert Oldfield (NSW, wk), Arthur Mailey (NSW), Clarrie Grimmett (SA).

Soon the quip went the rounds that England had missed a trick by not including Arthur Cook, the miners' union secretary and a contender in the right-wing press for being the most reviled man in Britain. He was, it went, the best bowler in the country because he had got a million men out for nothing. Cook retorted by saying that his side were still batting – though it was a near thing by this time with miners in some areas beginning to return to work, and poverty among his members growing by the day.

The likely length of the match occupied minds and filled column inches. The decision to play to a finish was not finally confirmed until a meeting of the Imperial Cricket Conference at Lord's the day after the Fourth Test had ended in another draw. There was concern that a timeless Test might make for tedious cricket, encouraging batsmen to bed in for days on end. One commentator wrote that he would be going on holiday for a fortnight on August 14, the day the match was due to start, but certainly hoped to see a few days of the finish. There was a cartoon depicting a billboard and a chap below it napping. 'Why suffer from insomnia? Come to the final Test and be cured,' said the caption. One feature-writing wag imagined play being suspended in November and being resumed in an untypically fine February, by which time both teams had completed their first innings, Australia reaching 1,015 and England replying with 1,001. A gossip column mused on what would finish first, the final Test or the coal dispute.

But the fact that one side or the other had to win merely increased the sense of anticipation. Competitions ran in many newspapers inviting readers to make various predictions. The bats used by Hobbs during the series were offered as prizes by his paper, the *Weekly Dispatch*. Entrants had to guess the runs scored by each side. In the *Westminster Gazette* readers had a chance of winning £250 for predicting the total number of runs. A London reader of the *Sunday Pictorial*, John Lawrence, a commissionaire in the City and former soldier who had been awarded the Military Cross and Croix de Guerre, won £2,000 (£153,000 a century later) for correctly nominating the leading batsman and bowler and the number of runs scored in the Third Test.

Opinion naturally differed about the likely destination of the Ashes. In Australia the consensus was that Chapman's elevation was high risk. Their public could hardly believe that some bloke from a posh private school (Uppingham) had been plucked from virtual obscurity for such a task and concluded that Carr, albeit another bloke from a posh private school (Sherborne), had been made a scapegoat by interfering selectors. The feeling was that the team would be captained by a three-man committee of Chapman, Hobbs and Rhodes. As for the inclusion of Rhodes, it was a striking commentary on the standard of English bowling. Panicky England had played into Australia's hands.

Despite doubts about Chapman, English observers were much more sanguine about their team's prospects. There was a natural agitation in the days before the match began, born of the fact that it had been 14 years since they had won a home Test against Australia – as it happened, in the first timeless match in another rain-affected summer in 1912.

Such was the mood that columnists like G Ward Price, a celebrated, opinionated journalist of the time, felt bound to offer the warning about misplaced priorities. He wrote his anguished polemic (quoted at the start of the chapter) after returning from a trip abroad. In the same column he wrote: 'When I got back to London last Sunday after six weeks' absence I found, indeed, the whole of England stirred. One topic held the nation's passionate attention, closely scrutinised and profoundly discussed. But this was not the coal strike; it was the problem: Should Carr have put them in?'

The few days leading up to the Test went by as normal in cricket. County Championship matches, then lasting three days, were played from Wednesday to Friday. Of the England twelve, the three faster bowlers Tate, Larwood and Geary were all rested by their counties and Hobbs did not turn out for Surrey at Weston-super-Mare. Kent had no fixture, meaning Chapman and Woolley could reach London early. Sutcliffe, Rhodes, Stevens, Hendren, Brown and Tyldesley all played and therefore could not travel to London until Friday evening.

Stevens, Hendren and Brown appeared in the match between Hampshire and Middlesex at Bournemouth (the latter two both made hundreds). They might have travelled together from the Dean Park ground to the station but thereafter would have to part company. MCC allowed a first-class train ticket for amateurs like Stevens but only paid for a third-class fare for the pros, Hendren and Brown. Australia had been playing a faintly ridiculous two-day match against a Public School XV at Lord's which ended on Thursday. They were already in town.

Whatever the opinions on the composition of the sides, they undoubtedly contained an abundance of great cricketers. Indeed, there were a few of the greatest cricketers of all time, no matter the era. No Test match before or since has had so many.

First, the England side contained four of the top six leading first-class run-scorers of all time, Hobbs, Woolley, Hendren and Sutcliffe, as well as the leading wicket-taker, Rhodes. In 2007 *Wisden Cricketers' Almanack,* which serves as an authority on such matters, came up with the wheeeze of naming the world's leading cricketers in each year from 1900. To do so, they assembled a panel of 16 cricket aficionados. There were 93 names on the list in all, and the Fifth Test at The Oval in 1926 contained nine of them, seven of them already anointed and two to be honoured in the years ahead. The Englishmen were: Rhodes (1909), Hobbs (1914, 1922, 1925), Hendren (1923), Tate (1924) and Larwood (1933). The Australians included: Gregory (1919), Collins (1920), Macartney (1921 and 1926) and Ponsford (1927). It was a different cricketing planet, of course, with only England, Australia and South Africa playing in those years. But that does not dilute the quality that was on display in this epic match. It was a cast list of stellar proportions.

The nation then, despite its woes, was enthralled. At last the great match had arrived, a fitting climax to the Ashes with the promise of nerves being shredded all the way. English cricket was, tantalisingly, on the verge of a magnificent achievement. Equally, more disappointment beckoned for a country torn apart and ill-equipped to take much more. It had taken seven years – and four years of world war before that – to reach this point and the road had been constantly harrowing.

2

BACK TO THE BEGINNING

We arrived hopeful and although we have been beaten we can take a punch on the nose without showing it. We congratulate the Australians who whacked us well.

Johnny Douglas

(comments to the Press, March 1921)

What is our task? To make Britain a fit country for heroes to live in ... Let us make victory the motive power to link the old land up in such measure that it will be nearer the sunshine than ever before, and that at any rate it will lift those who have been living in the dark places to a plateau where they will get the rays of the sun.

David Lloyd George

(speech in Wolverhampton, November 1918)

What a team the AIF were. Fearless, entertaining, hard to beat. They came to England on a wing and a prayer, most of them from the battlefields of northern France. Several potential members were unavailable, wounded, sent home, otherwise indisposed, which meant a few false starts. The party which eventually gathered in May 1919 comprised the cricketers in the Australian Imperial Forces, to give them their full title, remaining in the old country, the very best of men. They were precisely what was needed to lift spirits in England after the deprivations of the war. If they did not quite take all before them, they sowed the seeds for the period of overwhelming Ashes dominance that followed.

Five of them went on to be part of those sides. Of their 28 matches the AIF won 12 and lost only four. Derbyshire, alone among the counties, prevailed against the tourists. Herbie Collins was the leader, Jack Gregory the totem, Johnny Taylor and Nip Pellew the known quality, Bert Oldfield the complete unknown. Taylor and Pellew had both played in the Sheffield Shield inter-state first-class tournament before the war. They shared the qualities of being attacking batsmen and outstanding outfielders who were instrumental in giving Australian sides a daunting reputation at a time when fielding, for many, was a dawdle in the country.

Like Gregory, Oldfield had not progressed beyond club cricket at home but after impressing in the AIF trial matches he had, by late August, become a wicketkeeper-batsman with a big future. Collins took over as captain after the original choice, Charlie Kelleway, was sent home in some disgrace after a series of disagreements, which have never been fully explained. Kelleway was a contentious figure, a hard-nosed cricketer who made the most of his gifts, but another talent, for argument, badly affected his career. Seven years later, when the Ashes squad for 1926 was selected, his behaviour with the AIF seemed to tell against him.

Collins quickly showed that he was a top-notch captain. His elevation to the job embodied the difference between Australia and England. Collins had played a dozen first-class matches in the Sheffield Shield at home between 1910 and 1914, which made him the senior remaining player in the AIF party, but his army rank had never risen above acting corporal. It was unthinkable that a corporal, acting or otherwise, would have been put in charge of an England representative team.

Gregory was a marvel, a gladiator whose runs, wickets and catches captured the imagination of a public desperate to have their imaginations captured. Collins, lacking Gregory's physical grace, had an equal impact. Four players performed the double of 1,000 runs and 100 wickets in that first season after the war: Frank Woolley (1,082 and 128), Wilfred Rhodes (1,237 and 164), Johnny Douglas (1,178 and 136) and Herbie Collins (1,615 and 106).

All summer long, the Australia Cricket Board badgered England to send a full touring team the following winter and all summer long MCC prevaricated. They could probably sense where the future lay. Both countries had lost too many young men in the fighting, but England had suffered more grievously.

Only the AIF played three-day matches in 1919. The County Championship, organised with more determination than strategy, consisted entirely of two-day games. It was a welcome return but the quality was frequently poor. The verdict afterwards was grudging. 'In batting and bowling fresh talent is wanted and the half-and-half season that was hurriedly arranged for 1919 gave little chance to those cricketers who were youngsters when the war broke out and had had no opportunities for the finding of their game.'

Opinion among the counties about playing Australia was divided. All doubtless recognised the potential for defeat but some saw an opportunity to replenish their depleted coffers. Finally, in October, MCC sent a telegram to the Australian board which managed to be both courteous and curt: 'With reference to cable dated September 16 regret cannot contemplate Australian visit in 1920, but would endeavour to send a team in 1920-21, and would be glad to receive a visit of Australian team in 1921.'

The country was at the start of a long period of recovery, marked too often by discord. Although it is entirely coincidental, it is striking how often Australian cricket teams arrived in England to find themselves amidst a state of great industrial conflagration – which itself betrayed the sense of a nation ill at ease with itself. Soon after the Armistice was signed in 1918, the Prime Minister David Lloyd George delivered in Wolverhampton an uplifting speech which would soon become infamous. In effect, he promised to deliver a land fit for heroes.

By the following year the country's miners, many of them returned from the trenches, entered a prolonged era of dispute. Coal had been a vital part of the war effort; it was the essential reason for Britain's industrial might before it. The men who worked down the pits in unthinkably spartan conditions simply wanted a better deal. A bit of tender, loving care in place of being treated like owners' (and there were 4,000 of them) serfs.

The industry was in constant disarray, its future uncertain. Miners called for a reduction in hours and a return to pre-war wages. Lloyd George did what governments tend to do when faced with an intractable dilemma: procrastinate by setting up a commission of inquiry.

In June, at the same time as Gregory's feats were raising the spirits of Yorkshire and its miners, the commission chaired by Judge John Sankey reported. Had the recommendations subsequently been enacted by Lloyd George's government much of the continuing unrest which ensued, and never truly subsided for two decades, might have been averted.

Sankey's view was unequivocal. The coal industry, he said, should be nationalised. (In effect, he was recommending that nationalisation should continue since the government had taken control of the mines in 1916 at the height of the war.) It was a system that seemed to work for most – except the mine owners. Sankey also proposed a reduction in hours and an increase in pay. Lloyd George sanctioned the hours and the money but backed down from a fight on nationalisation and stored up trouble.

As the AIF party embarked in September for South Africa where they were to enjoy further triumphs, Collins was unequivocal in his assessment of Gregory. Waiting to board the *Ascanius*, he told reporters on the quayside that nothing would alter his conviction that Gregory was the best fast bowler in the world.

England would find out soon enough that he was bang on the money. Having postponed one series because they knew their team would not be ready MCC had little choice but to accept the next invitation. Disaster awaited.

England in Australia 1920/21

It started calamitously, and it was all downhill after that. In July 1920 Reggie Spooner, the popular Lancashire amateur, son of an archdeacon, was asked to lead the England side in the following winter's Ashes series. A month later he withdrew because of a knee injury.

This was immediately viewed as deeply worrying. Although Spooner was an untried international captain, he was generally held to be made of precisely the right stuff – amateur, splendid batsman, good leader. His career figures are nothing special but the *Who's Who of Cricketers*, a scholarly tome not given to hyperbole, says of him that 'he has come to be regarded as the supreme example of the amateur batsman of the golden age.'

Spooner's replacement was Johnny Douglas, who had already been named in the party. A sound argument could be made for suggesting that Douglas should have been captain in the first place. England had a thumping 4-1 success in the 1911/12 Ashes under his stewardship. True, he was captain then only because the designated captain, Pelham Warner, fell ill early in the tour and was confined to hospital for most of the trip but it was to all intents and purposes Douglas's triumph.

Douglas took an England team to South Africa in 1913/14 and won the Test series 4-0, thanks largely to Sydney Barnes taking 49 wickets in four matches. The bald fact was that Douglas had led England in ten Test matches of which they had won eight.

However, there was something about the cut of Johnny's jib that did not sit well with the MCC committee. Nobody seemed surprised when Spooner was asked to lead the party before Douglas. Indeed, when Spooner cried off the press coverage about his replacement was hardly cause for optimism. 'A notoriously ineffective captain,' said one. 'Opinions differ concerning the nicety of his judgement,' offered another. It did not augur well.

But Douglas wasted no time in accepting the position when it was eventually offered. One quality at least seemed to be much in his favour. It was agreed that Douglas never expected anything of his men that he would not take on himself. The team at his disposal represented about the best that English cricket could then provide. In bowling and fielding it was woefully inadequate.

There had been a period of comparative industrial calm in England after the tensions of the previous year. Export prices of coal had kept mining buoyant. As the touring party departed with its second-choice leader in late September, that was beginning to unravel. The miners demanded more money, the railwaymen likewise, as the cost-of-living easily outstripped wages. A so-called Triple Alliance was formed between miners, rail and dock workers. They would fight on a united front in future.

By the time the touring party reached Perth in November the crisis at home had been postponed again by government intervention (although unemployment had by now reached one million and would not fall below that figure for another 20 years).

Douglas's men had problems of their own. On arrival they were immediately quarantined for a week following an outbreak of typhoid on the boat, *RMS Osterley*. It could be said that they never recovered and they went on to lose 5-0, the first clean sweep in a five-match series. It is conceivable that England might have eked out a draw in a match or two. But Test matches in Australia were timeless. There were no drawn games between 1882 and 1947, a span of 72 Ashes matches, 39 to 33 in the home side's favour. It meant that for Douglas's men there was no hiding place.

After it was done, Douglas, his stiff upper lip intact as befitted an Olympic boxing gold medallist, was almost matter-of-fact in his assessment. Conceding that the Australians had 'whacked us well', he pointed out that the Englishmen were rather of the ancient order and that the Australians withstood casualties and hard work better. 'They are a powerful side and bat well right to number 11,' he said. 'Whereas we unfortunately had a tail, our last five practically being gifts.'

Both teams sailed back to England on the *Osterley*. They were all pals together, competing in deck games. 'But we refrained from the idea of introducing England v Australia into them,' said Jack Hobbs. 'We had for the time being had quite enough of England v Australia!' Perhaps this was just as well since the left-handed opening batsman Warren Bardsley won the quoits and Jack Gregory the tennis.

England all-rounder Percy Fender went to the Fancy Dress Ball on board as Rasputin, Bardsley as WG Grace, which presumably tested the ship's stocks of long false beards. Fender conducted an impromptu jazz band, Bardsley played saxophone for the first time (and for years afterwards performed regularly), the Lancashire jack-the-lad Cec Parkin kept everyone entertained with his knockabout humour.

By the time they disembarked, the industrial mood in the country had changed dramatically. Having decided not to follow the recommendations of its own inquiry two years previously, the government suddenly announced that the coal mines, which they had run since the war, would be returned to private ownership the following March.

The owners, faced with the collapse of the export market and with being self-reliant again, immediately imposed wage cuts and longer hours. But with the Triple Alliance in play, the miners were quietly confident that they could win the day and a better future.

A General Strike of the three unions was called. The miners' leaders pleaded with their counterparts to 'get on t'field' but they never did. Instead, the strike collapsed on April 15, before it started, when the unions disagreed over negotiating tactics. The day swiftly went down in trade union annals as Black Friday. The miners were on their own.

It is perhaps a peculiarity of the British way of life that only three days later on April 18, the front page of the *Daily Mirror*, then devoted exclusively to photographs, was dominated by the return of Douglas's men from Australia. More than 7,000 people were at Victoria Station at 10pm when the train pulled in – and this for a team that had been crushed. Had the Triple Alliance held together there would have been no train for them to greet. The homecoming of a heavily defeated team playing the country's favourite sport was considered more significant than the coal lock-out. Possibly, too, it indicated, long before it became a trite phrase, that there already existed a north-south divide.

There was barely time to draw breath before the next Test series had to be contemplated. From whichever angle it was viewed England had big problems.

England v Australia 1921

The man in charge of picking the England side was the one who had been forced to decline the captaincy a few months before, Reggie Spooner. He and his two fellow selectors, Henry Foster and John Daniell, met for the first time on May 23, with the First Test due to start five days later. It seemed that the fortunes of the country would be in good hands. Foster, one of the seven cricketing Foster brothers, was a former captain of Worcestershire. Daniell, at the age of 42, was not only captain of Somerset but was also a selector of the England rugby union team of which he had once been captain.

Gilbert Jessop, once a swashbuckling batsman who was by then an acute if benevolent judge, said that never before in his experience had the composition of the selection committee met with such general approval. 'This in itself is a happy augury and if it should so happen that once again Australia asserts her supremacy we may, I think, rest content that it will not be due to any lack of acumen in the committee room.' Four months later, Gilbert, the man known as the Croucher, might have had cause to revise that view.

The size of the task facing Spooner and his colleagues can be seen from the differences in the team picked by Jessop, who was presumably well-informed, and that actually chosen. Only four of the players were the same.

The captain was widely expected to be Charles Burgess Fry, who had been asked to lead MCC against the Australians at Lord's, a sure sign of the way the wind was blowing. Fry had led England to victory in the 1912 Triangular Series against Australia and South Africa. True, 11 years had passed and he was now 49 (eight years older than the chairman of selectors, Spooner), but he possessed a cachet not bestowed on any other English amateur cricketer. On the morning of the MCC match, starting the day before the selection meeting, Fry withdrew because of a leg injury. It was not to be the last time he cried off.

Spooner and Co gathered at 11am in London's Sporting Club and did not emerge until eight hours later. The chairman looked weary. After all the deliberations Spooner was able to announce only eight players who were definitely in the side for the Test at Trent Bridge and the panel had not decided on their wicketkeeper. It displayed a dithering and indecision which was to be the hallmark – the blemish – of the summer. Or perhaps they were simply too anxious to be seen to be decisive. As captain, they turned again to Johnny Douglas. 'The omission of Mr Fry's name will give rise to much discussion.'

It seemed that for the second series in succession Douglas was the second-choice captain, the third if we count the 1911/12 contest when he was called up to lead the side after Pelham Warner fell ill. Whatever his shortcomings, disloyalty to the cause was never among them.

What followed was utterly dispiriting for English cricket. There was some sympathy for a game still recovering after the war, but as the season wore on it was evident that the selectors not only lacked direction, they had no plan. The teams they picked ran into the first great pairing of authentically fast bowlers, Jack Gregory and Ted McDonald, by whom they were undoubtedly intimidated. It has been said that selectors, confronted with the combination of a weak pool from which to choose and a strong opposition, can appear to be basing their choices on sticking the pin on the tail of the donkey. Rarely has that been truer. Some may have mused that they might as well have been running the country.

Australia's players felt the effects of the continuing coal lock-out. During their second match against Lionel Robinson's XI at Buckenham Hall in Norfolk there was an early May cold snap and no fuel available to heat the players' hotel. Robinson, an Australian mining millionaire who had settled in England, secured the team half a hundredweight of coal and as Charlie Macartney recalled 'we drove home assured for once of a pleasant evening.'

During the First Test in Nottingham, the effects of the dispute were only too evident at the tourists' hotel. All the players were instructed to take a candle to light their room. It did nothing to diminish their chances in the match.

Early in July, coinciding with the Headingley Test, close to the heartland of the mining industry, the miners submitted. The owners immediately imposed pay reductions, which in some cases amounted to 50 per cent.

England picked 30 players in all during the series. There were 16 debutants, at least one in each match, seven of whom never played another Test. Only two men played in all five matches. From the start, England were grievously debilitated by the absence of Hobbs, their talisman and standard bearer, who sustained a thigh injury at the start of the summer and was then laid low by appendicitis, and to a lesser extent of Jack Hearne.

Some of the choices were bizarre. John Evans was a hero of the Great War who had escaped four times as a prisoner of war. But he had played little cricket since and had appeared in only two matches in 1921 when he was selected for England – an unbeaten 69 for MCC against the Australians apparently being the clincher. Not surprisingly he was all at sea in the Test at Lord's and was twice dismissed by the menacing McDonald. For the same match, the Hon. Lionel Tennyson was telephoned at his club at 1am – on the morning of the match – declared that he was honoured to play but might have foregone a couple of cigars and gone to bed earlier had he been given more notice. By the following match Tennyson was captain.

But the season was as notable for who did not play as who did. The selectors made no attempt to summon Sydney Barnes, still the best bowler in England who was laying waste to minor-counties batsmen. They jettisoned Wilfred Rhodes, who was to be called up as the saviour in 1926, after the first match. Some if not all the selectorial chaos could be put down to the fact the best eleven cricketers were simply not known because nobody had had a real chance to emerge after the enforced intermission.

That England avoided another 5-0 reversal might have been partly because of belated obduracy and, perversely, the home side ended the rubber scoring three centuries to Australia's one. But the 0-3 scoreline was also helped by the weather (in an otherwise sun-soaked summer, rain interrupted the last two Tests) and Australia's indifference as the proceedings wore on. Their captain Warwick Armstrong, in particular, conveyed the impression that he would rather be somewhere else.

Until the previous winter the countries had not met on a cricket field since 1912, a gap of 3,038 days, and the renewal of their competition was a reason for unbounded joy. But after ten Test matches in eight months, it was time for a break. The teams were tired of each other and England were no doubt fed up to the back teeth. A total of 50 players appeared in the two series, 34 of them for England, 16 for Australia.

England in Australia 1924/25

More than three years passed before the Ashes were contested again. England had regrouped. Not only had new players emerged, they were new players with huge talent and obvious purpose. The MCC party of 17 which left in September 1924, though seven of its members had taken part in the debacle five years earlier, went with hope in their hearts.

England had played two series in the intervening years, both against South Africa. They won 2-1 away in a dramatic affair in 1922/23 and then trounced their opponents 3-0 at home the following year. Another 16 players made their debuts during the 10 matches, which showed that English cricket was still trying to rediscover itself.

Those successes coincided with a brief resurgence in the country's largest industry. Coal exports burgeoned to record levels because of a strike in the USA and France's military occupation of the Ruhr, halting coal production there, which meant that British coal was needed throughout Europe. It was boom time again. The mine owners might have chosen to use this period to consider modernising their means of production. That they did not was a costly oversight.

After almost three years of plenty and a sense that the national mood was eventually shifting – that if it was not quite a nation fit for heroes it was not entirely an unfit one either – the mood darkened as 1924 wore on. By the time MCC landed in Fremantle in mid-October, crisis was again engulfing the United Kingdom. Another strike in the pits was avoided by a swiftly-negotiated wage rise but sales were plummeting, down by almost 25 per cent. It was not a sustainable position and everyone involved – government, owners, miners – knew it.

Political views became extreme. The repercussions of the Russian Revolution in 1917 led to warnings that the Bolshevik menace was present in Britain, and that in turn created fertile ground for fascist movements. It was inevitable in its way that this sort of unrest and uncertainty should extend to cricket and years later Arthur Gilligan, England's hugely popular captain on the tour, was exposed as a member of the Fascisti, the first official fascist organisation in Britain. Its aims were to stem what they perceived to be the communist tide. Thus, on the one hand, the left of the Labour party bellowed that fascism had infiltrated the Conservatives while, on the other, the right of the Conservative Party shrieked that Labour had fallen prey to communism. In both cases, they probably had a point. The fascists were xenophobic and anti-semitic but some of them, and this perhaps included Arthur Gilligan, merely (though dimly) wanted to protect Old England's glories.

He was a hugely popular touring captain, always socially amenable, but, still, patted gently on the back in a way that winning England captains in Australia are not. Gilligan's political exploits, it turned out, were well known. 'The Commonwealth Police kept half an eye on

Gilligan's activities to see whether he was carrying out any political work.' He was not, and it is difficult to see how he could have found the time, though he did write, anonymously and ill-advisedly, an article for the British Fascists' bulletin in which he suggested that it was essential cricket tours were run on fascist lines and that 'Bolsheviks and revolutionaries probably loathe the game.'

The bleak bulletins on the home front were accompanied by bad news from Australia. It was far from another meltdown and the matches were constantly close and engaging. But hope was extinguished: England lost the first three Tests and thus the Ashes again.

The third defeat was preceded by an almighty row in England of the sort cricket still finds itself embroiled in from time to time. This one was precipitated by knowingly controversial comments from the Lancashire bowler, Cec Parkin, which in turn provoked a response from Lord Hawke, one of the two *eminences grises* of the game (the other being Lord Harris). His lordship uttered a dictum that still resonates today, and it epitomised the chasm that still existed in English cricket

Parkin, a cheeky chappy who was immensely popular with the public and his fellow players, was full of good cheer, but he was also a man who spoke his mind. It is not difficult to conclude that he was one of those comedians with a tortured soul. After the First Test against South Africa in June 1924, which England won by an innings, he went into print to lambast his captain, Gilligan.

Having not bowled much in the second innings as South Africa mounted a rearguard action Parkin wrote in his column in the *Weekly Dispatch* that he had never been so humiliated in the whole course of his cricketing career. 'I can take the rough with the smooth with anybody but I am not going to stand being treated as I was on Tuesday. I feel I should not be fair to myself if I accepted an invitation to play in any further Test match.'

Needless, to say, although Parkin was comfortably top of the country's bowling averages, he was not invited to play in the next Test or ever again. It left him with a taste for continuing the argument and in early January 1925, the week before the start of the Third Test in Adelaide, which England needed to win to keep the Ashes alive, he burst into print once more.

Declaring that Jack Hobbs was the finest captain he had ever played under (in three matches for Players v Gentlemen) he lamented, 'but I suppose such an unprecedented thing as a professional leading England would not be tolerated for a moment.' The choice of captain, he said, must therefore fall on 'Mr Gilligan, the present one, Mr Douglas or Mr Chapman. As the Adelaide wicket is not so productive of runs as say Sydney or Melbourne I would risk Mr Chapman captaining the side under the supervision of Hobbs.' Since Gilligan was the appointed captain, Parkin must have known it was a moot point.

Lord Hawke seized his opportunity to reply at the Yorkshire annual meeting a few days later. After taking a pot shot at Parkin for his temerity in taking Gilligan to task he warmed to the theme. 'No more popular skipper has ever crossed the seas to Australia and to think that a man who calls himself a cricketer should write an attack on the England captain and at the same time should say the best cricketer he ever played under was Hobbs is beneath contempt. Pray God, no professional may ever captain England.'

Everyone who heard or read those words probably understood that Lord Hawke was not voicing a private opinion. These were the sentiments of all those who were at the helm of English cricket. Hobbs, by now, was virtually sanctified among a public who adored him, but even he was not deemed worthy enough to be captain. In extolling Chapman's virtues, Parkin may not have realised how prescient he was.

In many respects Lord Hawke, 63 years old by then, was, or at any rate had been, a moderniser but there was a red line which he was clearly not prepared to cross. He provoked a furore. The professionals with the touring team were unhappy and, according to a cable from *Reuters*, 'On reading the news they met and discussed the matter and they ask for the opportunity of saying they consider such a statement a disparagement of professionalism.' But that was as far as their protest got.

In an interview a few days later, Lord Hawke backtracked, but only a bit. 'Bless my soul! I never meant to hurt anyone's feelings, especially the professionals.' What he meant, he said, was that England would be in a bad way if she could not produce an amateur good enough to skipper the team in Test matches. 'Why, how could one possibly allow a professional to be captain over an amateur? Besides, think of the extremely awkward position a professional would find himself if he were captain.' And his lordship neatly turned Parkin's original protest around, suggesting that if he were to complain about Australia making 350 and not being put on to bowl what might he do if the captain were a professional with a professional interest in the game. 'No, no, no, to have a professional captaining a team with only one amateur in it. Ha, ha, ha.' Nothing was about to change any time soon.

England duly went down to habitual defeat in the Third Test and, indeed, Chapman had to assume the captaincy when Gilligan was injured and left the field. The desperately close margin of 11 runs enthused all England followers and still better was to come.

The jubilation when, deservedly, the tourists won the fourth by a wide margin was born as much of blessed relief as excitement. Unfortunately, there followed a further crushing defeat in the final match, which included a remarkable debut by another outstanding bowler, Clarrie Grimmett, who had been born in New Zealand. To some observers, especially Australian ones, it emphasised that Australia still reigned supreme. Yet there were now reasons to suppose that things really might get better. And soon.

1920/21

First Test, Sydney

Australia 267 (Collins 70, Hearne 3-77) and 581 (Armstrong 158, Collins 104, Kelleway 78, Macartney 69, Bardsley 57, Taylor 51, Parkin 3-102); England 190 (Woolley 52, Gregory 3-56, Mailey 3-95) and 281 (Hobbs 59, Hearne 57, Hendren 56, Kelleway 3-45, Gregory 3-70, Mailey 3-105)
Australia won by 377 runs

This was a notable occasion, the first Ashes Test for eight years four months. There was a world record crowd. Seven of Australia's team, including those five from the AIF side, and four of England's were making their debuts. When England restricted the opposition to a first-innings score that was probably at least 80 short of their aspirations it was tempting to think that all might go well after all. The feeling did not last long. By the end of the second day Australia led by 123, at the end of the third by 409.

Warwick Armstrong, captain for the first time, and Herbie Collins scored centuries. At 32 Collins was the oldest Australian to make a hundred in his maiden Test. One of his nicknames was born in this match. He was dubbed Lucky Collins because he was dropped three times in the first innings, twice in the second. Australia's remained the highest second-innings total for no more than two Test matches when they themselves overtook it. Faced with a mountainous 659 to win, England did well to hold out until the 103rd over. The writing, however, was on the wall.

Second Test, Melbourne

Australia 499 (Pellew 116, Gregory 100, Taylor 68, Collins 64, Bardsley 51, Howell 3-142); England 251 (Hobbs 122, Hendren 67, Gregory 7-69) and 157 (Woolley 50, Armstrong 4-26)
Australia won by and innings and 91 runs

Already staring at defeat after Australia's first innings, hapless England were then caught on a sticky wicket. Pellew and Gregory registered their maiden hundreds to put the home side in command. The gloveless, left-handed Gregory was 'very brilliant'. With conditions in his favour, he then bowled with irrepressible force. Bouncers came aplenty and Strudwick, one of the least capable batters, was struck three times in successive balls.

There really was nowhere for them to turn. It was Hobbs' sixth Test century, his third in successive innings at Melbourne. England were badly handicapped by the absence of Hearne with lumbago. But their fielding was poor and it never improved. Arthur Mailey was not required to bowl an over in the match, but he was soon to make up for that.

Third Test, Adelaide

Australia 354 (Collins 162, Oldfield 50, Parkin 5-60) and 582 (Kelleway 147, Armstrong 121, Pellew 104, Gregory 78*, Howell 4-115, Rhodes 3-61); England 447 (Russell 135*, Woolley 79, Makepeace 60, Douglas 60, Mailey 5-160) and 370 (Hobbs 123, Russell 59, Hendren 51, Mailey 5-142, Gregory 3-50)

Australia won by 119 runs

The match aggregate of 1,753 runs remains a record for an Ashes Test. To Mailey went most of the spoils as well as the unwanted distinction of being the first bowler to concede 300 runs in a Test match, and he remains alone in doing so twice. A return of 10 wickets made it worthwhile and Gregory, who bowled nearly as many overs in the match, was full of menace. Woolley, batting serenely, was struck in the back and laid out. Two balls later he edged to slip.

A new fast bowler, Ted McDonald, arrived to partner Gregory for the first time, though their potency was, as yet, unclear. England had their moments to stay in touch but when Kelleway was missed in the slips before he had scored in the second innings and went on to bat for seven hours the game was up. This time round, the tourists needed a relatively modest 490 to win and, thanks to Hobbs making the sixth century of the match, did not immediately capitulate. The tour was then interrupted briefly when a shipping strike meant England could not travel to Tasmania. In some ways, it may have made them feel at home.

Fourth Test, Melbourne

England 284 (Makepeace 117, Douglas 50, Mailey 4-115, Kelleway 3-37) and 315 (Rhodes 73, Douglas 60, Fender 59, Makepeace 54, Mailey 9-121); Australia 389 (Armstrong 123*, Gregory 77, Collins 59, Bardsley 56, Fender 5-122, Woolley 3-56) and 211 for 2 (Gregory 76*, Taylor 52*)

Australia won by 8 wickets

Arthur Mailey's figures remain the record in a Test innings by an Australian bowler, and he undermined England's tenacious response after they had won the toss for the first time in the series. Makepeace, at the age of 39 years and 173 days, was the oldest batsman to score a maiden Test century, though he was superseded nine years later by Andrew Sandham and Ted Bowley, both a few days older.

There was more to Makepeace than that. He is one of only 12 male players to have played internationally for England at both cricket and football (Clare Taylor is the only woman). And he played for clubs, Lancashire and Everton, that won respectively the County Championship and the First Division. He stands alone on that quartet of achievements: capped at both sports and also appearing in club teams that won their respective championships. Makepeace was, in addition, one of three players in this England side who played cricket and football professionally; Patsy Hendren and Harry Howell were the others. None of this could disguise the magnitude of a defeat in which Australia again scored much more quickly than their opponents. When their captain, Armstrong came out to bat, Herbert Strudwick, England's wicketkeeper, said 'there was a demonstration the like of which I have never seen before. Never have I heard such cheering.'

Fifth Test, Sydney

England 204 (Woolley 53, Kelleway 4-27, Gregory 3-42) and 280 (Douglas 68, Mailey 5-119); Australia 392 (Macartney 170, Gregory 93, Fender 5-90) and 93 for 1 (Bardsley 50*)
Australia won by 9 wickets

Gregory added three wickets, 93 runs and six catches to take his totals for the series to 23, 442 and 15, respectively. His number of catches, the majority taken at slip, has yet to be overtaken in a five-match Test rubber.

Mailey took his wicket tally to 36, a five-match Ashes series record for Australia until 2005. Macartney's innings was the highest of his seven Test hundreds. These individual achievements meant an overwhelming triumph for their team, enabling Australia to prevail by an unprecedented margin of 5-0 (though it was to become almost commonplace in the early part of the following century).

1921

First Test, Trent Bridge

England 112 (Gregory 6-58, McDonald 3-42) and 147 (McDonald 5-32); Australia 232 (Bardsley 66, Woolley 3-46) and 30 for 0
Australia won by 10 wickets

This match, the 100th between the sides, also marked the ascent of a formidable, genuine fast-bowling partnership. Gregory and McDonald were irresistible. The match – probably the series – was effectively done after the opening half hour when Gregory, generating pace and bounce, took the first three wickets in an over. In McDonald he had a perfect foil.

There was no coming back. Australia led by 55 at the end of the first day, and on the second their speed merchants pummelled England once more. The embodiment of the mauling was a fierce Gregory bouncer which hit Tyldesley in the face and rolled on to the stumps.

Second Test, Lord's

England 187 (Woolley 95, Mailey 4-55, McDonald 4-58) and 283 (Woolley 93, Tennyson 74*, Gregory 4-76, McDonald 4-89); Australia 342 (Bardsley 88, Gregory 52, Durston 4-102) and 131 for 2 (Bardsley 63*)
Australia won by 8 wickets

The England selectors made six changes and banked on generating popular acclaim by recalling CB Fry, as near to a national institution as 1921 permitted. On the eve of the match, Fry withdrew, citing his lack of form. Thus was the disarray prolonged. Of the four debutants in the match, three never played another Test.

The brightest part of the match for England was the form of Woolley whose two nineties were as elegant as they were controlled and explained why he was never, ever left out of England sides, even in a crazy summer like this.

Third Test, Headingley

Australia 407 (Macartney 115, Armstrong 77, Pellew 52, Taylor 50, Parkin 4-106, Douglas 3-80) and 273 for 7 dec (Andrews 92, White 3-37); England 259 (Douglas 75, Tennyson 63, Brown 57, McDonald 4-105) and 202 (Mailey 3-71)
Australia won by 219 runs

At last embarking on a policy of reducing England's tail, the selectors were confounded when Hobbs, returning after injury, had to withdraw on the first afternoon with appendicitis which needed immediate surgery. The seven changes included the captaincy, with Tennyson taking over from the faithful Douglas and batting bravely and belligerently.

It was to no avail. Australia enjoyed their eighth successive win at a canter, a sequence unsurpassed until 1984 when West Indies had 11 wins in a row. Macartney's hundred was his fourth in consecutive first-class innings. It was Australia's only century in the series.

Fourth Test, Old Trafford

England 362 for 4 dec (Russell 101, Tyldesley 78*) and 44 for 1; Australia 175 (Parkin 5-38)
Match Drawn

Just the six changes and two debutants for this match as the selectors sustained their apparent theory that if they gave enough players a go some might prove capable. Play was washed out on the first day, which was to be the cause of huge embarrassment for Tennyson on the second. With only 40 minutes play left he declared the innings. Unfortunately for him, under regulations introduced nine years earlier 100 minutes batting had to be available to the fielding side in a two-day match which this now was.

A further 25 minutes were lost while the point was cleared up and when the teams returned there was a further breach, this time of the Laws, when Armstrong bowled his second successive over, having also bowled the last before the interlude. Collins batted for 4 hours 50 minutes for his 40, facing 340 balls, a model of self-denial, to deny England a shot at victory. It remains the slowest of all Test innings above 30.

Fifth Test, The Oval

England 403 for 8 dec (Mead 182*, Tennyson 51, McDonald 5-143) and 244 for 2 (Russell 102*, Brown 84, Hitch 51*); Australia 389 (Andrews 94, Taylor 75, Macartney 61, Parkin 3-82, Douglas 3-117)
Match Drawn

Though the phrase had yet to be minted, few matches can have done more to bring Test cricket into disrepute. By the afternoon of the third day proceedings had descended to farce. It mattered not that 471 runs were scored in the day. Armstrong retreated to the outfield and let his team organise itself, picked up a newspaper – 'to see who we're playing', legend has it – and runs were served up on a platter.

Whilst the Test still had some life, Mead made the highest innings by an England batsman in a home Test, a figure which stood till Eddie Paynter hit 216 against Australia in 1938.

1924/25

First Test, Sydney

Australia 450 (Collins 114, Ponsford 110, Tate 6-130) and 452 (Taylor 108, Richardson 98, Collins 60, Tate 5-98, Freeman 3-134); England 298 (Hobbs 115, Hendren 74*, Sutcliffe 59, Gregory 5-111, Mailey 4-129) and 411 (Woolley 123, Sutcliffe 115, Hobbs 57, Freeman 50*, Hendry 3-36, Mailey 3-179)
Australia won by 193 runs

Hobbs and Sutcliffe opened against Australia for the first time and shared two century partnerships, 157 and 110. But it was to little avail as Australia piled up runs. Ponsford became the sixth Australian to score a hundred on his debut. Turned inside out by the magnificent Tate at the start, he was then protected from the strike by his captain, Collins, until the menace subsided.

Taylor and Mailey's second innings partnership of 127 remained the record for Australia's 10th wicket against England for 89 years. England's total of 411 was the highest in the final innings of a Test and remains so in an Ashes match. The match went to seven days and was the first to have eight-ball overs (aimed at increasing the number of overs bowled in a day), an Australian experiment which lasted intermittently until 1979/80.

Second Test, Melbourne

Australia 600 (Richardson 138, Ponsford 128, Hartkopf 80, Taylor 72, Gilligan 3-114, Tate 3-142) and 250 (Taylor 90, Tate 6-99, Hearne 4-84); England 479 (Sutcliffe 176, Hobbs 154, Gregory 3-124) and 290 (Sutcliffe 127, Woolley 50, Mailey 5-92, Gregory 4-87)

Australia won by 81 runs

Responding to Australia's mountainous total, made at four runs an over, England's opening pair, Hobbs and Sutcliffe, put on 283 and batted throughout the third of the seven days the match lasted, the first time this had occurred. Their team-mates did not perform so creditably. Sutcliffe was the first England batsman to score two hundreds in an Ashes Test (Bardsley had previously done so for Australia 15 years earlier) and the first England player to score three successive hundreds in Test cricket.

There was another, less celebrated record. Bert Hartkopf, a Melbourne doctor and leg-spinning all-rounder, scored 80 in the first innings and was dropped, never to reappear. His innings remains the highest for Australia by players to have won only one cap. England pushed Australia but when Collins closed the match down with a defensive fields and negative bowling, designed to rest Gregory until the second new ball, they were flummoxed. The attendance for the match was 236,258. Two matches in, and Tate, England's most important bowler, had already bowled almost 168 overs (or 224 measured in six-ball overs).

Third Test, Adelaide

Australia 489 (Ryder 201, Andrews 72, Richardson 69, Kilner 4-127) and 250 (Ryder 88, Kilner 4-51, Woolley 4-77); England 365 (Hobbs 119, Hendren 92, Gregory 3-111, Mailey 3-133) and 363 (Whysall 75, Sutcliffe 59, Chapman 58, Kelleway 3-57, Mailey 3-126)*

Australia won by 11 runs

For the third successive time Australia won the toss; for the third successive time the match went into its seventh day. At 119-6, Australia were in deep trouble but Ryder's innings effected a full recovery. This was assisted in great measure by injuries to both Tate and Gilligan, who had to leave the field at Australia's lowest point and were followed not long after by Freeman. As debilitating as this was at the time, perhaps the most pertinent pointer for the future was that Chapman took over the England captaincy for the rest of the match.

Going in towards the end of the second day, England changed their batting order but quickly lost two wickets. Hobbs, batting at five, made his second hundred of the rubber. Overnight rain before the fifth day told against both sides as the wicket dried. Australia lost their last seven wickets for 39 runs but

England, too, had to negotiate a difficult surface for much of the rest of the day. England scored 215 runs on the sixth day and ended it at 348-8, 27 short of victory with the injured Gilligan and Freeman in occupation. Agonisingly, England lost match and Ashes, but if there was a crucial turning point in the long-awaited rehabilitation this was probably it.

Fourth Test, Melbourne

England 548 (Sutcliffe 143, Whysall 76, Kilner 74, Hobbs 66, Hendren 65, Mailey 4-186, Kelleway 3-70); Australia 269 (Taylor 86, Kilner 3-29, Hearne 3-77) and 250 (Taylor 68, Tate 5-75)

England won by an innings and 29 runs

Gilligan won the toss for the first (and only) time in the series. Hobbs and Sutcliffe marked it with their third three-figure opening stand, and Sutcliffe became the first batsman to score four hundreds in a single rubber. England had learned the value of a short tail – seven of the top eight passed 40. When rain stopped play on the second day the crowd impatiently invaded the pitch which assuredly did not help to mollify the surface. By the fifth morning the pitch had eased completely, but Tate was irresistible in a spell of 4-21 and the last six wickets went for 60. Cue relief and anticipation.

Fifth Test, Sydney

Australia 295 (Ponsford 80, Tate 4-92, Kilner 4-97) and 325 (Andrews 80, Kelleway 73, Oldfield 65, Tate 5-115); England 167 (Grimmett 5-45) and 146 (Grimmett 6-37)*

Australia won by 307 runs

A breathtaking catch by Oldfield, anticipating a fine glance by Hobbs down the leg side, knocked the stuffing out of England from the start of their reply. Clarrie Grimmett, a 33-year-old leg spin and googly bowler from Dunedin (New Zealand were not yet playing Test matches), ran through the tourists in both innings, and his match figures on debut stood as the best by an Australia bowler for 47 years. Although Sutcliffe failed in both innings for the first time his aggregate of 734 runs at an average of 81.55 was a record.

Australia's second innings might have been curtailed more quickly, but they displayed immense resolve down the order. The magnificent Tate took his haul of wickets for the series to 38 and his number of balls to 2,528, both still the highest by an England player in the Ashes.

3

THE START OF THE TOUR

The Cabinet were informed that racing had already been stopped. There was general agreement that cricket should not be stopped.
Cabinet Minutes
(May 1926)

Our team is mostly to be composed of new men. They are presently being kept hidden away in cellars. Our fast bowler – I mention this in confidence – is WK Thunder. He has never been known to smile except when people refer to Mr Gregory as a fast bowler.
JM Barrie
(luncheon speech in London, April 1926)

There had been nothing quite like it before. The train carrying Australia's cricketers chugged into Victoria Station at 10pm on April 18. Throngs packed the platform and lined the streets outside. Police had to hold them back. Conservative estimates of the crowd size put it at 30,000; the more liberal count nudged it to 50,000.

The tourists, *en route* from Dover where they had arrived after leaving their boat at Naples and travelling through continental Europe, had been besieged by young autograph hunters. They were warned what to expect on reaching Herne Hill but were still astonished at their greeting. 'I don't think that ever in the annals of cricket either in Australia or here a team has been given such a welcome as we were given today,' said Sydney Smith, Australia's seasoned manager, who had seen everything. At Victoria small boys armed with autograph books mingled with excited Australian sailors. 'On with the Kangaroos, on with the Wallabies, on with the diggers,' the servicemen kept yelling. And the Englishmen present, who vastly outnumbered them, simply laughed uproariously.

Such a gathering represented the end of the long first part of the propaganda campaign which had been waging for months about the 16th Australian visit to England. Phoney wars, in which supporters and sometimes players, trade jocular insults and improbable predictions, have long since become a staple factor in the build-up to Ashes series. In the duller encounters they have often proved the most enjoyable element. But 1926 saw the first shining example of the phenomenon.

A few bullish remarks made by the Surrey captain Percy Fender warmed things up nicely. Speaking to an audience in London he suggested that Australian cricketers 'do certain things that are not in our game.' There was no elaboration, but there was no need. Australia immediately assumed that Fender was accusing the team of gamesmanship or worse, and when the team left Melbourne a few days later the accompanying officials queued up to deprecate Fender. It was all lovely stuff, grist to the mill of any self-respecting reporter of gossip.

This all had something to do with cricket's blanket popularity but also with the 14 long years that had passed since England had last won the Ashes. In three successive series since the proper war, the First World War, they had been swept aside. Now there was renewed hope.

When the Aussies reached the Hotel Cecil on The Strand, there was an impromptu press conference at which Smith and the captain Herbie Collins spoke. One of the stories in the preceding months about which much had been made was the Australian Cricket Board's decision to ban wives from joining their husbands on tour. A reporter asked Smith what would happen if one of the players married an English girl during the tour. A hypothetical question, said Smith, which he had better not answer.

What made this joyous assembly the more remarkable – but possibly the reason for it – was that the country was on the verge of a crisis which threatened to tear it apart. It had been nine months (or maybe five years) in the making, another type of phoney war, running virtually parallel with the increasingly excitable prognostications about the cricket. People wanted to dwell on the imminent Test series rather than think about the real catastrophe round the corner.

In July 1925, with mine owners once more demanding increased hours and reduced wages for their workers, the government averted another bitter confrontation by subsidising the industry for nine months. This agreement was due to run out on 30 April 1926. The Australians arrived slap bang in the middle of it all.

A Royal Commission which had been established during the uncomfortable period of peace produced recommendations but no commitment. The colliery owners and the miners were again on a collision course. But this time the miners had the support of their fellow members in the Trades Union Congress who themselves were feeling the pinch of lower pay and a higher cost of living. This time they really were in it together. The workers' plight was worsened by the country's return to the Gold Standard. The Gold Standard was used to measure the value of sterling (and most of the world's other major currencies) by a specific weight in gold and helped to ensure fixed exchange rates. It was abandoned at the outbreak of war but the pressure to return to it was almost constant afterwards in Conservative circles, where it was seen as an essential part of Britain's standing in the world. The eminent economist John Maynard Keynes urged the government to stick to the system which had prevailed since the war; this would allow the United Kingdom to keep control of its internal credit system. But the Chancellor of the Exchequer, Winston Churchill, disagreed. When he announced the return of the Gold Standard early in 1925, sterling was pegged at its rate in 1914. This overvalued it by at least 10 per cent and the results proved disastrous. Almost 75 per cent of British coal in the last three months of 1925 cost more to produce than it was worth. Employers responded by imposing wage reductions. That led to the accusation that the workers had been sold out for the benefit of the City and its financier pals. One joyous night at Victoria Station was not enough to conceal the whiff of rebellion.

As a cricket buff Stanley Baldwin, the Prime Minister, did not easily let the affairs of state, even at this crucial juncture, interfere with his interest. Baldwin had led the Conservatives to a landslide General Election victory in late 1924 after several years of unstable or minority governments, and his position therefore was secure, if subject to regular criticism bordering on disparagement from a right-wing cabal in his cabinet many of whom possessed neither his moderation nor his vision.

If Baldwin was determined to try to end the industrial strife, he was equally intent on ensuring that he had time for cricket. One evening shortly before the Australians arrived, Baldwin's close confidant Tom Jones, the deputy cabinet secretary, dashed to see him in Downing Street after a failed meeting with the mine owners. Jones found that the Prime Minister wanted merely to discuss the foreword he had written that weekend to a book on the history of matches between Eton and Harrow (Baldwin was a Harrovian). Potential revolution must not be allowed to impede the general order of affairs – and nobody then, except perhaps the most committed Bolshevik, considered it remotely strange that the match between the two schools should be at Lord's. Baldwin regularly attended Worcestershire matches when he was back home in his constituency and stood beside the sight screen wearing his Panama hat, pipe ruminatively in mouth, so he could be sure to see the ball's movement.

Two days after the tourists landed, a luncheon was held in their honour in London's Criterion Restaurant. With the subsidy to the mine owners about to expire and with lock-out notices already posted outside collieries, Baldwin found the time not only to turn up but to deliver a speech. The main offering was given by the author and another cricket fanatic, JM Barrie, a whimsical little piece in which he suggested that the England team was to be composed mostly of new men who were hidden in cellars. The fast bowler was a chap called WK Thunder and the batting of such impressive talent that Jack Hobbs would be 12th man. The audience lapped it up. Barrie was crazy about cricket and ran his own team for years. It was called the Allahakbarries and featured many fellow authors including Rudyard Kipling, HG Wells, Arthur Conan Doyle, PG Wodehouse and AA Milne. Even as Barrie spoke, Milne was putting the finishing touches to the first stories of his most famous fictional character, Winnie-the-Pooh, which were about to be published.

Baldwin proposed the toast to 'Our Australian Guests'. He made a joke about cricket and rabbits both having been exported from England to Australia but that rabbits had somehow not found their way into the Australian cricket team. It brought the house down. Probably it was one of those occasions when you had to be there. The PM also held out a hand of sympathy to the chairman of selectors, Pelham Warner. 'I want to ask him not to allow his nerves to be rattled by the Press barrage under which our opponents are advancing to fight us. I can assure you I have passed through those barrages unscathed.' To compare the scrutiny which Warner had to bear with the daily examinations of his own response to the approaching industrial cataclysm said something, at least, about Baldwin's devotion to the game.

Anticipation of the 1926 series had begun as soon as Arthur Gilligan's team left Australia in March 1925. There were no Test matches in England that summer so the Ashes dominated sporting conversation. The Ashes, that is, and Jack Hobbs, the most popular sportsman in the country. Hobbs had many great summers, but 1925 was probably the acme, the year that he scored 3,000 runs, 14 hundreds and surpassed

WG Grace's record of 125 first-class centuries. The whole country was in thrall to Hobbs as he eventually equalled the record in Taunton and went past it the next day.

The euphoria which greeted this achievement showed that football's grip on the nation, though hardly inconsiderable, was not yet relentless. Huddersfield Town won the League championship for the third time in succession and Bolton Wanderers the FA Cup Final, then by far the most prestigious match of the year, against Manchester City, who were also relegated. But there was quite as much attention when Yorkshire won the County Championship for the fourth consecutive season. Teams in the northern outposts thus dominated in both major sports, the same northern outposts where the effects of strikes would be most keenly felt. For all that thousands were flocking to professional football each week, it was generally sensed that cricket remained the national sport and that the matches against Australia were its apex. Who would pick the England team? Who would lead it? Arthur Gilligan was the man in possession, so to speak, but his spark seemed to have been extinguished. Up in Nottingham Arthur Carr was having the season of his life, booming hundred after hundred – without taking any attention away from Hobbs – and leading ten professionals who thought the world of him.

The major topics of conversation in both countries surrounded these two subjects: selectors and captaincy. Australia had to act first in both cases. Its board appointed three selectors in October: Clem Hill, the former Test batsman and the Test record runs scorer, in addition to the players Herbie Collins and Jack Ryder. It virtually guaranteed that Collins would be captain and Ryder would be in the touring party.

On the penultimate day of the year, Australia announced the first 12 of the 15 players it intended to take. Collins was duly nominated as captain and Ryder was also included. The others were:

> Warren Bardsley, Charlie Macartney, Tommy Andrews,
> Bill Ponsford, Jack Gregory, Johnny Taylor, Stork Hendry,
> Bert Oldfield, Arthur Mailey and Clarrie Grimmett.

As so often, it was not so much who was in as who was out that exercised most of the reaction. It was pretty clear that Australia's bowling resources were depleted for the time being, not helped by Ted McDonald having decided to make his home in England. But they had left out the all-rounder Charlie Kelleway, who was in form. He scored 99 not out in the trial match early in December and on the day the selectors met was in the middle of an innings of 145 not out in a Sheffield Shield match in which he also opened the bowling.

His non-appearance in the squad served as a distraction relished by the English Press. They were being scurrilous in suggesting that he was still at loggerheads with various cricket associations at home and that it all went back to the Australian Imperial Forces side in 1919; but it was not based solely on gossip. During a Sheffield Shield match after the original 12 were picked, Ryder was subject to intense barracking as he went out to bat.

It left the selectors in some disarray. The intention was that Collins and Ryder would rubber-stamp the remaining members of the party at a match between New South Wales and Victoria in Sydney in which they were both playing, with the endorsement of Hill in Adelaide. But Hill had to be sent for to attend in person. Despite the populist uprising Kelleway did not make the final cut. Australia added three players: Arthur Richardson, a dependable batsman and medium pace off-break bowler, Bill Woodfull, who made a hundred in the game, and John Ellis, reserve wicketkeeper. Finally, as an afterthought they included Sam Everett, whose nine wickets for New South Wales in the fixture they were watching persuaded them that his raw, youthful pace was needed as support for Gregory. Suddenly 23-year-old Everett was being proclaimed as being the new fast bowling sensation. Gregory himself was reported as saying that Everett would soon be the greatest fast bowler that Australia had ever produced.

While England's Press was mocking the Australian indecision, the Aussies in turn poked fun at the Mother Country's old-fashioned ways. In discussing the selection made by Hill and company, the *Melbourne Age* pushed at an open door to deride the policy which dictated that an amateur must always captain England, the corollary being that a professional must never do so. Naturally, the *Age* alighted on Hobbs as an obvious candidate. 'His many years of fine performances on the field have not made him acceptable as a cricket captain, the one post for which his qualifications could not be excelled. English conservatism sometimes appals.'

MCC was moving slowly to decreeing how and by whom the teams for the Ashes series would be picked. It was in no hurry, and its committee was not about to be cajoled by the Press. The Press on the other hand was determined to cajole. Towards the end of February, the London evening paper, *The Star*, got wind that the selection committee was about to be appointed and said that it was already cut and dried with HDG Leveson Gower – Shrimp to his chums – John Daniell, despite his part in the debacle of 1921, and Arthur Gilligan already certain to form the panel. This proved to be one of those speculative non-exclusives which the popular papers, engaged in bitter circulation wars, were vigorously pursuing. Had mobile phones been invented they would undoubtedly have bugged that of the MCC president, Sir John de Robeck (who was also Admiral of the Fleet). When the Board of Control of Test Matches met the afternoon following the story, Sir John said it contained not a word of truth.

After what the meeting minutes described as prolonged discussion, the initial selection panel was agreed. Pelham Warner would be its chairman with Arthur Gilligan and Percy Perrin as the other members.

*

The Selectors

Pelham Warner

History has hardly been kind to Plum Warner. In Duncan Hamilton's lauded biography of Harold Larwood the author pulls no punches: 'Put simply, Warner was a bastard.' The academic Derek Birley was less shrill but quite as critical in his seminal work, *A Social History of English Cricket*. Birley cast Warner as a mildly ridiculous figure who refused to move with the times and was alarmed by the Bolshevik threat.

Another academic, Marina Warner, on the other hand, brings not only the rigour of a distinguished historian but the sensitivity of a devoted granddaughter to her nuanced assessment: 'Plum's self-effacing yet poised, slender yet impressive figure embodied history for me, not only a chapter of cricketing history, but many loops to do with England and abroad, with ideas of about where one belongs and who one is: he was the pattern of an English gentleman, and everything about him was indeed absolutely cricket. Yet his life shows wonderfully that what that meant was very complicated, and this too was like the game.' Such assessment recognises that her grandfather might have been a flawed character, but was he then not like us all? And was he not also a man of his times?

Whatever he did before and after, Warner's life, like Larwood's and Douglas Jardine's, will forever be associated with, possibly defined by, the Bodyline series of 1932/33 and the lasting damage it inflicted. It would be pointless to suggest that Warner played a neutral part in it because his attitude as the tour manager of, at best, pusillanimity, helped to ruin cricketing lives, and therefore real lives, and change the direction of the game. Partly (mostly) as a result of Bodyline, it has come to be perceived that Plum was as adept at watching his own back while readily finding backs belonging to others into which a blade might be nimbly plunged. The 1926 series itself provided an early example of duplicity. Warner behaved badly towards Arthur Carr, saying one thing, doing another. And as we shall see from his private correspondence, he did that while making sure to protect his own interests.

He was skilful at deflecting criticism and, in print at least, adroit at the avoidance of giving it. However, in 1926 he was still largely esteemed. The clear conflict of interest posed by his dual jobs as cricket correspondent of the *Morning Post* and being chairman of selectors was, by and large, buried under the oak floor of the Lord's Long Room. And as for that other conflict – the side you were on, if or when the General Strike took place – there was obviously no debate, internal or otherwise, for Warner.

The men who played with and against him – and this is not wholly unimportant – gave the impression that they liked him. Jack Hobbs, who was not quite as benevolent in his opinions of others as is often assumed for such a kindly man, was unstinting in his praise: 'the best captain I ever played under'; 'a wonder, always alert, always cheery, and always acting with fine judgement'; 'he was one of the most popular men who ever played the best of games.'

Patsy Hendren, whose cause as a young professional Warner had championed, remained devoted all his life. And Bert Strudwick, Hobbs' best friend in cricket and team-mate at England and Surrey, was barely less gushing. Discussing the match in which Warner's Middlesex beat Surrey at Lord's in 1920 to win the Championship in Warner's last match he said: 'Mr Warner was carried off the field shoulder high! He had a most wonderful reception and no man deserved it more.' Allowing for the blandishments of ghost-writers these are encomia which would not be bestowed without the genuine sentiment that Warner had done right by them.

Wally Hammond, for another, remained devoted to Plum throughout his career. This was certainly in part because during the 1926 series, in which he might well have played, Hammond lay perilously ill in a Bristol nursing home suffering from an illness contracted on an MCC tour of West Indies the previous winter. Warner was a regular and solicitous visitor. It was Warner who arranged for MCC to pay some medical bills, it was Warner whose support for Hammond never wavered.

Warner's prime weakness as a man (and as a journalist, it would be worth wagering) seems to have been that he wanted to be all things to all men. He was quite willing to say one thing to your face and behave quite differently behind your back. This much became wholly apparent during the selections of 1926; in its way it foreshadowed his devious and chronically weak behaviour during and after Bodyline seven years later. It was his way of doing business: he liked to be liked. Marina Warner was alluding to this trait in her affectionate tribute.

He was a product of his times in so many ways, yet in others not quite a conventional establishment figure. Warner was born in Trinidad, where his father was attorney general. He was the youngest of 21 children his father had by two wives. His mother was Spanish. The family came to England shortly after Plum's father died, and his life thereafter, though money was short, was one of privilege: Rugby School and Oxford University, Middlesex and England. That he loved cricket and (most) cricketers cannot be questioned. He devoted his entire life to it, player, journalist, administrator.

Warner led the first official MCC team to Australia in 1903/04 and came back with the Ashes. Named captain again for the 1911/12 series he fell dangerously ill, was committed to a nursing home for six weeks and never played a single match in the series. He played that final Championship game for Middlesex in 1920 when he was carried from the field at Lord's by his fellow players as the county he led defeated Surrey to become the champions for the first time in 17 years.

He should certainly not have been chairman of selectors given his other role as critic, and he was not reappointed the following year for that very reason. For all that, the general feeling was that the job had been entrusted to the right man, one who knew the game and its players inside out. Warner's reputation may not have travelled well, which may be deserved, though it is doubtful if those who sit in the stand at Lord's which bears his name give it a moment's thought.

Arthur Gilligan

Any brief search of old newspapers for Arthur Gilligan reveals his missionary zeal for cricket. He was forever visiting club dinners or presentation evenings to dole out cups and extol the virtues of the game. There is nary a mention of his misguided support for Fascism in the 1920s. It seems to have been a brief flirtation and one that he probably fell into because the Bolshevist threat at the same time was perceived to be all too real. If you were not a communist, becoming a member of the British Fascisti might have made a perverse sense. Unfortunately it clouds all judgements of him.

Gilligan was that rarity among amateurs, a genuine fast bowler. Usually they left the pros to do the heavy lifting. He was, too, a menacing big hitter from any position in the order, the state of the match never influencing his approach. He was all but finished as a proper big-time player by the time he was called up to the 1926 selection panel. Still captain of Sussex until 1929, his career was derailed when he was hit over the heart and knocked out while batting for Gentlemen against Players in July 1924.

There is no rational long-term medical condition which might result from such a blow, delivered by the Worcester veteran Fred Pearson who was barely above slow-medium, but Gilligan was never the same player again. Maurice Tate, Gilligan's opening bowling partner for Sussex and England, was fielding in the slips that day and tried to revive him. He recalled that the accident 'prevented Gilligan from remaining the best fast bowler and all-rounder in the world. I saw a terrible bruise over his heart and there is no doubt that he should have retired.'

For a couple of seasons Gilligan was properly quick, and he and Tate were formidable. At the start of the 1924 summer Gilligan was made England captain and in the First Test against South Africa, in which Herbert Sutcliffe, Percy Chapman and Roy Kilner were making their Test debuts, the pair were responsible for dismissing South Africa for 30. The overwhelming win was marred by the reaction to it of Lancashire spin bowler Cec Parkin, who promptly ended his own Test career by castigating Gilligan's handling of the attack.

Although Gilligan continued to play after his injury at The Oval his effectiveness was diminished. That much was apparent in Australia in the winter of 1924/25. After the triumph against South Africa, Gilligan was the obvious choice to lead the Ashes campaign, but 10 Test wickets at almost 52 runs each indicated a bowler in rapid decline. His demeanour in Australia – endlessly genial, readily available for the myriad social engagements – made him an extremely popular captain. Losing England captains in Australia tend to have that edge over their winning counterparts.

By the time 1926 dawned, Gilligan was sometimes mentioned as the possible captain, perhaps in deference to the fact that he was in effect still in office (there had been no Test matches since the Australia tour). If that was not a viable proposition it surprised nobody that he was nominated for the panel. It made much sense: he was close to many of the players likely to be discussed, he had his ear to the ground on the county circuit and he had recent experience of the Australians. Whether he remained a fully paid-up member of the Fascists by then – he probably did – it was not difficult to work out where his sympathies lay in the industrial struggle. He was not about to join picket lines outside Yorkshire pits.

Like Warner he was most definitely a man of cricket. Like Warner he would become President of MCC, and like Warner he joined the media. In Gilligan's case this was not only as an author but as one of the first popular radio commentators. He formed with Vic Richardson, the Australian batter, an amusing double act. Audiences loved them for many years. Gilligan always stayed loyal to Sussex where he espoused the game.

Percy Perrin

Percy Perrin was quite untypical of the amateur cricketers of his generation. The family wealth allowed him to be educated at preparatory and boarding schools, but it was the source of the money that set him apart. His father ran a pub in the East End of London. From the profits of that, Samuel Perrin invested in property and in turn Percy increased the portfolio.

To everyone in the game he was Peter, which came from the French diminutive of his surname. In the early days of his career as an Essex batsman Perrin, having taken over from Samuel, organised the pub staff around his days at the cricket. When the property business multiplied in the years before the war he bought a Rolls-Royce. He was independently wealthy in a way which by then eluded most of his fellow amateurs, though some of them may have considered him to be a London geezer.

There were two features of Perrin's cricket on which his peers agreed. The first was the wide recognition that he was the best batsman never to have played for England, and as the scorer of 29,709 first-class runs over 32 years he would probably still be chosen for that particular uncapped eleven today. Only three players not to have played a Test – Alan Jones, John Langridge and Les Berry – have scored more runs in the County Championship.

The second aspect peculiar to Perrin was the respect in which his judgement of cricketers was held. He might not have played in Test matches, but he had a rare understanding of what it would take for others to succeed in them and cricket people instinctively knew that.

The summer of 1926 was his first as a selector, but he was on the panel throughout the 1930s when he and Warner were sidekicks, and chairman in the last year before the Second World War. Perrin was a quiet and shy man but he was not afraid to deliver telling verdicts on cricketers. He was the first to travel to all points on the map to inspect a player's credentials, rather than simply rely on the bush telegraph. It was inconvenient for him to be made captain of Essex in 1926 when he was 50 but he played as often as he could, missing matches to ensure he could attend to his selectorial duties. Often on his travels around England, he was, somewhat bizarrely, accompanied by the journalist, author and baronet, Sir Home Gordon, who thought so highly of Peter Perrin that he dedicated his memoirs to him and then wrote a generous tribute to him in the same volume. Gordon attempted to sum up his friend's qualities as an observer. 'He will watch a bowler and in a terse phrase express exactly what is lacking to render him notably better. More than anyone else, he can appreciate the effect that a man's temperament will have in the long run on his batting.'

The panel was ready for someone like Perrin in 1926. He did not always win the day and although at the last fateful selection meeting he was in favour of removing Arthur Carr as captain, his favoured replacement was not Percy Chapman but Greville Stevens. But it was Perrin alone who, when cornered by the Press, was willing to speak up about the real reasons.

It was nothing to do with illness, it was because Carr was out of form and he had to go. There spoke a publican's boy from the East End.

*

The trio was mandated to appoint two professionals, one from the north and one from the south, to supplement their deliberations. This was an unprecedented move greeted with genuine joy by all sections of the Press. Jack Hobbs and Wilfred Rhodes were duly co-opted with full voting rights. This quintet would choose the captain. It showed that MCC meant business.

After a few days of glad-handing the Australian party was into its stride. Or it would have been had circumstances permitted. Circumstances did not permit. They were hampered by both the poor weather, which curtailed their practices at Lord's, and in short order the General Strike.

Three days after he was talking cheerily at the Criterion of Australian rabbits, Stanley Baldwin met miners and owners. Nothing gave. Baldwin wanted a compromise, most of his cabinet were intent on confrontation to the end. Hopes of averting the crisis rose and then faded. Neither side was in the mood for flexibility; the government could not afford to extend a subsidy that had already cost £23m (£1.2 billion a century later).

The threat of industry coming to a halt was regularly entwined with the menace of communism. Anne Perkins said in her outstanding book *A Very British Strike*: 'In the newspaper headlines and, consequently, in the public mind, the threat of national crisis and of Communist insurgency – indeed the threat to England herself – were duly conflated into one alarming story.'

Yet life went on. The front page of the *Westminster Gazette* on April 28 tells us how. Its main story on a day when there seemed to be reasons for believing that sense might after all prevail carried the headline:

MINE STOPPAGE TO BE AVERTED
OWNERS' CONCESSION ON PREMIER'S PLEA

It made clear that negotiations were continuing but, in any case, there were other matters of import. The story alongside was about the touring Australians:

FIRST MATCH TODAY
ON AN OLD ENGLISH VILLAGE GREEN
REAL SPIRIT OF CRICKET

The match being referred to was the Australians' gentle opener at Maidenhead against Minor Counties. Midnight oil (in the absence of coal!) continued to be burnt, to no avail. By May 1 the coal subsidy ran out. There was no going back now and although the weekend intervened, the miners were officially locked out and the strike was on.

Nobody seemed to have a clear policy on what should happen to cricket, but an emergency meeting of the Cabinet (they were all emergency meetings by then) signalled its desire for fixtures to continue, not least since all horse racing had been cancelled. MCC was similarly inclined and sent a message to the *British Gazette*, hastily cobbled together as a government newspaper in the absence of most of the other papers: 'The committee have no desire to dictate to either the Counties or to cricketers but believe that both may be desirous of an opinion. They recommend the Counties to carry on their programme as well as circumstances permit, although owing to transport difficulties some matches may have to be reduced to two days or even abandoned, and although their elevens may be much weakened owing to the absence of some cricketers on public duty. They suggest to cricketers that they should be guided by a sense of public duty rather than by affection for their counties but they strongly recommend that the best possible elevens should be put into the field against the Australians as on those occasions cricketers may, out of courtesy to our guests, legitimately obtain leave from public duties.'

This message was not sent to the *British Worker*, the emergency newspaper published by the TUC during the strike. Nor was there the slightest thought, it may be noted, that anybody associated with cricket might sympathise with the cause of the strikers. At least eight members of the England team were likely to be professionals and perhaps three, even four, of them from Yorkshire, heart of the entire dispute. Among those who did their 'public duty' during the strike was Percy Chapman who was at Folkestone Docks loading and unloading. Thousands of volunteers like him stepped up, having been loosely organised by local committees during the nine months of the subsidy, for the government knew what might ensue when the time came and had established the Organisation for the Maintenance of Supplies. In the two worlds of them and us, cricket, its masters casually asserted, was part of the us.

Amidst the turbulence the Australians were left to fend for themselves. They awoke on the morning of the match against Minor Counties at Maidenhead to the gloomiest skies in London where they were staying.

It was practically dark at 9.30am when they left for the ground. From the rain-ruined draw at Maidenhead, which set the tone for much of the tour, they managed to reach Leicester where they encountered more rain. Australian manager Sydney Smith was at the MCC meeting which urged the game to continue, but nobody was about to help them travel from A to B, or more pressingly, from Leicester to Leyton where they were due to play Essex the following day. Smith was ruefully phlegmatic in his tour report.

'To add to our further difficulties a General Strike was declared on the last day of the match at Leicester with the result that I had to go to a great deal of trouble in securing the necessary motor cars to take the team to London so as to be in readiness for the game at Leyton (a distance of about 110 miles) the next day. We left Leicester about 7 in the evening and arrived at our headquarters in London just before midnight, our luggage arriving about an hour later. The next day taxis had to be taken to Leyton for the Essex match but on the following two days these were unprocurable, and, to give some further idea of my difficulties, I might state that it took me nearly two hours on the second morning of the match before I was able to secure motors to take the team to Leyton.'

But the cricket battled through with a cussed cheerfulness. The weather was more of an obstacle than the strike. The tourists had much the better of a rain-ruined draw at Leyton where Bill Woodfull marked his debut on English soil with a double century. In the next weather-hit match at The Oval against Surrey, with the General Strike in full swing and public transport at a virtual standstill, there was still a crowd of 10,000 on the first day. Woodfull scored another hundred. It remains the only example in first-class matches in England of a batsman reaching three figures without a boundary – although Woodfull's last scoring shot in his 118 was a four.

Only one County Championship game was directly affected by the lack of transport. Hampshire went to Birmingham with only eight players and bowled on winning the toss. The missing trio did not turn up at all for the first day's play and when they did arrive there was no play on days two and three.

The strike officially lasted for nine days from May 3 to May 12, when the Trades Union Congress caved in. Some workers, especially railwaymen, stayed out for much longer and many others were not welcomed back. Throughout it the BBC played its first prominent role in the life of the nation. Winston Churchill recognised the immediacy of wireless, especially in the absence of newspapers, and tried to cajole Baldwin to commandeer the airwaves. John Reith, the BBC general manager, resisted. The day before the strike collapsed Baldwin emphasised the independence of the BBC, but the fact remained that during it Ramsay MacDonald, the leader of the Labour Party, and Randall Davidson, the Archbishop of Canterbury, who would have put forward a view opposing the government, were denied the opportunity to broadcast.

Employers used the strike as a stick with which to beat some of those who walked out and now wished to return. The miners were intransigent and rejected terms offered by Baldwin, which promised an amalgamation of pits, a welfare levy on profits and a national wages board. Not that the owners, more stubborn still, were minded to make any concessions. The miners were left once more to fight a lone battle.

A century later, the episode is portrayed still as a very British affair – viz cricket's part in it – but the end brought total victory for the government, and the workers felt betrayed. Left-wing commentators continue to write about it in dismayed terms. Baldwin tried to introduce a conciliatory tone, but his Cabinet were in rampant mood. Legislation reducing the power of trade unions would soon follow. True, there was some progress around this time in broadening the right to education and in nutritional health, but all in all it did not much feel like a land fit for heroes.

In the light of this, the contest for the Ashes took on yet more significance. The country was essentially broke, unemployment was still rising steeply in many areas, society was divided, but the Ashes ... well, the Ashes were a panacea. The England captain was finally announced to muted fanfare the very day the strike was called off. Many names had been bandied around month after month. Arthur Gilligan had his friends, but even they must have conceded he was a non-starter. Then there were the Hon Frederick Calthorpe, John Bryan, Johnny Douglas, Percy Fender and, late in the day, the Minor Counties captain Michael Falcon. Several newspapers, out of mischief, carried letters which asked the question 'Why Not Hobbs?' but they knew the answer to that. And in reality the chosen name was a statement of the obvious. Arthur Carr of Nottinghamshire was the man to lead England in the Test series. He would be up against the player widely considered to be the most masterful captain of all, Herbie Collins.

4

ARTHUR CARR – ENGLAND'S CAPTAIN

Right-hand bat, medium-pace bowler

Born: 21.5.1893 Tonbridge, Kent
Age on 1.5.26: **32**
County: Nottinghamshire

Record at start of 1926

Tests: 10, debut 1922/23
199 runs @ 22.11, HS 63

F/c matches: 219, debut 1910
10.774 runs @ 32.94, HS 206
19 wickets @ 37.00, BB 3-14

*There was no side to Arthur Carr. He brought his honesty and
forthrightness to every aspect of his life.*
Peter Wynne-Thomas
(Carr biography, 2017)

*Because speaking as I have found – and speaking the truth –
I cannot pretend that all cricketers are clean-limbed, noble
Englishmen on the verge of sprouting wings.*
Arthur Carr
(Memoirs, 1935)

In the depths of the winter before the momentous 1926 season, Maurice
Tate, England's premier bowler, was ambling along Brighton seafront.
He was startled by a cry from a chap sitting at the wheel of his car in the
middle of the road. 'Cheerio, Maurice!' Tate turned round and there was
Arthur Carr. They chatted for a few moments and after inviting Tate for
a spin Carr said: 'What sort of wicket do we want at Nottingham for the
First Test?'

Whether this meeting was by accident or design – Carr might simply have wanted some sea air, but to find it he had to drive nearly 60 miles from his new home in Walton-on-Thames without his young family – the question indicated Carr's confidence that he would be anointed England's new captain. It had long since become an exalted, much-sought after position, and by then it was also the topic of constant, heated speculation, some of it informed, much of it quite the opposite.

Carr had put himself at the forefront of the selectors' minds (whoever the selectors were to be) in the preceding season. Captain of Nottinghamshire for the seventh successive year, he had led a team otherwise comprising entirely of professionals to fourth place in the Championship. He had also scored 2,388 runs at an average of 51.95, making him comfortably the leading amateur batsman, and taken 28 catches, mostly at slip. As he himself later put it, 'Altogether I was pretty well set for the captaincy of England in 1926, and it would be affectation to pretend that I was surprised when it came my way.' Other names, of which there were many, were touted almost solely in the interests of entertaining newspaper columns, although equally with England's selectors (whoever they may be) you could perhaps never be sure.

That it would all end in accusation and recrimination, and that Carr's life would be irrevocably affected for the worse by what ensued, does not alter the judgement that he was a more significant figure in English cricket than most accounts have usually allowed. He was captain for the bulk of what counts still, for many reasons, as one of the most epic of all Test series. And he was an outstanding captain, both tactically and as a leader of his men, who steered Nottinghamshire in 397 matches across 16 seasons from 1919. Only WG Grace and Lord Hawke have captained in more first-class matches. Carr was an architect and persistent defender of Bodyline, the game's most controversial episode, and he was the mentor and faithful supporter of one of England's most legendary fast bowlers, Harold Larwood, its chief exponent. He was also cussed, obstinate, opinionated and extremely partial to a drink, a good-time Charlie – a fondness he shared with his successor, Percy Chapman. 'I am not boasting – heaven forbid – but I do not think that anyone in big cricket has ever had more rows than I have had.'

Probably alone among England captains, Arthur Carr's character was enshrined, if briefly, in a best-selling novel. In *Loom of Youth* by Alec Waugh, written in 1917 when the author was only 17, he is portrayed as Lovelace major, the heroic all-round sportsman at Sherborne School, renamed as Fernhurst, where both Waugh and Carr were pupils.

'On a raised dais was the Sixth Form table. In the middle, haughty, self-conscious with sleepy-looking but watchful eyes, sat the captain of the house, Lovelace major, in many ways the finest athlete Fernhurst ever produced, who had already got his county cap and played rugger for Richmond. Gordon had seen him bat at Lord's for the Public Schools v MCC and before he had come to Fernhurst, Lovelace had been the hero of his imagination; ambition could hardly attain a higher pedestal.'

Hopeless academically, Carr was indeed, like Lovelace, an exceptional schoolboy athlete, captain of rugby, hockey and gym – everything except cricket. He was also a competent horseman. But it was as a cricketer that he made his lasting reputation, good enough to be selected for the Public Schools XI v MCC at Lord's, which was, rightly or wrongly, a pretty big deal. Carr scored 2 in his only innings and took 1-46 with his medium-pace bowling. The match was notable chiefly for an innings of 144 by someone even more prodigious at sport than Carr, Max Woosnam, who has belatedly come to be viewed in some quarters as Britain's greatest sportsman. Cricket was the least of Woosnam's talents. He won two Olympic medals, gold and silver, for tennis at the Antwerp Games in 1920, a Wimbledon mixed doubles title in 1921, soccer international caps for both England amateur and full teams, was a scratch golfer and made a maximum break of 147 at snooker. In addition it is said that he once beat the silent screen legend Charlie Chaplin at table tennis, using a butter knife instead of a bat. If that is true, it suggests that Chaplin was probably as inept as Woosnam was competent.

Carr arrived at Sherborne via Eton where he lasted two terms before being expelled for misbehaviour, the first indication of the defiant streak in his character which would dominate much of his life. His cricket began slowly but blossomed as he progressed up the school. The event which would shape his life was the decision in 1908 by Arthur's father, Philip, to move the family to Rempstone Hall in Nottinghamshire, a palatial mansion which had its own cricket ground. The primary reason for the move was for Philip to join the Quorn Hunt, one of the oldest and most eminent foxhound packs in the world. Riding with the Quorn for a huntsman was like playing at Lord's for a cricketer. For Arthur it soon meant a residential qualification to play cricket for Nottinghamshire.

The family was extremely wealthy. Philip Carr was a stockbroker who was the son of a stockbroker, who in turn was the son of a city merchant. These generations of Carrs had all made serious money (when Philip died in 1928 he left almost £177,000 in his will, around £14m in 2024 values). They lived in some splendour, they had myriad servants and kept a string of racehorses. The family all rode to hounds. It might have been expected that Carr would join the family firm but his father indulged him. By 1926 Carr was one of the few amateurs to have truly independent means.

His career in big cricket began early. In 1909, the year after the move, he played for the county second XI. The following year, still only 17, he made his debut in the County Championship, against Gloucestershire, barely a month after playing for Sherborne against Tonbridge. It was an unsuccessful appearance, opening the batting and dismissed for 1 and 0, both times by the left-arm spinner Charlie Parker, who was approaching his peak. As we shall see, Carr might have had cause to reflect on that 16 years later when, crucially, he decided to leave Parker out of his England team on the morning of a Test match, though the conditions seemed to demand his inclusion.

By 1912 Carr had an assured place in the Nottinghamshire side when he was available and in 1913, 20 years old, he made his maiden first-class century in a Championship match against Leicestershire. It was a sparkling innings, full of fierce driving and he and the ex-miner Garnett Lee shared a partnership of 333, then the second highest for Notts' second wicket. In all, Notts added 363 in 185 minutes on the second day and Carr's innings of 169 lasted a little more than three hours. 'His off driving was so well-timed that the ball gathered speed as it approached the boundary.' The innings contained a six, 20 fours, nine threes and seven twos, and Notts made a total of 507-3 from 121 overs against an attack which contained the 20-year-old George Geary and Ewart Astill, both of them in their different styles accomplished performers. Carr had arrived.

It was intended that young Arthur would eventually join the Army, but the Army would not have him. By his own account he tried and failed to join several different regiments, let down by his academic shortcomings, but he was eventually enlisted as a reserve in a cavalry regiment. When the war started he was called up. Unlike so many hundreds, thousands, of his contemporaries, Carr survived the conflict. He was lucky. He was on horseback in the melée at the Battle of Mons and was mentioned in despatches during an early engagement on the Somme. Yet in his volcanic memoir, *Cricket With The Lid Off*, which is largely occupied with settling scores, he barely mentions his wartime service.

When cricket resumed, Nottinghamshire did not have an abundance of amateur riches from which to choose their captain and were turned down by a few potential candidates. Carr's circumstances had changed. He was married in a hurry in early 1917 while home on leave, and six months later his wife Ivy gave birth to a son. His father granted Arthur an allowance 'to allow him to keep his family in the style to which they were accustomed.' It meant he was the only viable choice remaining to be the county captain. There was one string attached: the deal for him to play cricket was struck with Philip on the understanding that Arthur would become England captain. As it happened, he was a natural. He sought the advice of the gnarled old pros in his first years, most often George Gunn, and made a point of saying so, but he also had nous and empathy, two desirable but elusive qualities in captains – and he could play a bit.

Even in his first months he was reported to be 'setting a good example in bright batting and smart fielding.' It was a learning curve for him as a batsman. Not until 1921 did he make 1,000 runs in a season for the first time, but thereafter it became routine. One of Carr's most significant qualities was that he did not let the captaincy affect his batting style. That he was an amateur almost certainly helped. He represented, perhaps embodied, the other side in an unequal society. The Roaring Twenties – nightclubs, jazz, gin and flappers – was in full swing for some like Carr and his class, and his booming drives seemed to come with an invitation to a party. His audacity was breathtaking, evoking comparisons with Gilbert Jessop, Edwardian symbol of attacking strokeplay.

Playing for the North against the South at Scarborough in 1922, Carr's 65 contained six sixes, including two struck into the stands, in successive balls from Frank Woolley. In 1925 he made a thunderous 206, his career best, against Leicestershire in a little under two-and-a-half hours. Veteran observers said it was like old times, redolent of the Golden Age. A rapid 54 on a Saturday evening at Lord's in mid-August was greeted with unbridled, poetic joy.

'The cricket at Lord's would have been all serene and mellow as befitted an August afternoon except that Carr came out to bat when the clock struck five. Then did the bright sun overhead find itself challenged, for as everyone knows Carr will have fireworks wherever he goes. His bat seemed to blossom like Tannhäuser's staff, but into crackling flame, rips raps and snapdragon.'

The writer was Thomas Moult, later to become President of the Poetry Society. It is perhaps unfortunate that Carr did not bat on to his hundred, for the purple prose society might have offered Moult life membership. In any case Carr's innings that day was rather overshadowed by Jack Hobbs' 91 not out at Taunton. For a month and nine innings, a span which seemed interminable, the country had waited for Hobbs to equal WG Grace's record of 125 first-class centuries, and now here he was on the cusp of achieving it (though he would have to wait until Monday). It put even Tannhäuser's staff in the shade.

If his exploits and the descriptions of them made it possible to think that Arthur resembled a Greek God, he did not. He was stocky, prone to putting on weight, with a high forehead, which made it look as though his hairline was receding long before it finally gave up the ghost. He had muscular forearms, the size of hams, which made him look like the progeny of a blacksmith rather than a stockbroker, and he had a round face and bent nose (broken in the nets) which tended to suggest that he was growling even when he was smiling.

That Carr was an inspiring captain seems to have been taken for granted by 1926. As the seasons went by he impressed the professionals, most of whom accepted as part of their lot that they would be led by an amateur. His handling of the young Harold Larwood exemplified his approach. Larwood respected him instantly and quickly came to revere him. 'From the very first day I bowled under his orders, Mr Carr has been most thoughtful on my behalf. I have never made a suggestion to him on the field to have turned down without a thought. Nobody but myself knows how much I owe to Mr Carr ...'

Under Carr's guidance, Notts were among the main challengers to a dominant Yorkshire, who won the title four times in a row from 1922 – runners up in 1922 and 1923, sixth and fourth in the following two years. Carr was the only amateur. Notts did not have (nor did they encourage) the parade of August gents who generally occupied middle-order batting positions in the southern counties.

There was a series of testimonials to his qualities:

'He has the disposition, temperament of a fine captain.'

'He is one of those who thinks out his cricket. He can appreciate the lessons of experience – a thing that one of England's recent captains never did.'

'His captaincy was shrewd and his courage beyond all question.'

Carr's natural instinct, as in his batting, was to attack, but he could be hard-nosed if he felt the match situation warranted it. At The Oval in 1923 he was barracked relentlessly by the home supporters when he delayed his declaration until a few minutes after tea, thus meaning two breaks in play in quick succession and almost certainly consigning the match to a draw. It went down badly with most of the Press who wanted perpetually positive cricket. 'People who pay the piper, if not expected to call the tune of the County Championship, are entitled to something more than a travesty of the game and if this sort of thing continues nobody will have the hardihood to protest that the football season comes too soon as an interloper.'

But the view of Patsy Hendren, who had been round the block a few times, was much more persuasive as the speculation about the captaincy for the Ashes intensified. He said of Carr that he had the knack of inspiring his side. 'His cavalier treatment of petty nothings stamps him as a man who will leave a lasting impression in cricket history. When he says a thing he means it and he takes good care that everybody understands what he means. That is a quality that has characterised nearly all our great cricket leaders.' There could hardly have been a more glowing reference had Carr penned it himself.

Still, it is fair to ponder whether he would have been England captain had the absurd amateur-only system been discarded. Probably not, though that could have been said of most of the others who came before. Hobbs, the world's greatest batsman and a hero to almost all, seemed eminently qualified, and the list of veteran professionals behind him was fairly extensive: Frank Woolley for one, Jack Hearne for another, a litany of shrewd Yorkshiremen and Lancastrians. But given the constraints, Carr was a popular choice. Perhaps he should have been appointed before he was, in place of Frank Mann in 1922/23 for MCC's tour of South Africa (when he went as a member of the party) and of Arthur Gilligan in 1924 and 1924/25. At last given the job when he was almost 33, he seemed to be at his zenith, he had served a long county apprenticeship and knew all the players likely to be under his command. If an amateur it had to be, then he was the one.

Nobody could fully foresee how it might all unravel, but the confrontational aspect of Carr's personality suggested there might be trouble ahead. Unlike the chairman of selectors, Plum Warner, his champion and later his nemesis, Carr, as Hendren mentioned, meant what he said and was frequently prepared to say it. It was not especially that he went out of his way to put others' noses out of joint, but he did not mind doing so if he felt it necessary, spurred doubtless by his privileged status in life but also an innate bloody-mindedness. Carr's biographer, Peter Wynne-Thomas, among the most eminent of cricket historians and a Notts specialist, came to admire him the more he delved – while recognising his faults – as demonstrated by the quotation atop the chapter.

At the outset, then, there was a general feeling that the selectors had done not only the right thing but the only thing. Plum Warner wrote a charming letter to Carr.

'My dear Arthur, I have had some talks and correspondence with other members of the Selection Committee and we all agree in thinking you are the man to captain England in the Test matches this year. I wish you all the best of luck and my sincere congratulations. I know you will do well, as you have the right spirit towards, and appreciation of, the game. I will announce your appointment to the newspapers on Thursday evening next.'

Had the series been played in sunshine throughout, then it might have turned out differently. But three of the matches in which Carr was England captain were badly rain-affected, ensuring there was no realistic chance of a finish. The game was also going through one of those periods – there are plenty of them – where the bat was in the ascendancy over the ball and three days was simply not enough time for a proper game to unfold. Carr batted only once in the series, making a desultory 13 from 56 balls, but he was out of form and also short of runs in the County Championship either side of that innings. As the season wore on, Press and public obsession only intensified, as did the scrutiny of the captain. Carr was undeniably under pressure.

His season reached its nadir in the Tests at Headingley and Old Trafford when, weather apart, almost nothing went right for him – apart from the fact that England did not lose either match. Even before the Leeds match, Carr began to have doubts about his position which he expressed privately to the selectors. How relieved he must have been to receive more messages from the solicitous Plum. First a telegram: 'Nonsense. Your captaincy and fielding worth 100 runs an innings and you will get going soon. Love from Plum.' Then a letter which was unequivocal in its praise, bordering on the fulsome. Carr might have smelt a rat.

It said: 'My dear Arthur, You will have had my telegram. You are the best captain we have had for ages and you are worth 100 runs an innings. Go to a net, get someone to bowl nothing but half-volleys for 20 minutes and I bet you anything you like you will get plenty of runs in a few days. Cheer up, old fellow. We all have the greatest confidence in you and I wouldn't be without you for anything. Don't worry for a minute, I beg of you, please. A captain like you is worth many, many runs. Love from yours affectionately. Plum'

Nobody in cricket, least of all Warner, would have been unaware of Carr's capacity for roistering. The first of his two career double-hundreds, in 1921, was made at Leyton against Essex in June. He had had a fairly poor trot and thought that the way out of it was a night on the tiles. Off he drove to Brighton, 72 miles away, after the first day's play and had more than a few. Nursing a hangover the next morning he returned to the game, went to the pavilion bar and sank three double whiskies and soda in short order. His 204 that followed lasted little more than four hours.

Carr seems to have been what has become known as a binge drinker. He might go weeks without a drop but as he said: 'I am the sort of person who never does things by halves. If I play cricket I want to play the best cricket or none at all. If I have a row I want to have a proper row. If I have a night out I want to have a real night out.' As he did on hearing the news of his selection for the 1922/23 tour of South Africa when he was captain of North against South in a late September festival match at Eastbourne. Carr informed the waiter after dinner one evening that when he ordered a ginger ale he also wanted a brandy in it. Before long Carr was plastered. Someone contacted Frank Mann who drove from London to Eastbourne the next day to remonstrate. Arthur was inordinately proud to be, by then, 'beautifully sober' and assured Mann of his intention to behave in South Africa.

He did not quite keep his promise. Asked to deliver a speech at a dinner in Johannesburg he rose to his feet and promptly announced, fuelled by port and brandy, that half the South African team would not get into the Notts side. A row ensued and instead of apologising, Carr doubled down and laid a bet of £50 that South Africa would not beat Notts the next time they met. Nor did they. Notts won by three wickets the following year.

These were still the early days of motoring, and the laws against driving under the influence were at best hazy until 1925 when it became an offence to be found drunk in charge of any mechanically propelled vehicle on a public highway. But it was difficult to enforce and there was not much will to do so. For someone of Carr's predilections, drinking and driving were natural partners and he was in constant scrapes.

It is not certain that excess alcohol was always involved but with Carr it could never be ruled out. He missed a day of one Championship match after being involved in a collision on the way to the ground. In another accident he drove into the back of a lorry, hit a telegraph pole and then ran off the road when a tyre burst. He came to view as a bad omen the green Morgan he bought to celebrate his elevation to the captaincy.

On May 14, two days after the General Strike ended, his appointment was officially announced by Warner, the chairman of selectors. Carr, who was playing for Notts at Trent Bridge waved from the dressing room to elated supporters. 'I have realised the ambition of my life,' he said. What could possibly go wrong?

5

HERBIE COLLINS – AUSTRALIA'S CAPTAIN

Right-hand bat, slow left-arm bowler

Born: 21.1.1888 Darlinghurst, New South Wales
Age on 1.5.26: **38**
State: New South Wales

Record at start of 1926

Tests: 16, debut 1920/21
1,262 runs @ 48.53, HS 203
4 wkts@ 60.25, BB 2-47

F/c matches: 146, debut 1909/10
9,145 runs @ 41.19, HS 282
175 wickets @ 21.15, BB 8-31

Collins is perhaps the best living captain. Let all the previous 'A1 at Lloyd's' county or international captains rest.

Arthur Gilligan
(Collins's Men, 1926)

We are confident – that is all I wish to say about prospects. To tell you the truth I am about fed up with the word prospects. I can say, however, that although we are confident we believe we shall have some very hard games.

Herbie Collins
(Press Conference, April 1926)

Herbie Collins was a man of few words and many nicknames. He led by deed and example, by knowing his men, their abilities and their limitations. To them he was Herbie or Bert, sometimes Mauldy, the Australian way of denoting left-handedness, occasionally Nutty for reasons unknown. To the public and Press, especially in England, he was Lucky or Horseshoe to signify his perceived excessive share of good fortune. When Collins and his team arrived in 1926, Horseshoe had taken root as the preferred sobriquet. Somehow it matched his face, too, long and oval.

Horseshoe had confirmed his credentials as a captain on the Australian Imperial Forces tour seven years earlier when, as Acting Corporal Collins, he had been thrust into the job. The team had proved hugely popular thanks to the positive way they played, and their captain was outstanding as leader, batsman, bowler and athletic cover fielder. A young, untried team lost only four of 28 matches and Collins' double – he scored 1,615 runs and took 106 wickets – marked him out as a formidable cricketer. He was a slight figure, around 5ft 7ins, weighing less than ten stones, a batsman of the sort that Australians might describe as nuggety, and he bowled slow left-arm spin with a fast arm ball that swung, in an era when all-rounders were a common breed.

Australia's captain had little in common with his opposite number, Arthur Carr, apart perhaps from an affinity with horses. Herbie did not ride them, however. He backed them. Actually, he was said to be prepared to bet on anything except cricket. Collins was born into a lower middle-class family in the Sydney suburbs and left his state school at 15. What he did for a living in those early years of the 1900s is unrecorded, and in newspaper memoirs about his life Collins writes only of his sporting exploits. He made his way up grade cricket where he played in the same team as Alf Noble, Australia's greatest all-rounder, and Victor Trumper, her greatest batsman. The relationship that Collins forged with them, Trumper in particular, was to be vital to Collins' continued progress. Collins had many failures, but Trumper saw there was something in his cramped, unorthodox style which could take him places.

In the winter Herbie played rugby, first the union code and then, briefly but spectacularly, rugby league. Collins played only four first-grade league matches at inside-centre, but he won the Grand Final with Eastern Suburbs. Eventually, still only 24, he gave up both rugby codes, deciding that he had a better chance of playing representative cricket. He was undoubtedly correct, but the journey was slow. If it had not been for Trumper's backing his career in big cricket might have ended before it had really begun.

By the time he went out at Hobart to open the innings for New South Wales against Tasmania in February 1913 he had played 30 innings as a top-order batsman at an average of 21. It was a non-competitive match in the sense that it was not part of the Sheffield Shield competition, but it was designated as a first-class fixture. Collins proceeded to score not only his maiden first-class century but went on to make 282 and shared a fifth-wicket partnership of 168 with his mentor Trumper in under an hour. The size of the innings meant that the weakness of the opposition did not much reduce the attention it brought him. He was invited on a private tour of the USA which included Charlie Macartney, Warren Bardsley and Arthur Mailey. Collins was not yet part of the elite, but he was on its fringes. The following season, his fourth with New South Wales, he made another hundred against a New Zealand touring team and then, at last, came his breakthrough, 111 in a Shield match against South Australia. Trumper's faith in his protégé had been rewarded.

And then came war. Collins signed up for the Australian Army in 1915 but was bizarrely rejected for active service because of a weak chest. Instead, he was sent to Egypt and then to France as part of the Service Corps. Considering the carnage around him, he spent a largely uneventful three years. Fate intervened in November 1918, the week before the Armistice was signed, when Collins contracted bronchial pneumonia. He was sent to England to recuperate, and he was still in the country when the idea of a tour by a side from the Australian Imperial Forces was first floated.

When Charlie Kelleway, a veteran of 15 Tests, was forced out as captain of the party, his replacement was quickly found. Captaincy was the making of Herbie Collins as a cricketer. It made him a better player. It completed him. Yet in truth, nobody could have foreseen it. Charlie Macartney probably spoke for many when he said: 'Collins was a very modest performer, and most people little dreamed that he would develop into a successful leader, first of the AIF team, then of New South Wales and finally of Australia.' It begs the perennial question of what qualities make a cricket captain. Collins was certainly not a leader outside the game as his humdrum, unsettled career demonstrates. But give him ten men under his command and it was as if he knew instinctively how to get the best out of them.

He had to wait to become Australia's captain. When Test cricket resumed, although captain of a strong New South Wales team, he was overlooked, partly because he had not played in Tests before. Warwick Armstrong, known as the Big Ship, 41 years old and almost 20 stones, returned by right as a player. His experience (he had played in 40 Tests and seven Ashes series) demanded that he also be the big potato as captain. But the selectors' vote was close, and Collins was made the vice-captain. He took immediately to Test cricket, scoring 70 and 104 on debut in the First Test against England at Sydney in December 1920. Dropped multiple times in both innings, his good fortune immediately prompted new nicknames.

Collins had two successful series as one of Australia's opening batsmen under Armstrong before assuming the captaincy unexpectedly. He was the leading scorer in his maiden series with 572 runs, adding a second hundred in the Third Test. On the way to England immediately afterwards, accompanied by the England team, the Australians disembarked at Toulon and proceeded post-haste to the gaming tables of Monte Carlo where Collins was in his element. The party netted £100 after entrusting Herbie with their cash. He missed two Tests in the subsequent series with a broken thumb, but on his return for the Fourth Test he played the innings which most encapsulated his style. For the first time Australia were under some pressure, and Collins batted 11 minutes short of five hours, facing 340 balls in making 40 before being seventh out to ensure there was no chance of an upset.

Following the England tour in 1921, Australia embarked for South Africa. On the voyage Armstrong injured a leg, then contracted malaria and he played no part in the three-match series. Collins, captain by default, seized his opportunity. Although the first two Test matches were drawn, Collins scored 203 in the second in Johannesburg. This was also the match in which Jack Gregory made 119 from 81 balls in 85 minutes, reaching his hundred in 70 minutes, which remains the fastest Test century in terms of time. Australia dominated the final Test to take the series – and Horseshoe Collins was their captain as of right.

When the party returned home, Collins had a living to make. Australian cricketers were all nominally amateurs with jobs outside the game. (Much of the English press insisted on appending to them all the prefix Mr, as they did with English amateurs.) Until then Collins seems to have avoided the necessity. The Army had kept him for three years and for the tour of England the players were paid £400 with a £300 bonus at the end – when the average wage in Australia was £300 a year. Eventually, Collins had to find work, and he did so in horse racing. He was a familiar face on Sydney courses as a punter, and he was hired as a stipendiary steward. Quite what his qualifications for the role were, except as a regular visitor to the bookmakers, does not seem to have been a question that was asked at interview. It was to be the start of an uneven career in and around racing from which he never truly prospered.

That a man like Collins can appear a natural leader at a sport as complex as cricket, having the backing of so many different personalities in the dressing room, yet be so often at sea in the world at large, is one of those imponderables. There is no answer, not really, other than a pat response that he knew of cricket but not of life. The formative influence at the Paddington club of Noble and Trumper should probably not be underestimated. Noble was a hugely astute captain who rarely missed a trick and knew how to play several as well. He had led Australia in three Ashes series and after losing the first recovered to win the next two with deceptive ease. Trumper, master batsman, was also one of life's natural gentlemen. Collins came under their tutelage when he was only 16 years old and playing in top level club cricket, the Sydney first grade. It was the right age for a cricketer to be exposed to such impressive guidance.

Herbie also had the ability to be self-contained as a cricketer. He did not let the extraneous noise – real or imagined – affect him, and he was a strong enough personality to trust his own game. There was nothing classic or elegant about him as a batter. He nudged and glanced many of his runs; the drive was an alien art form. But he had the most prized assets for anyone in the top order: putting a high price on his wicket and sensing the state of the game. In his unwieldy way, sometimes with a bat so non-horizontal as to alarm compilers of coaching manuals, he never gave it away easily. It was the sort of batting that only a mother could love and then only if she were blindfolded and turned away from the action.

Arthur Gilligan, his counterpart in the 1924/25 series, admired him hugely. The quotation at the start of the chapter from *Collins's Men*, his record of the 1926 tour, sums it up, but there was more from a man who had seen Collins close-up: 'A good, thoughtful, scheming captain, who too is a judge of cricket, inspires his men with confidence in a manner which cannot be put into cold print. Collins, I feel sure, has this power. Even if his men think he has made the wrong change of bowling, or, put otherwise, the right change at the wrong time, they will support him and back his judgement as against their own, right up to the uttermost limit. This is, at all events partly, what is meant by confidence in a captain.' Small wonder, having to contend with this kind of mastery, that Gilligan's men had lost so heavily to Australia in the 1924/25 series.

Of the players under his command none respected Collins more than Arthur Mailey, the maverick spin bowler who would remain his loyal, lifelong friend. Mailey thinks that Noble's approach left Collins an enduring legacy and that the 1919 AIF side, 'one of the strongest teams in the history of Australian cricket', was his greatest achievement.

'Collins was one of the most undemonstrative yet one of the richest characters in Australian cricket, during my playing career at any rate,' said Mailey in his wonderfully knockabout but perceptive memoir *10 for 66 And All That*. 'His faults to me were virtues. His so-called weaknesses faded away or were set in true perspective for me by the richness and fine quality of his nature. Herbie never complained, never moaned. His philosophy seemed to provide an antidote for bad luck. Indeed, frowning fortune to this little, possum-eyed Australian was just another incident that would be of no account when a new day dawned.'

In that lovingly respectful paragraph Mailey paid proper tribute. Noble, Collins' mentor, could not quite bring himself to be so generous. His assessment is at best grudging, perhaps trying to avoid comparison with himself. Instead, in his chronicle of the 1926 tour, *Those Ashes*, Noble chooses to compare Collins directly with Armstrong not by scrutinising their captaincy credentials but by contrasting their very different physical shapes. 'Collins is the direct antithesis of Armstrong whose massive, burly appearance is almost overpowering in its effect on the senses. He is short and spare of body and therefore fails to impress the ordinary onlooker when compared with his herculean predecessor.'

If that is a masterclass in damning with faint praise, even Noble has to admit that there was another school of thought, one that tended to prevail among most in the cricket fraternity: 'Regardless of this, however, many of those who had become accustomed to Collins' leadership ... were quite certain that though lacking in size he was mentally much more richly endowed than nine-tenths of his contemporaries, as well as his predecessors.' Noble insisted on being sizeist as well.

Whatever his physical stature, Collins was still a considerable figure when he reached England in April 1926. The team had left their ship *Otranto* at Naples, travelling overland for 10 days from there to Paris – though this time there was no diversion via Monte Carlo. In Paris Collins laid a wreath at the Tomb of the Unknown Soldier, and then the team finally set off for the Mother Country. Collins, first mobbed by small boys and then surrounded by the Press, delivered his platitude, though he genuinely did simply want to get on with it. Horseshoe could not quite have known what to expect.

Jack Hobbs and Herbert Sutcliffe

Jack Hobbs

England

Right-hand bat

Born: 16.12.1882 Cambridge
Age on 1.5.26: **43**
County: Surrey

Record at start of 1926

Tests: 43, debut 1905
3,898 runs @ 58.17, HS 211
1 wicket @ 165, BB 1-19

F/c matches: 600, debut 1905
42,796 runs @ 47.23, HS 266*
107 wickets @ 24.63, BB 7-56

Herbert Sutcliffe

England

Right-hand bat

Born: 24.11.1894 Summerbridge, Yorkshire
Age on 1.5.26: **31**
County: Yorkshire

Record at start of 1926

Tests: 10, debut 1924
1,037 runs @ 79.76, HS 176

F/c matches: 246, debut 1919
14,407 runs @ 44.19, HS 255*
5 wickets @ 25.00, BB 2-24

Hobbs and Sutcliffe were not quite yet an imperishable double act. But they were well on the way there, a solidifying force at the top of England's batting order whose general frailty still gave the selectors cause to fret. Hobbs, dear old Jack, was naturally a certainty in anyone's book, and if there were still some sniffy reservations about Herbert, who did not score his runs quickly enough for some, the weight of those runs was truly overbearing. They first opened the innings together for CI Thornton's XI against MCC South African Touring Team at Scarborough in September 1922, England v The Rest by another name. Hobbs had declined the invitation to tour; Sutcliffe, to the surprise of many, had not been selected. Thus were they almost thrown together. Nobody could have foretold, of course, but they gave notice of what was to come by putting on 120 in an hour and a half – Hobbs out first for 45, Sutcliffe going on to 111. 'Hobbs and Sutcliffe gave their side a splendid start,' said *The Times*. 'Hobbs was missed from an easy chance in the gully off Macaulay when he had made eight runs; otherwise his batting was very attractive. Sutcliffe was especially good on the off side and scored at a far greater pace than his more famous partner.' The *Sheffield Telegraph* reported: 'Sutcliffe's batting was positively brilliant, he overshadowed even Hobbs.'

The pair were next together for the Players against the Gentlemen at Lord's in 1923 – parted at nine in the first innings, 45 in the second – but it was the young shaver, Greville Stevens, who took the plaudits in that match by scoring 122, opening for the amateurs. The first Test match in which Hobbs and Sutcliffe opened was against South Africa in 1924, Sutcliffe's debut at long last at the age of 29. As they walked to the wicket, Hobbs, in his 35th Test, said: 'Play your own game,' words which Sutcliffe remembered forever, and they put on 136.

They never really looked back. By the time Herbert came along, Jack had already enjoyed several fruitful partnerships – with Tom Hayward and Andrew Sandham at Surrey and Wilfred Rhodes for England, to name but three. But there was something about his association with the younger Yorkshireman that set it apart. Their styles complemented each other and there existed an extraordinary mutual belief apparent from the very beginning.

Hobbs on Sutcliffe: 'He has the temperament for a big occasion, if ever anyone had. We gave each other confidence; I had every trust in him for his successes far outnumbered his failures. He was a good judge of the game and many a time we had a word together as to the line to adopt against particular bowlers. On one occasion after a bowler had sent up an exceptionally deadly over and had beaten me twice, Herbert walked along to me and said, "Stick at it, Jack, he can't keep that up." That's where Herbert is so great; if he was beaten he would go on playing his natural game, quite unruffled, just as if nothing untoward had happened.'

Sutcliffe on Hobbs: 'It was a source of strength for me to see Hobbs take his stance at the wicket. When I walked out with him, I gained confidence and that confidence was increased by almost everything he did. There was his free and graceful stance, there was the exactness of his run calling and overall there was this delightful batsmanship. I felt that this man, who was for so many years the outstanding figure in outside sport, was a scientific wonder. There he was as easy and as comfortable at the start of a Test innings as at any time, and there he was determined to carry out the advice he gave to me – determined to play his own game.'

Perhaps the chief difference between them was that Sutcliffe recognised his limitations as a batsman and played within them and that Hobbs had no limitations. The deep impression they had made in the previous two years made them the first and obvious choices for 1926. In nine matches and 13 innings they had made 1,276 runs together – it would have been ten matches but in their wisdom the selectors dropped Hobbs from the Fourth Test against South Africa in 1924 because he had not yet committed to make himself available for that winter's Ashes tour.

They were both from distinctly working-class, honest backgrounds, similar in their outlook. Jack was born in Cambridge, the eldest of 12 children, and his father, after working as a slater's labourer, became professional at Fenner's ground and then groundsman at Jesus College. Along with two brothers, Herbert was brought up in Pudsey, near Leeds, by three aunts after his father died when he was four and his mother when he was 10. Church was central to the early lives of both the Hobbs and Sutcliffe families. Jack played his first organised cricket for his choir's team. Herbert and his two brothers worshipped every Sunday at Pudsey Congregational Church, and his first team was from the Wesleyan Church in the nearby village. They both knew what it was to go without.

Hobbs was already a national treasure when their association began, as good a batsman, probably better, after the age of 40 than before it. He had already achieved more than enough to confirm his place in the annals of greatness. But in Sutcliffe he found the perfect sidekick. As in all successful partnerships in all walks of life their association was built on trust. This was reflected in their uncanny ability to steal quick singles, without a look and nary a word. Bill Woodfull, who first encountered them in 1926, thought it remarkable.

'How much did they owe to their perfect understanding and ability between the wickets? They never neglected the single and what was good enough for them should be good enough for you. Complete understanding is necessary for such remarkably consistent exhibitions of judgement, for neither was quite as much at home with other members of the side.'

Together they were never either statistically or aesthetically better than in 1926. They opened together seven times, and the only time they put on under 50 was in the First Test at Leeds when rain curtailed them at 32. Three times they shared a partnership of above 100, and the first-wicket average was 118.67. Hobbs had achieved a status accorded few individuals, before or since, when the rubber began. His demeanour and his manner made him both respected and loved. People rooted for him. Had a poll been conducted to nominate the most trustworthy man in England, he would have walked it.

He compiled his runs with a quiet authority, a sound defence allied to a wide range of attacking strokes, all of them pleasingly executed: he seems to have been the very embodiment of that tenet of superlative batsmanship – see it early, play it late. Hobbs scored his 100th century in 1921, but in 1925 he reached a new plateau. The nation was enraptured by his pursuit of WG Grace's record of 125 centuries, and it was made the more gripping because Hobbs kept them waiting.

Flocks of reporters followed him wherever he played – Hove, Gloucester, four times at The Oval – and his top score was 54. It took a month and nine innings before finally at Taunton in mid-August he equalled and then immediately surpassed the total. The feat dominated the front pages of the papers that carried news and the inside pages of those that did not. Shrimp Leveson Gower, one of the old buffers running English cricket who had been Hobbs' captain at Surrey 15 years earlier and was eventually knighted along with Hobbs in 1953 for services to cricket, went on the radio to reflect the feelings of a nation.

'WG loved the game, he played the game and during his era he placed cricket on a pedestal which can challenge any other game or sport for fairness and integrity. Hobbs has done the same and is doing it today. That is where I would like to compare these two great masters. I believe that if WG were alive he would be the happiest of all to think that his mantle had fallen on the shoulders of so great a cricketer and so great a gentleman as Jack Hobbs.' Telegrams reached Hobbs at Taunton variously addressed to: 'The Greatest Cricketer in the World' and 'Superman, Taunton'.

For all his formidable powers, Sutcliffe was held in nowhere near that level of affection by the public in 1926 or afterwards. The warmth that embraced Jack eluded Herbert (he was never given an honour which seems bizarre and frankly insulting now). It was a different kind of relationship. He was already universally admired for his own qualities, his grit and imperturbable nature, but that was not quite the same as being loved as Jack was. Nothing, but nothing, disturbed his composure or even ruffled his hair. Herbert was always immaculately turned out, his creams a perfect fit, elegantly worn. He walked off the pitch after scoring a hundred in the most trying circumstances as though he had been doing nothing more strenuous than reading the paper.

His batting was built primarily on understanding the value of his wicket: he only had one, and he was determined to preserve it. Yet his tenacity was matched by a peerless ability to play to his strengths, the push through point off either foot, the wonderfully crisp off-drive which was as good-looking as the man himself, as if to demonstrate that he had style as well as determination, and the ferocious hook against short-pitched bowling, always the perfect counter-punch but hugely difficult to pull off.

Like Hobbs he had an enduring county opening partner, in Percy Holmes, and like Hobbs his own prowess prevented his extremely capable lieutenant from winning the international acclaim he might have done had the other not existed. Sutcliffe's entry into Test cricket was glorious, a masterclass in fierce accumulation. In his first series against Australia he scored 734 runs, a record, and at the start of the crucial 1926 summer his Test average was 79.77, with five hundreds and four fifties in 14 innings.

It is impossible to overstate the importance of Hobbs and Sutcliffe to England's cause in 1926, or indeed in any of the series in which they played. In the autumn of that year Herbert's first son was born and was named William Herbert Hobbs after his father, himself and his close friend and ally. They played much cricket separately from each other, of course, but they are inextricably linked and it is difficult to think of one without the other. Forever Hobbs and Sutcliffe.

Jack Gregory

Australia

Left-hand bat, fast bowler

Born: 14.8.1895 Sydney, New South Wales
Age on 1.5.26: **30**
State: New South Wales

Record at start of 1926

Tests: 18, debut 1920/21
992 runs @ 39.88, HS 119
79 wickets @ 27.94, BB 7-69

F/c matches: 96, debut 1919
4,496 runs @ 36.55, HS 130
448 wickets @ 19.35, BB 9-32

For a brief, compelling moment Jack Gregory was the greatest cricketer on the planet. He appeared unheralded and unknown, as if from nowhere, to perform the mightiest deeds. Perhaps he should have been borne in on time's winged chariot.

Gregory arrived, in every sense, as a member of the Australian Imperial Forces party which toured England in 1919. He was a key to both their success and popularity. He took 151 wickets, scored 1,008 runs, held 45 catches, not quite a proper double because it contained four fixtures that were not first-class. The match against Yorkshire at Sheffield in June confirmed his emergence. He took 13 wickets (6-91 and 7-79), his victims including Herbert Sutcliffe (in his first season), George Hirst, Wilfred Rhodes and Percy Holmes. And with the match on a knife-edge he made a calm 41 not out, the leading part in a last-wicket partnership of 54 which won the game. The British public were hooked.

Gregory was a giant of a man, standing well above six feet and with a large, powerful frame. He was born in Sydney – he was a relation of Dave and Syd Gregory, the former Australia captains – and after leaving school where he established a reputation as a hurdler he went to Queensland to work on farms. Early in 1916, with the war intensifying, he joined up as an artillery gunner in the Australian Imperial Force and was eventually made a lieutenant. Everything about Jack Gregory – even the name – evoked a kind of romantic ideal. He exuded a zest for life which was reflected in his cricket. From a run-up of around 20 yards, he generated explosive pace, gaining in speed as he approached the crease and with a final, powerful leap in the delivery stride. His bowling was not without subtlety, but pace was his chief ally. Gregory batted left-handed without gloves or box, and it followed that he did not believe in hanging about, hitting down the ground with belligerent frequency, the ball usually skimming over the turf. As a fielder he was fleet-footed with hands that seemed to demand the ball lodge in them.

Following his initial exploits in England he was a shoo-in for Australia's Test team, one of seven debutants in the eleven which in December 1920 won the first Test to be played for nearly seven years by 377 runs. But it was Gregory's second appearance that propelled him to the pantheon. Batting at number nine he scored 100 from 115 balls and then brought England to their knees by taking 7-69 from which there was to be no recovery.

In the third match of the series Gregory began his fearsome partnership with Ted McDonald. They were the first truly intimidating fast-bowling pair, and for a couple of years they were the hottest thing in cricket. Gregory was muscular, strong; McDonald was lithe, rhythmical. They were both decidedly quick. It was not until 1921 in England that they entered their pomp and overpowered England from the start. The first morning of the First Test at Trent Bridge, the first in England for nine years, set the tone. Gregory took a little while to settle, but after being driven for two fours in his first over he responded with three wickets in five balls. England were 18-3 and never recovered. Gregory and McDonald each took eight wickets in the match, and England, it is fair to say, were running scared. Between them they took 46 of the 71 wickets to fall to bowlers in the series, but it was the apprehension, the fear that they instilled, that remained in the minds of observers.

On the way home from the Ashes, Australia went to South Africa where Gregory set a batting record which still stands. In the Second Test at Old Wanderers he scored a century in 70 minutes. Nobody has yet batted less time to reach three figures. The 67 balls that it took remained a record until beaten by Viv Richards 64 years later.

He married a Miss Australia, Phyllis von Alwyn, and their wedding in Tasmania generated huge crowds. The happy couple were mobbed by fans before and after the ceremony, and later hundreds waited outside their hotel for a glimpse of them. It was truly a celebrity wedding.

Gregory featured little in domestic first-class cricket, and his entire Sheffield Shield career spanned a mere 11 matches. He played in all the Tests of the 1924/25 series against England, and if he was less penetrating as the series went on, missing McDonald who had emigrated to England to play club cricket, he made decisive incursions to give Australia an early lead. In the season before the 1926 tour, as business occupied his attention, his cricket was largely restricted to playing for his club side, Paddington, but there was no question about his inclusion in the party. He was injured almost from the start, but it was not diagnosed as shin splints until much later. Yet Gregory hobbled on heroically. There were bursts of excellence, but he was not the valiant, irrepressible Jack of yore, a man who could probably have shifted mountains.

6

STARTING AND STOPPING AGAIN

The reception given to our friends could hardly have been more enthusiastic had a Nelson or Wellington reappeared and if newspaper reports are to be believed the Australians may well be excused if they felt somewhat embarrassed by the crowds that seem to pursue them in every street.

R.H. Lyttleton
(cricket essayist, one of five sons of the fourth Lord Lyttleton to play first-class cricket, The Spectator, May, 1926)

Our business is not to triumph over those who have failed in a mistaken attempt. It is rather to rally them, together with the public as a whole, in the attempt to restore the well-being of the nation.

Stanley Baldwin
(Prime Minister, radio speech, May, 1926)

As the day approached, excitement swept a careworn country. Expectation piled upon anticipation. The newspapers, involved in fierce circulation wars, whetted appetites, sensing how much they longed to be fed. Nottingham, venue for the First Test, was at fever pitch.

Most shop windows in the city carried pictures of the teams, the Commonwealth flag fluttered willy-nilly, and people were said either to be tapping the barometer, looking up at the heavens, or parading outside the teams' hotel hoping for a glimpse of their heroes inside. One report said, without any intimation of exaggeration: 'About 25,000 people are expected at the match which is the chief topic of conversation in the city, even among the miners, and their dispute – there are five collieries within the city boundaries – has paled into insignificance before the visit of the Australians.'

The Test and who might play in it were the subjects of reams of opinion, comment, punditry and speculation. Sometimes a fact was thrown in, usually gleaned from scorecards. England's selectors, as was their wont, were saying nowt. To an extent it seemed perfectly designed to take minds off what was happening in the nation at large. In some ways, too, it felt like a denial of reality.

The end of the General Strike had been just that; it had not ended the distrust, the feelings of abandonment and betrayal sensed by millions of people while the rich grew richer and their gay lives became gayer. The miners continued to be locked out, and although every day brought news of a potential settlement none came. The fact that no coal was being produced and imports were taking their time to arrive began to affect almost every manufacturing industry. Reductions in hours and wages became the norm in the cotton factories in Lancashire, the shipyards on Tyneside, the potteries in Stoke, the bootmakers in Northampton, the steelworks in West Wales. The London clubs, whether of the night or gentlemen's variety, seemed unaffected.

Among some of the toffs there was an unmistakable sense that society's imbalance needed attention. Dudley Carew was a 22-year-old journalist, educated at Lancing College, who was embarking on a career with *The Times*. He decided to write a book about the 1926 cricket season, based on matches at various grounds. It was not quite a novel idea but it was in its infancy. Carew undertook his summer-long tour partly to mix with those people a man from his background would never usually meet – 'the less fortunate products of what we call our democracy'.

It was a lesson taught by the war, the faith in comradeship that emerged in the trenches. 'He did believe,' wrote Carew of himself, 'in the land that was going to be fit for heroes to live in.' But as Carew pointed out it had not gone according to plan. The rich, he suggested, had got richer and his own prosperity 'has forced him into an unreasonable hatred of the well-fed and the rich of whom of course – and the knowledge burns into him night and day – he is one.' Carew, who would eventually become the long-serving film critic of *The Times*, learned on his tour that England's people, diverse as they were, had qualities in common.

'Not the least of which is their devotion to a game which does not pander to their cravings for money or sensation but which satisfies their unconscious need for beauty, and transforms them from men with rents to pay and children to feed into boys whose whole happiness depends upon the hitting of a boundary or the fall of a wicket.' Cricket was, for all, a unifying force in a wretchedly disparate country.

Prime Minister Stanley Baldwin was determined to avoid triumphalism after the collapse of the strike. Equally, he was keen to stress that the government had won and the workers had lost. The broadcast speech he made on the evening of the surrender, in which he appealed to employers to be generous, was calculated to douse the flames of conflict, but it hardly addressed the imbalances in the country he governed. If anything was going 'to restore the well-being of the nation' it would have to be cricket. The British Broadcasting Company was established in 1923, and Baldwin was therefore the first Prime Minister able to use the wireless regularly. He not only recognised its power to influence – the number of wireless sets was growing rapidly and licences now exceeded two million – but was also a natural. Anne Perkins, his biographer, said he was a genius of radio because he spoke from the heart.

The end of the strike almost exactly coincided with, and virtually submerged, a court case which profoundly affected all professional cricketers. On May 13 the Appeal Court decided that the veteran Kent batsman James Seymour must pay income tax on a substantial part of the proceeds from his benefit match. The decision bestowed legal precedent and threatened to blight the retirement of many long-serving players like Seymour.

The match had been played as part of the Canterbury Festival in 1920 and had been a huge success (though poor Seymour was run out without scoring in the first innings when the crowd was at its largest). The takings on the gate came to £939 (more than three times Seymour's wage from the county). When the Kent committee released the funds, Seymour bought a fruit farm in Marden, Kent, his home village. The Inland Revenue then demanded their share of the gate money – at least 30 per cent – upon which Seymour appealed to the Income Tax Commissioners and won, and when the Inland Revenue took its case to the High Court he won again. But the Revenue was determined to pursue the action and the King's Bench of the Appeal Court found in its favour by 2-1. The legal costs meant that Seymour faced ruin. Benefits of all professionals in future would be subject to much closer scrutiny by the Revenue and a great deal less benefit for the player.

Cricket at large was spurred into action. MCC voted initially to pay 20 per cent of the costs of the original appeal, and though that left Seymour still potentially in serious financial trouble it demonstrated that the governing body might after all have a heart and soul. No doubt it helped Seymour that he played for Kent. It was Lord Harris's county, he knew and liked Seymour and at the age of 75 he still had considerable clout at

Lord's. He also urged the other counties to contribute to the legal fund. The game and all the professionals playing it waited to see if Seymour would appeal to the House of Lords. If he did and lost there would be nowhere else to turn. Seymour, 46, was still playing for Kent, and if he was downcast by the Appeal Court verdict he did not let it show on the field. Two days after the decision he made 60 against Gloucestershire and followed that with 71 against Hampshire.

Generally, little cricket was taking place. The game might be able to beat a bunch of recalcitrant strikers but the weather was a different matter. By the time the teams arrived in Nottingham for the Test, Australia had played 12 fixtures. They could not be said, however, to be match fit. Their travel arrangements for the opening three weeks of the trip had been necessarily chaotic, and all but one of their games had been interrupted by rain.

They were also afflicted by illness and injury. Stork Hendry (he had four forenames but he was Stork to everyone) was laid low with scarlet fever at The Oval in early May and would not return until late August; Bill Ponsford went down with tonsillitis a week before the First Test, had to be admitted to hospital, was out of action for three weeks and according to Sydney Smith, the tour manager, it was much longer before he returned to normal. More importantly, Jack Gregory, the team's talismanic fast bowler, was carrying a leg injury – what has become known as shin splints – which restricted him to short spells. That was not to be the end of their misfortunes.

The public flocked to watch them – 28,000 at Lord's on the first day of the Middlesex match, 20,000 at Sunderland for the opening of their match against the minor county Durham. Out-of-work miners, allowed reduced entry, packed the stands at the Ashbrooke ground. Only four matches produced higher receipts for the tourists. Smith was effusive about the fixture: 'As in 1921 the match against the second-class county, Durham, was a great success and such a match should always occupy a place in the fixtures for Australian teams in England.'

There was just enough play everywhere to allow England's selectors to gather an informed opinion of what might constitute their best team. Most of the conjecture was about who might be the bowlers. There were two or three significant performances. Greville Stevens, the Middlesex all-rounder, and Percy Chapman, the Kent batsman, each played two opportune innings against the tourists. At Lord's Stevens made 77 for

MCC and 149 for Middlesex. Chapman scored 51 for MCC and then 89 for the South of England at Bristol, which was the more important since it was billed as a Test trial. Crucially, their efforts were watched by the chairman of selectors Plum Warner in his other day job as cricket correspondent of the *Morning Post*. He was impressed: Stevens had 'cool judgement and the temperament fitted for a big match', Chapman 'played magnificently in a most brilliant innings.' Between those innings, Chapman also scored a blazing 159 for Kent against Hampshire.

But the most pertinent display came from Fred Root, the hitherto unsung Worcestershire bowler. He had been little more than a journeyman seam bowler for much of a career that began with Derbyshire in 1910, but by 1926 he had become a master. Root had gradually refined the art of late in-swing bowling on a leg stump line and allied it to accuracy: what had come to be known as leg theory. In 1925 he took 205 wickets and in the early part of the 1926 season did enough to be chosen for the North of England against the Australians at Birmingham. It was still quite something for a Worcestershire player to be selected to play in a Test match. The county were habitually at the tail end of the Championship and despite Root's double-century haul in 1925 they could still manage only 16th place, nosing ahead of Glamorgan. New Road, Worcester, was not high on the selectors' places to visit.

On the second evening and third morning of the Birmingham match the 36-year-old Root, who had already appeared in 160 first-class matches, made an overwhelming case to make his England debut as he mesmerised the opposition. His field comprised four men near the bat on the leg side, two of them behind the wicket, with a mid-on and deep square-leg. The short-leg fielders were so close as to be called the 'suicide club'. Thus were the Australians ensnared. Root took 7-42 from 28 overs (while the new lad on the block, Harold Larwood, also took three wickets in the match). Arthur Carr, already named as captain of England, was so anxious not to allow the opponents another sight of his new secret weapon that Root did not bowl any of the 28 overs the North sent down in the second innings.

Nor did he play in the match at Lord's which followed immediately, England v The Rest, though it was in effect an extremely late trial, a kind of Possible Probables against Probable Possibles with some in both categories not called up. The team for the Test, now only four days away, was announced on the last afternoon. Carr and Hobbs, as selectors, had to leave the field to take part in discussions. Rhodes, along with Hobbs one of the two professional players to be nominated as selectors, was otherwise engaged playing for Yorkshire against the Australians in Bradford. It might conceivably have reduced the northern influence in the discussions. George Macaulay, the Yorkshire fast-medium bowler who was in superb form and had been hotly tipped to be included, was omitted from a team that seemed designed not to lose. Warner was overheard saying that Macaulay had injured a thigh, but he did not miss any matches and had seven times taken five wickets in an innings by early June.

The side contained only three specialist bowlers in Root, Maurice Tate and Roy Kilner with seven batsmen, two of whom, Frank Woolley and Jack Hearne, could be counted as all-rounders, as indeed could Kilner and to a lesser extent Tate. Herbert Sutcliffe was doubtful having strained a thigh while batting in the North of England match, and his Yorkshire opening partner Percy Holmes was named as his replacement should he prove unfit. Carr was down in the batting list at number eight. The eleven entrusted with the first stage of reclaiming the Ashes was:

> Jack Hobbs, Herbert Sutcliffe*, Frank Woolley, Jack Hearne,
> Patsy Hendren, Percy Chapman, Roy Kilner, Arthur Carr
> (capt), Maurice Tate, Fred Root, Herbert Strudwick (wk).
> 12th man Andrew Sandham *Percy Holmes to play if unfit

Of the batsmen, only the amateur Chapman was in his twenties and four of them were over 35. One who might have broken into this inner sanctum could not be considered. Wally Hammond, not quite 23, lay gravely ill in a Bristol nursing home having contracted a serious, unidentified disease, apparently following a mosquito bite on MCC's tour of West Indies earlier in the year. Hammond needed 12 operations. The season of 1925 when he scored 1,818 runs had seen him start to fulfil his vast promise, and he had embellished that on the Caribbean trip with another 732. But he had arrived home looking like a ghost, had shed weight alarmingly and the question was not whether he would recover in time to make the 1926 Test team but whether he would recover at all. The suspicion has grown over the years, given all but irrefutable credence in David Foot's meticulously researched biography, that he had contracted a sexually transmitted disease in the West Indies.

It was the last Ashes series for 25 years not to feature either Hammond or Donald Bradman – with both playing in the next seven series, up to 1946/47. On the first day of the Trent Bridge Test, while Hammond remained seriously ill, the 17-year-old Bradman was finishing a match for his hometown club of Bowral against Moss Vale in the final of the Tom Mack Cup which they won by an innings and 338 runs. To be played to a finish, the match had taken place over five weekends and across the first three of them Bradman had compiled a score of 300 in his side's 672 for nine. Weeks later he was invited to the New South Wales nets.

England's preferred eleven was, as Aubrey Faulkner said in the *Westminster Gazette*, a team without risk. But was it capable of taking 20 wickets to win a Test match? Faulkner was one of the contingent of newspaper cricket writers who were ensuring that they not only reflected public interest in the series but fuelled it. Like many of the others he was himself a former cricketer, a redoubtable all-rounder who, a century on, can still lay claim to being the greatest produced by South Africa. Of the other ex-players, Warner was probably the most illustrious as a man who had captained England to an Ashes victory. But he had a significant Australian rival in Clem Hill, the leading run-scorer in Ashes history, also a former Test captain and the chairman of the Australian selectors. Hill was recruited by the *Daily Mirror* with appropriate hullaballoo. Two former captains and current chairmen of selectors, now in opposition as reporters on the series, promised to be an engrossing contrast in style and content.

The cast list also included Monty Noble, invariably called Alf, another former Australia captain, who was providing syndicated columns for a variety of regional papers. The *Daily Express* mischievously signed Charlie Kelleway, controversially omitted from the touring party, to supplement its respected reporter, William Pollock. *The Times* was represented by Arthur Croome, new to the cricket correspondent's job (though his articles were unsigned in line with the paper's policy of anonymity), and the *Daily Telegraph* by Colonel Philip Trevor. At *The Guardian* Neville Cardus was seven years into the job as its correspondent and had already begun the transformation of cricket writing into something approaching an art form. The middle-market papers tended to employ career reporters. Frank Thorogood at the *Daily News* had established a reputation for the cricket annual he edited for the paper. Robin Baily managed, by and large, to perform a delicate balancing act at the left-wing *Daily Herald*.

The popular Sunday papers, the *Weekly Dispatch*, *Reynolds's Illustrated News* and *The People* augmented their coverage with star columnists from the England team, Hobbs, Tate and Hendren respectively. They continued to appear despite an edict from the MCC committee in February that any selected player 'does not contribute a report or statement of any kind to the Press until the end of the season.' A fortnight before the First Test, Tate gave the selectors a nudge about who he would prefer to open the bowling with him for England: 'We should all rejoice over the form of Macaulay who has surely bowled himself into the position of a certainty for the First Test match.'

In addition to Hobbs, the heavy-hitting *Dispatch* was able to parade the poet Thomas Moult as a colourful match essayist and the former England cricketer BJT Bosanquet as an expert commentator. One of the most interesting and occasionally trenchant Sunday men was Frank Mitchell of the *Sunday Pictorial* who had played Test cricket for both England and South Africa, rugby union for England and had also won a Cambridge blue for putting the weight.

Most of them made haste to Nottingham. They were exercised by the fact that the teams were staying in the same hotel, the Victoria Station. If this was unusual, there was one aspect of the match which was unprecedented. The England players would use the same dressing room, the distinction between amateurs and professionals having been suspended at long last. It meant that Carr and Chapman would change with their team-mates and walk out onto the field from the same gate. The initiative had come from MCC at Warner's behest, with the crucial support of Lord Harris whose ubiquity was unchallenged, and the other grounds could only follow suit. It was not a change that yet applied to county matches. Maurice Tate said he was unconcerned by the 'snobbery side of the operation' but welcomed the change because it ought to improve the England team's effectiveness. 'Every little helps and we must use every little to help us to beat Australia. Clearly if the amateur captain and the other amateurs mix with the professionals in the dressing room they are thus provided with a greater number of opportunities for discussion.' Indeed, they would. It is a wonder that England had ever won a match under the old system.

On the morning of the match, Baily summed up the mood of a nation: 'None of the 109 Test matches played in the past by England and Australia has been awaited with such intense interest than the one that will begin half an hour before high noon at history-laden Trent Bridge.'

Australia announced their team:

> Herbie Collins (capt), Warren Bardsley, Charlie Macartney, Johnny Taylor, Tom Andrews, Bill Woodfull, Jack Ryder, Jack Gregory, Arthur Richardson, Bert Oldfield (wk), Arthur Mailey.

Like England's team it was long in batting and cricketing maturity. The 22 men who went out at Trent Bridge had a combined average age of 35.90, England's side marginally the older. Five players were over 40, nine over 35 and only two in their 20s. They remain the oldest two sides to have played in the same Test match. England would have been older still but Sutcliffe, 31 years and seven months, was declared fit, meaning that Holmes, 39 years and seven months, was not required.

First Day

If the phrase damp squib had not already been 400 years old it would have needed inventing for what took place. A damper squib can rarely have spluttered. Carr won the toss soon before 11.30am upon which it rained. It stopped around noon and after waiting for a mower to leave the outfield, the 1926 Ashes series finally began at 12.12pm. Hobbs and Sutcliffe came out to bat and Gregory opened the bowling for Australia as he had five years previously when it was clear from his first over that England faced huge trouble. There was no such peril this time, and Hobbs took a single from the fourth ball. Macartney shared the new ball with his left-arm spin, as if to emphasise that things were not what they used to be.

Although Macartney had opened the bowling for Australia in six Test matches between 1908 and 1911 (as spinners often did then), he had bowled only 11 overs in his seven Ashes matches since the war. The batsmen quickly settled, and in Macartney's first over Hobbs hit a no ball for four. Sutcliffe cover drove Gregory for four in the bowler's fourth over for his first boundary and the pair scampered singles, as they always did. There was a minor alarm when Hobbs only just made his ground in completing one of them. At 12.58pm, 46 minutes into the match, it rained again and off they went.

To coincide with the opening day, disappointing as it was, the Ashes themselves were on display in their little terracotta urn. Not at the match, however, but at Westminster in an exhibition of decorative art opened by the Duchess of Buccleuch. They had been loaned by Lord Darnley who, as Ivo Bligh, captain of the 1882/83 team to Australia, had been presented with the trophy in an amusing gesture by a group of Melbourne women. The urn and its ashes had since stood on his lordship's mantelpiece in Kent. It took a little while for them to become the symbol of the contests between England and Australia and for the mystical name to be conferred. It is not really known what the Ashes in the urn comprise, though a burned bail is usually preferred in most imaginations. In reporting the Westminster exhibition, *The People* offered a more prosaic suggestion. The Melbourne ladies 'bought a little urn and filled it with ordinary ashes from the hearth and presented it to Mr Bligh.'

Nottingham was packed to the rafters, and all hotel rooms had been booked long ago. As much doubtless as he would have liked to be occupying one of them, Stanley Baldwin was in Chippenham attending to problems beyond the recapture of the Ashes. He delivered another of his deceptively rousing, well-crafted speeches in which he referred to the alien heresy besetting the British labour movement. 'We will do our utmost to instil hope and faith in the future,' he said, 'and to create a real brotherhood in the minds of employers and employees alike. One of the tragedies of the present time is that owing to the events through which we are passing, the purchasing power of the nation is being diminished daily.'

Late in the afternoon at Trent Bridge, the rain cleared and although Carr tried to persuade Collins that conditions were playable the Australian captain stood his ground. The captains being unable to agree, the umpires, Robert Burrows and Frank Chester, were summoned and immediately signalled the end of play for the day.

Close: England 32-0 (Hobbs 19, Sutcliffe 13)

From such slender pickings all the newspapers managed to make the Test their main story on Sunday morning. The Prime Minister's speech on the future of the country had second billing.

It was gloriously sunny on Sunday, the rest day, and the Australians visited the Duke and Duchess of Portland at Welbeck Abbey. The tourists were uplifted when walking through the house to see a portrait of the racehorse Carbine, one of the greatest of Australia's sporting heroes. Carbine won the Melbourne Cup carrying a record weight and prevailed in 33 of his 43 starts before becoming equally successful at stud. There was hardly an Australian alive at that time who had not heard of Carbine. The Duke of Portland bought the horse and imported him to England where he continued his successful career as a sire of champions.

Having been thus invigorated, the party were denied the opportunity to let it be reflected in their cricket. It rained all day on Monday, and on Tuesday, the third and final scheduled day, the match was quickly abandoned. The commentators started to grumble about the absurdity of trying to finish Test matches in three days, and almost everyone agreed with them. Except for many administrators associated with the county clubs, that is. Extended Test matches would impinge on the Championship programme and deprive several clubs of their best players for longer.

No-one was more strident than Sydney Smith. 'If your cricket rulers don't agree to play out the next series of Tests after the farcical business at Trent Bridge – well I shall be surprised,' he said. 'There is only one thing standing in the way, the claims of the counties. Up till now the counties have been narrow-minded. They must learn to think imperially instead of locally and set aside six days, Saturday to Friday for each Test. After all these Tests are the biggest things in cricket and they should be done in a big way. At present they are ruined.'

He was only warming to his theme. Australia were clearly miffed because they thought England were guilty of sharp practice. 'Several things have irritated Australia,' Smith said. 'For one thing your policy of keeping your bowlers secretly for the Test, the policy of having "mystery men", the policy of diplomatic colds. You may say you were merely trying new men and not hiding the others. It comes to the same thing. We did not play the real South of England, nor the real North. The star bowlers were missing. Why should we come all these thousands of miles to play half-finished games? That is the point. Can you wonder that out in Australia they are exasperated into saying that unless the matches are played to a finish – which means six-days games – it is not worthwhile arranging a tour.'

Strong words with which it was difficult to disagree. In the absence of much cricket to report, thoughts soon turned to the next Test. Hobbs, in his Sunday column, waxed lyrical about 21-year-old Harold Larwood. The great batsman had already been dismissed three times in the season by the tyro fast bowler, for 16, 6 and 2, twice bowled, once caught behind. 'He has come into his kingdom early.' How early would be known soon enough.

Jack Hearne

England

Right-hand bat, leg-break bowler

Born: 11.2.1891 Hillingdon, Middlesex
Age on 1.5.26: **35**
County: Middlesex

Record at start of 1926

Tests: 23, debut 1911/12
806 runs @ 26.00, HS 114
30 wickets @ 48.73, BB 5-49

F/c matches: 378, debut 1909
22,840 runs @ 43.09, HS 234*
1,286 wickets @ 22.89, BB 9-82

On New Year's Day 1912 in Melbourne, Jack Hearne scored his maiden Test century. At 20 years 324 days he was the youngest England player to do so until Denis Compton, who was 20 years 19 days when he made 102 at Nottingham in 1938. It could, perhaps should, have heralded the start of a stellar international career for Hearne. This never quite transpired and that innings in an eight-wicket England victory, which levelled the series and set them on the way to a thumping series win, remained his only Test hundred.

Hearne was thought of highly enough to be chosen for three Ashes tours, and his compact batting style was buttressed by his profitable if erratic leg spin. Joe Murrell, who kept to him for many years at Middlesex, said: 'You can have 'em all, here and overseas. When he was pitching the leg-break "Nutty" Hearne was away on his own.' The difference in his averages for Test and first-class cricket for once tell a story. In Tests he averaged in the mid-twenties with the bat and high forties with the ball; in first-class matches it was almost the reverse, early forties with the bat, mid-twenties with the ball.

His cause was hindered by poor health. On the 1920/21 Ashes tour, for example, he was laid low by lumbago during the Second Test and took no further part in the tour. In 1926 he was chosen for the First Test because of the lingering doubts over the side's batting – the team included eight batsmen of whom three were all-rounders – but the match was restricted to 47 minutes in which Hearne took no part and he fell ill soon afterwards. He missed 10 Middlesex matches, and the selectors dared not risk him again. Hearne was overtaken in the panel's thinking by his amateur Middlesex colleague Greville Stevens.

Throughout his long career, Hearne was known as Young Jack Hearne – and often described as such in newspaper reports – to distinguish him from Old Jack Hearne. The pair who might or might not have been distant cousins both played for Middlesex, overlapping for six years from 1909 until the outbreak of war.

Harold Larwood

England

Fast bowler

Born: 14.11.1904 Nuncargate, Notts
Age on 1.5.26: **21**
County: Nottinghamshire

Record at start of 1926

Tests: 0

F/c matches: 21, debut 1924
361 runs @ 24.06, HS: 70
74 wickets @ 18.72, BB 6-17

Like many fast bowlers, Harold Larwood's rise was meteoric. One minute he was down the pit, the next on the Nottinghamshire ground staff, then in the county eleven and before you knew it in the England team at Lord's. He was 21 years, 224 days old when he made his Test debut on 26 June 1926, and his first Test wicket was one of the greatest batsman of all, Charlie Macartney, who edged Larwood to slip, undone by the pace and fierce bounce.

Larwood owed his rapid ascent to sheer talent, explosive pace which raised more eyebrows for being delivered from such a small frame (he was just above 5ft 7ins) and careful, shrewd handling by his Nottinghamshire captain, Arthur Carr. Perhaps Larwood was fortunate to have Carr, also England captain, championing his cause in the selection committee, but Carr knew whereof he spoke since the lad had taken 73 wickets in 1925. Larwood himself put it thus: 'It is a very big thing for a fast bowler to feel quite sure that his captain will never bowl him to death and that even if it is a losing match, he will not keep him on an over too long. Also, it is a most heartening feeling to have, that if one feels a bit off-colour one could go to the captain and say so without being suspected of shirking one's job. From the first day I bowled under his orders Mr Carr has been most thoughtful on my behalf. I have never made a suggestion to him on the field to have it turned down without a thought.'

The mutual respect and admiration between the pair were evident from the start of Larwood's career, when Carr had already been on the county circuit for years. In a way they helped to change each other. Carr's admiration was boundless: 'He was born with a natural talent not given to one bowler in ten thousand, his command of a cricket ball is extraordinary, his accuracy amazing.' Carr recalled the boy's unworldliness when he first went to play for Notts in London (against Surrey in August 1925). In the vestibule of a London hotel, 'having viewed the passing pageant of life for some time in astonishment, he turned to another Notts player and asked, in his youthful innocence of the ways of this wicked world: "Are *all* these women for hire?"'

It was Carr who introduced Larwood to beer. Whatever his other virtues as a captain he had formed the idea, which he breezily promulgated, that: 'All really fast bowlers need beer to help keep them going. You cannot be a great fast bowler on a bottle of ginger-pop or a nice glass of cold water.' Thus was Larwood assisted in the honing of his craft.

Carr, Pelham Warner and the other men charged with choosing a team to recover the Ashes probably recognised that they needed something beyond even the highly skilled, metronomic reliability of Maurice Tate and George Geary to put doubt into Australian minds. Fred Root's leg theory was the option they initially alighted on. Larwood bowled with real fire in the match for the North against Australia, but Root's spectacular figures rather relegated him. Another selection panel at another time would have summoned Larwood immediately. The damage that could have been done by his pace, allied to the control of Tate and one of the others, seems obvious in retrospect. Larwood was the fastest bowler around – in the series and in England generally. But he needed the pitches, too, and the right weather, and Warner, who knew cricketers, also felt that he must not be overworked. They erred on the side of caution – omitting Larwood from the Third and Fourth Tests despite his steady contribution at Lord's – until their hand was forced for the deciding match.

Plenty happened to Larwood in subsequent years, much of it beyond his control, but in that riveting 1926 series he was the new kid on the block, the fresh hope. He remains the embodiment of the absurd image of how to find a truly fast bowler in England in a certain era: shout down a pit and one will emerge into the light. (Launching a search in an Amazon warehouse does not have quite the same resonance). That is essentially what happened to a lad who was brought up in Nuncargate, a Nottinghamshire pit village, was a pit pony boy at 14 and working the night shift hewing coal in an underground tunnel about three feet high when he was 17. When he was 19, Larwood walked five miles from his home to the nearest station, another two miles from the station in Nottingham to Trent Bridge and then bowled in a trial net where they could not believe that this scrawny kid could bowl at all, let alone like the speed of light.

Charlie Macartney

Australia

Right-hand bat, slow left-arm bowler

Born: 27.6.1886 West Maitland, New South Wales
Age on 1.5.26: **39**
State: New South Wales

Record at start of 1926

Tests: 30, debut 1907/08
1,658 runs @ 36.04, HS 170
41 wickets @ 25.00, BB 7-58

F/c matches: 207, debut 1905/06
12,879 runs @ 46.16, HS 345
327 wickets @ 21.85, BB 7-58

The wonder of Charlie Macartney in 1926 was not that he was batting with such utter magnificence but that he was batting at all. Macartney's life and career, like so many others, was torn asunder by the war. He joined up in 1915, was sent to France in 1916, served with the 3rd Division Artillery and in June 1918 was awarded the meritorious medal for gallantry under enemy fire. The listing merely said: 'No. 18380 Warrant Officer, Class I.3 C. G. Macartney, Artillery.'

Between bombardments Macartney made occasional visits to England to play cricket, although he missed the AIF Tour in 1919 because he wanted to go home after the death of his father. By then his experiences in the battlefields of northern France had altered his life and his outlook. Never an outgoing man off the field, he became brooding and introspective. He missed some cricket in the early 1920s, and in late 1924 he suffered a nervous breakdown. Neither the condition nor its probable genesis was spoken of much at the time.

Macartney was himself deliberately but understandably evasive on the subject. He barely touched on it in his cricketing memoirs. 'The English team under the captaincy of AER Gilligan came to Australia in October 1924, but owing to a severe illness I was unable to appear against them after the first match with New South Wales in November. Evidently, this illness had been on me for some considerable time, as I had no desire to play cricket ... and my doctor told me I had to drop out.' He excused his absence by saying he had a septic ulcer on his leg. But he still gave a hint that all was not well. 'It is impossible to play cricket successfully unless one's mind is on the game. Once the mind gets tired, a complete rest is necessary.'

He did not play cricket for a year. Yet when he resumed he was simply marvellous. When he was on the cricket field, especially at the crease, it was as if the cares of the world, the woes inflicted by the war, were behind him. Macartney's career was divided by the conflict in another way. Before it, his batting too often flattered to deceive while his left-arm spin bowling ensured he was almost always sure of his place.

But he made an early impression which never faded. Alf Noble, shortly to become Australia captain, first saw him in a coaching session at Macartney's school. 'There was nothing to distinguish him from hundreds of other boy cricketers except there was an extraordinary air of confidence about him, rarely developed in one so young.' Having seen him bowl – 'he tossed up a slow which turned about six inches from leg and shattered my stumps' – and then bat – 'his strokes were made with a confident audacity all round the wicket and there was an artistry even in his immaturity' – Noble concluded that Charlie 'was the greatest schoolboy cricketer I have ever seen.' His judgement was proved to be correct a thousand times over.

Macartney had a bearing that set him apart, a noticeable self-belief which was also spotted by the England batsman, Ken Hutchings, on England's 1907/08 tour to Australia. Having seen the way he carried himself on the field, especially when batting, Hutchings called him the Governor-General. The name stuck for the rest of Macartney's career but did not become truly apposite until the 1920s.

Macartney played in 21 Tests before the war, had 34 innings, averaged 26.64, scoring one century, at the 25th attempt, and took 34 wickets at 26.0, including 11-85 in the 1909 Test at Headingley (how he liked Headingley). When he began playing Test cricket again in 1920 after a gap of eight years, he appeared in another 14 matches, averaged 69.56 with six more hundreds but took only 11 more wickets at 32.36. He opened the bowling in nine of his 35 Tests, four in 1909. Sparingly used when Jack Gregory and Ted McDonald were in their pomp in the early 1920s, he was needed again by 1926, when McDonald had made his exit, and took the new ball in the first three Tests. His spinners were quick through the air, and in helpful conditions they turned significantly.

But it was his batting that placed Charlie Macartney on another plane. He knew how good he was and liked to recount the story of his wife overhearing a conversation between two schoolboys. One of them asked: 'Why do they call Mac the Governor-General?' and the other replied: 'Because he's so cocky.'

Macartney believed it was his duty to show the bowler who was the boss, the Governor-General if you like. Never was Charlie more dangerous than when he was dropped early in an innings, for he took that to mean it was his day and that he should exact a full toll – witness Trent Bridge in 1921 against Nottinghamshire when he escaped on nine and made the fastest 300 then seen, and the Headingley Test in 1926 when he was put down by Arthur Carr on two and proceeded to a century before lunch in an unforgettable exhibition.

As with all properly great batsmen, it was not that Macartney scored quickly or that he put the most skilful bowlers in his pocket, it was that he made it all look so darned easy. There was a casual grace to his plundering of attacks, a certainty that it would happen. He had a wonderful career, and in a series notable for the outstanding performances of senior players the exploits of the 40-year-old Macartney in 1926 crowned it.

Herbert Strudwick

England

Wicket-keeper

Born: 28.1.1880 Mitcham, Surrey
Age on 1.5.26: **46**
County: Surrey

Record at start of 1926

Tests: 23, debut 1910
223 runs @ 8.25, HS: 24
55 catches, 12 stumpings

F/c matches: 617, debut 1902
6,102 runs @ 10.87, HS: 93
1,155 catches, 243 stumpings

Bert Strudwick was in at the beginning of a debate that continues still and will probably never end. Indeed, he might have been its catalyst. Struddy was a magnificent wicketkeeper, but he had trouble distinguishing one end of the bat from the other. The concept of a wicketkeeper who could bat a bit was not quite novel. Dick Lilley, Strudwick's regular predecessor as England's wicketkeeper, had Test and first-class batting averages above 20, scored 16 hundreds and was generally considered to be the best behind the stumps as well. But there were not many like him. Generally, the keeper kept and that was that.

In 1926, as the country fretted constantly about regaining the Ashes, Struddy's inability to score runs became of growing concern. To strengthen a potentially fragile batting order it was regularly suggested that England needed a wicketkeeper/batsman rather than a wicketkeeper/passenger. When Strudwick had a poor game behind the stumps in the Second Test, putting down a string of chances and being untypically untidy, there were suggestions that the time had come. But the selectors held their nerve then, backing his undoubted class with the gloves and cheerful presence in the dressing room. Finally with the decisive Fifth Test looming, their patience gave way and they summoned George Brown of Hampshire, as they had done five years earlier when Australia were plundering the English at will, and who was now in the form of his life. As we shall see, however, Struddy was not quite yet done.

He was practically born to wicketkeeping. As he himself told it, he was 10 years old and practising with Mitcham Church Choirboys when Miss Wilson, a daughter of the Vicar of Mitcham who was supervising the lads, spotted his predilection for running into the stumps from cover to take the ball at the bowler's end when it was thrown from elsewhere in the field. She suggested, given his safe hands, that he should take up wicketkeeping, and that was that. He was first invited for a Surrey trial when he was 16 and recalled years later that having been asked to bring everything with him he consulted his non-cricketing father about what everything should mean. Young Bert pitched up at The Oval not only with pads and gloves but bat, stumps and bails. Initially rejected, he was eventually taken on two years later when he had grown a little.

His first-class debut was in 1902 in an early-season encounter at Crystal Palace against London County, the short-lived *ad hoc* team led by WG Grace. Strudwick acquitted himself well enough behind the stumps but was out twice for nought. Bowled by Grace himself in the second innings, the great man told the youngster that he would have given him one for off the mark had he realised the boy was on a pair. Strudwick barely heard him, for he was off to watch the replayed FA Cup Final between Southampton and Sheffield United which was being played that afternoon on the other side of Crystal Palace. (Surrey lost by 196 runs and Sheffield United won 2-1.)

By 1903 Strudwick had made the wicketkeeper's spot his own, taking over, slightly to his discomfiture, from Fred Stedman, who many judged to be the better keeper. They were probably wrong because that season Struddy broke the record for the number of victims in a season with 93 and was selected as second keeper in the MCC party to tour Australia under Pelham Warner. He did not play in any of the five matches in the series, and Lilley's presence meant he had to wait for another seven years and 24 Tests before making his debut in South Africa on New Year's Day 1910, four weeks short of his 30th birthday.

Like so many others he would have played more cricket but for the intervention of the First World War, but he was lucky to have a career either side of the conflict. When cricket resumed so did Struddy, and he was then England's first choice.

On uncovered pitches that were invariably untrustworthy after rain he stood up to most bowling. He had perfected his method long ago by persuading his brother one winter to throw him balls as hard as he could either side of the wicket. Usually he was without pads. He never paid similar attention to his batting which probably explained a career average of 10.88 and a highest score of 93. But bowlers trusted him, and Maurice Tate, for one, refers often to his brilliant catches down the leg side.

Strudwick was Jack Hobbs' best friend in cricket. They roomed together on tour and usually joined the rest of the team after travelling overland to Marseilles. For a while, Hobbs lived in a house owned by Strudwick. Bert and Jack were long-term golfing partners; it was Struddy who introduced Hobbs to the game on the MCC tour of South Africa in 1913/14 when they had to dash from the course at Port Elizabeth because of an impending storm.

Strudwick's record of victims stood for almost 50 years. He was also almost certainly the first cricketer to appear on television and to be seen in two places at once. In an experiment conducted at the Baird Television Company six images of Struddy were seen on a screen in the room next door as he played shots and scored runs. There were, of course, several reasons for not believing what they were seeing.

Bert Oldfield

Australia

Wicket-keeper

Born: 9.9.1894 Alexandria, New South Wales
Age on 1.5.26: **31**
State: New South Wales

Record at start of 1926

Tests: 10, debut 1920/21
428 runs @ 32.92, HS 65*
13 catches, 14 stumpings

F/c matches: 48, debut 1919
2,540 runs @ 26.456, HS 129
161 catches, 109 stumpings

The art of stumping was taken to new heights by Bert Oldfield. His record of 52 victims in Test matches has never come close to being overtaken in getting on for a century. He stumped at least one batsman in 30 of his 54 Tests, in addition to taking 78 catches. Oldfield was a model of neatness, precision and speed. His chief collaborator in the enterprise was Clarrie Grimmett, on whose behalf he made 28 stumpings. There has never been a more frequent scoreboard line in Tests for this particular mode of dismissal than 'stumped Oldfield, bowled Grimmett.' In 37 matches together they hunted as a pair.

Oldfield was also a member of that brigade of keepers who did not assume that stentorian demands were the way to persuade umpires to support their cause. If he was not exactly making a polite inquiry, nor was he attempting to bark orders. This was part of the natural character of a quiet, dapper chap. He was fortunate to be there at all. Serving with the 15th Field Ambulance in France during the Great War he was caught in the bombardment in the Battle of Polygon Wood in September 1917 when a shell exploded. Three of his mates died, but Oldfield was found several hours after the attack, semi-conscious and partly buried. Having somehow survived, albeit with shell shock, he was invalided to England and shortly afterwards took his place in the great Australian Imperial Forces team which began the period of the country's dominance over England on their tour in the summer of 1919. Oldfield had played only club cricket at home before the war, meaning, unusually, that he made his first-class debut in England. But he quickly made an unexpected mark with the AIF team, and a cricket career was born.

After only one Sheffield Shield match back home in December 1920 he was selected two weeks later for his Test debut in the country's first international match for eight years. He did not quite make the place his own with the pre-war keeper Sammy Carter soon winning selectorial favour again. But by the time of the 1924/25 series Oldfield was the undisputed first choice, and by 1926 he was vying with the English wicketkeeper, the other Bert, Strudwick, to be considered the best wicketkeeper in the world and often winning the debate.

This long-awaited series did not go according to plan, either for Oldfield or for Australia. The spinners on whom he depended so much for his living were kept quiet in frequently wet conditions, and accordingly he could offer neither Grimmett nor Arthur Mailey the assistance to which they had become accustomed. That Gregory was playing while injured, making his contribution negligible, further reduced Oldfield's ability to influence events.

Oldfield was among the first wicketkeepers – along with Strudwick – to recognise that the job needed specific preparation. He eschewed the steaks-in-the-gloves favoured by previous custodians and instead had a rigorous regime of taping his finger joints to which he then applied stalls and wore two pairs of chamois leather inner gloves.

Two pieces of Oldfield's handiwork have frequently been called as evidence when assessing his greatness. Both involved Jack Hobbs in the 1924/25 Ashes series, one a stumping, the other a catch. In the Fourth Test Hobbs had reached 66 in an opening partnership of 126 with Herbert Sutcliffe when Jack Ryder, bowling at fast-medium, sent one down the leg side which Hobbs failed to reach. 'I swear I wasn't out of my crease more than a split second,' Hobbs recalled. 'The bails were off and I knew what the answer would be to the confident How's That.' In the next match Hobbs was out to the fourth ball from Gregory, 'I was perfectly happy gliding that leg side ball. I was off the mark as every batsman yearns to be. This was my relieved thought. I was all wrong. Bert Oldfield made some five or six yards of ground, and going towards square-leg like a hare, or a kangaroo on the leap, he took the ball with an outstretched hand.' Forgiving the excesses of Jack's ghost-writer, you can still form a picture of the threat Oldfield posed.

Oldfield stayed awhile in England after the 1926 series and did not leave until late November. He was mixing in rarefied circles by then. At one reception he was introduced to the Duke of York – the future George VI – who said: 'My brother tells me he was nearly killed with hospitality when he was out in your country. I trust they will be more merciful to the Duchess and myself.' At which point the Duke's brother, the Prince of Wales and future Edward VIII, pitched up and said: 'I wish I was going to Australia again with my brother.' Bert Oldfield had come a long way from Polygon Wood.

Patsy Hendren

England

Right-hand bat

Born: 5.2.1889 Turnham Green, Middlesex
Age on 1.5.26: **37**
County: Middlesex

Record at start of 1926

Tests: 17, debut 1920
1,048 runs @ 41.92, HS 142
1 wicket @ 27.00, BB 1-27

F/c matches: 379, debut 1907
24,018 runs @ 47.09, HS 277
40 wickets @ 51.17, BB 5-43

For a batsman of such prodigious gifts and achievement Patsy Hendren took his time to get going. He did not score his maiden first-class hundred until his 90th innings in his sixth season. The delay until his maiden Test century was less protracted but involved a severe mauling at Australian hands before he finally made it at the 17th attempt. Many careers have foundered on that sort of procrastination.

The difference between his early and late careers is marked. He made his Middlesex debut at the age of 18 in 1907, and in the eight seasons between then and the start of the First World War in 1914 he scored 5,636 runs in 225 innings at an average of 27.49 with six hundreds. Ho-hum might have been a considered verdict. For the purposes of symmetrical comparison his next 225 innings between 1919, when cricket resumed, and July 1923 yielded 11,387 runs at 59.93 with 37 hundreds (and 38 fifties). Wow might have served as a reasonable reaction.

There was much more to come. As there was much more to Hendren than being a statistical colossus. He was the clown prince of cricket. It was not simply that he played with a smile on his face, he carried others along with him so that they too, team-mates and supporters alike, had fun playing and watching. He was an inveterate practical joker whose stunts were the more amusing for having the air of spontaneity.

In a match at Geelong on the 1920/21 England tour of Australia, he had to chase a ball to the boundary from deep third man. He bent, seemed to pick it up, and threw it in whereupon it burst – for it was an apple – much to the amusement of crowd and team-mates but to the evident displeasure of the captain for the match, the Yorkshire amateur Rockley Wilson.

A favourite Hendren trick which never seemed to pall was to play the ball down in front of him, pretend to dash down the pitch for a quick run and having taken two steps, dash back into the crease with an innocent look on his face.

It was the physog that did it. Patsy Hendren had a face that launched a thousand quips. It was round and cheerful with a long upper lip and harboured harmless mischief, giving him the look of a beardless leprechaun, a throwback to his Irish roots. He was deadly serious about his cricket and his football, as a professional career of 30 seasons in one and 20 in the other amply demonstrated, but he played them with a lightness of heart that belied his background.

Hendren had a poor but loving childhood in Brentford where his parents had emigrated from Ireland a year or two before his birth. His given names were Elias Henry, but he swiftly became known as Pat because of his Irishness. By the age of 14 he was an orphan, and his brother Denis, seven years older, took on responsibility for the household. The boys had learned both cricket and football by playing street games near home. Patsy followed his brother in joining the Turnham Green club, and there he was initially discovered as a prospect.

Perhaps he was in the right place at the right time. He met WG Grace at Turnham Green, was spotted by the pioneering cricket photographer George Beldam who visited one day, was interviewed at Lord's by the great wicketkeeper Gregor MacGregor, the Middlesex captain, who took a liking to him and when he needed a champion after early setbacks found one in Plum Warner, MacGregor's successor.

Hendren was fond of pointing out that he had received no coaching as a cricketer, and while he clearly absorbed much from watching others, that might have explained his unorthodoxy. It took him a while, but eventually he came to know when and what strokes to play. He probably made more cross-batted shots than most, and his fearsome hooking from in front of his eyebrows became a trademark. But he was also a forerunner of the powerful slash from outside leg stump through the covers aided by quick hands and strong wrists. His defensive mode also depended on a little bit of improvisation, compensating for the shortness of his legs in getting forward by having arms stretched far out in front of him.

By the time he fully established himself in the 1920s he was Murph to his team-mates but always Patsy to the press and an adoring public. He was not alone in disintegrating before the unprecedented pace of Jack Gregory and Ted McDonald in 1921, but it was a torrid period as he made scores of 0, 7, 0 and 10, bowled in the first three. He was dropped for the rest of the series, but the weight of his batting for Middlesex ensured he was eventually recalled.

In 1923 Hendren scored more than 3,000 runs for the first time which included 13 hundreds. In 1925 he played the leading role in one of the greatest run chases of all time. Middlesex, set 502 to win by Nottinghamshire captain Arthur Carr, fell to 66-4. But Patsy stayed, finished on 206 not out, shared an unbroken 271 for the seventh wicket with Frank Mann, and Middlesex won by four wickets.

Hendren was a great run-scorer and a greater character, 'the man, beyond his actual prowess, who evoked some special response in all who knew him.'

Warren Bardsley

Australia

Left-hand bat

Born: 7.12.1882 Warren, New South Wales
Age on 1.5.26: **43**
State: New South Wales

Record at start of 1926

Tests: 36, debut 1909
2,238 runs @ 39.26, HS 164

F/c matches: 222, debut 1903/04
15,600 runs @ 50.32, HS 264

When a biography of Warren Bardsley was finally published, 67 years after his death, it was called *The First Mr Cricket*. He trained harder and longer than his team-mates, he was usually first to the ground and frequently last to leave. He was besotted with the game. If his preparation was meticulous, his way of life was equally fastidious: he was a non-smoking, vegetarian teetotaller. His one concession to letting the good times roll was that he played the saxophone.

In 1912 most of Australia's leading players refused to make the tour of England because of a pay-and-conditions dispute with the board. Bardsley joined the party. He may have been ambivalent about the row, but the simple truth was that he could not bear not to play. He made four Ashes tours in all, starting in 1909 when he became the first player to score two hundreds in a match. Only eight players have since performed the feat in an Ashes Test.

The figures show that he was more reliable abroad than at home: 1,368 runs at 45.6, compared to 1,101 at 35.52. Charlie Macartney who knew him better than most and played with him in 94 first-class matches, said: 'I really think that Warren was a far better player in England than in Australia. He certainly exhibited a larger variety of strokes in the Old Country than out here, and I have often remarked that the Australian public has never seen him at his very best.' But between 1909 and 1926 he was usually selected, appearing in 41 of his country's 44 Test matches. And his overall first-class record was formidable, containing 53 centuries, a record number until Donald Bradman came along and surpassed that figure and a few others.

Bardsley was named after Warren, the tiny New South Wales town, 300 miles north west of Sydney, where he was born. To his mates, from an early age, he was usually Curly. He was not a cricketer truly formed in the outback because the family moved to Glebe, a small town three miles from Sydney, a year later.

At Forest Lodge Superior Public School, where his father William taught for 40 years, Warren developed the diligence and dedication which were the hallmarks of his career.

He was a left-handed batsman in an era when they were still much the exception. The only left-handers to have had substantial Test careers before him were Joe Darling and Clem Hill. Bardsley was as upright at the crease as his bat was straight, with a powerful drive and the alertness to move back and force the ball off his legs. His ability to flourish in England was, it was suggested, born of his days as a boy practising on the damp, early morning grass at Forest Lodge.

He started playing in the Sydney First Grade competition when he was 17, made his first-class debut for New South Wales when he was 21, nudged the selectors with 108 against the touring MCC in early 1908 and finally persuaded them to choose him for the party to tour England in 1909 with three centuries in six innings, topped by his career best 264 in a trial match for an Australia XI against the Rest of Australia. Australia defied the odds of a wet summer to beat England, and in the final Test, the Ashes if not the rubber secure, Bardsley made his imperishable entry into the record books with scores of 136 and 130. In none of the previous 104 Test matches had a batsman made centuries in each innings.

Although he subsequently scored two Test hundreds against South Africa (and one of those was in England in the 1912 Triangular series), Bardsley had to wait 17 years and 34 innings to repeat the feat in an Ashes match. A few seconds of film survive of his great unbeaten innings of 193 at Lord's. There is not much: a square-cut and running a couple of singles. Cricket historian and archivist David Frith who unearthed the footage said: 'They caught it just in time to save that square-cut. No matter how well someone describes something, you see the reality on film. That's the truth.' Bardsley presented the bat he used in the innings to Cornelius King, a page-boy at the Hotel Cecil where the team were staying.

Bardsley courted unpopularity at home when he did not enlist in the Australian forces during the First World War as did so many of his colleagues. It is posited as a reason for his not being considered as Australia's captain in the 1920s. Herbie Collins staked his claim in the Australian Imperial Forces tour in 1919, and he had also done the hard military yards in France.

As it turned out, Bardsley was to get his shot at the leadership when Herbie Collins suddenly fell ill. Thus, in quick succession he became the oldest Australian player to make a hundred and to captain the team: those are two records of his that remain unbroken.

Bardsley was not married until the age of 62 in 1945. Cricket had long been his mistress, and he continued playing club cricket until his fifties. He was briefly the national selector before the Second World War. It took almost a century for another Mr Cricket to come along in Mike Hussey, another left-handed batsman. But Warren Bardsley was the original.

7

FEAST OF RUNS AT LORD'S

The President informed White that the committee had seriously considered the question of dismissal and that in deciding to take a more lenient view they had, to a large extent, been influenced by the good account of his work generally.

MCC Committee minutes, July 1926
(considering the behaviour of the Lord's groundsman)

Ackroyd was sitting as I had left him in the armchair before the fire. His head had fallen sideways, and clearly visible, just below the collar of his coat, was a shining piece of twisted metalwork.

Dr James Sheppard
(The Murder of Roger Ackroyd, June 1926)

Amid the deprivation and the travails of 1926, popular culture exerted a welcome, distracting grip. It was not left to the Ashes alone to provide succour. The BBC began playing a wide range of music including jazz, as if recognising that it was indeed the Jazz Age (though the closest real live jazz got to the UK at the time was probably Jack Hylton and His Orchestra). When the Australians were departing Sheffield after another frustratingly rain-stricken match against Yorkshire they arrived at the station to find their train was delayed. The team unpacked their portable gramophone in the waiting room and sang along to the records. They included the year's biggest hit, *Valencia* by Paul Whiteman's orchestra (Hylton was the British version of Whiteman) and *It's a Long Way to Tipperary* 'with its memories of days that will never be forgotten,' said the *Sheffield Independent* which reported the impromptu concert.

The wireless was at the start of its long love affair with the British public, and for the next 25 years or so would have its exclusive attention. Plans were unveiled to build seven new transmitters dotted round the country. A night out at the pictures was also increasingly a favourite entertainment of the masses. Talkies were a year away, but this was the height of the silent cinema: huge purpose-built emporia, some with seating for 2,000, were going up in cities and large towns around the country. It was the first golden age of the film star. The biggest was Rudolf Valentino, though Douglas Fairbanks, Lon Chaney, Mary Pickford, Lillian Gish and the Englishman Charlie Chaplin were not far behind. Another Englishman, Ronald Colman, was also hugely popular and appeared in one of the year's highest grossing films, *Beau Geste*. Colman, the epitome of the suave English gent, was among a coterie of acting expatriates who played for the Hollywood Cricket Club and transferred his skills to the screen when he starred as Raffles, the gentleman thief (or 'amateur cracksman' to give him his official sobriquet, which makes him sound much more of a toff), who also played cricket for England. The cricket scene in the film is a forerunner of astonishingly unsuccessful attempts to portray cricket in the movies. The founder of the Hollywood Cricket Club actually did play cricket for England. C. Aubrey Smith appeared in what became the inaugural Test between England and South Africa in 1889 (though no-one knew at the time that it was a Test) long before going to Hollywood.

Among the films released for general distribution in late June 1926 was one simply called *The First Test Match*. It was a 1,200ft short – about 14 minutes running time – on the Nottingham match, which itself had lasted 46 minutes. The producer, Claude Soman, must have rued the day he set up his cameras. The documentary, however, was well received. The cinema magazine, *The Bioscope*, said it was 'a sparkling and very enjoyable little film of a dull and disappointing event'. Sadly, there are no copies in existence, for it included some slow-motion shots of Jack Gregory's bowling action as well as showing the players behind the scenes.

'There are also one or two humorous touches,' said the reviewer. 'One in particular, that of some ducks playing in a pool on the ground, which follows the subtitle "The Third Day's Play", is sure of a laugh.' Claude Soman was not quite finished with cricket. Four years later he wrote and produced a film called *Ashes*. It was not about the 1930 series but, according to the *British Film Institute*, a futuristic story about a slow-moving cricket match that begins in 1940 and finally finishes in 2000. It featured as 'a cricketer' Dar Lyon, the Somerset wicketkeeper.

Horseshoe Collins and his team finally escaped from the Sheffield waiting room and crossed the Pennines. No sooner had they arrived in Manchester than Collins was forced to defend the robust opinions of his manager Sydney Smith about the way England were running, or in his view ruining, the tour. Collins sounded as though he had been hung out to dry in what he referred to as 'the Smith Incident'. He suggested that everybody's motives had been misconstrued.

'Such things are regrettable, however, for they cast doubt on the sportsmanship of our team. Anybody who knows the spirit of our fellows knows how unfair that is. But we are guests of the home country and such reports have put us in a very difficult position. There is nobody more British than the Australians and you could not have a more sportsmanlike team than our fellows.'

The spat, confected as it was, soon receded when the cricket resumed. Smith and Collins probably suspected that anyone who might be able to do something about their grievances either did not care or was not listening. The tourists completed their preparations with two matches before the Second Test. A comfortable innings victory over Lancashire, who would be crowned as County Champions later in the season to end Yorkshire's run of four titles, contained a scintillating Macartney hundred and 11 wickets for Mailey. It seemed to have come at exactly the right time. A rain-shortened, two-day draw against Derbyshire at Chesterfield lasted long enough for the tourists to score 373 from 102 overs. They were running into form.

England were also beset by small, local difficulties. Wilfred Rhodes, appointed to the selection panel to general approval, was not being allowed free rein to do the job. Yorkshire, his employers, issued a statement to the effect that they were not standing in his way, which automatically suggested that they were. Rhodes had missed a couple of selection meetings when he was required to play and could not make the journey from Yorkshire to London in time. Plum Warner, chairman of selectors, sent a telegram to Fred Toone, Yorkshire's punctilious secretary, saying it would be valuable for Rhodes to be present at Test matches. Toone, whom Rhodes by then disliked intensely, replied publicly, saying that the Yorkshire committee did not want to do anything to hinder the selectors but considered that when a team had been selected Rhodes should continue searching for potential Test players. Essentially, of course, this meant not that he should be combing the highways and byways to visit various county matches but that he should be playing for Yorkshire and seeing if there were anyone in the opposition ranks who might fit the Test bill. It can only be speculated what Rhodes thought of this arrangement but when Toone was awarded a knighthood a few years later, he refused to send a note of congratulation.

In the event Rhodes was able to attend the meeting to discuss the England team for the Second Test, since Yorkshire were playing Middlesex at Lord's (he went wicketless in 31 overs). Given the curtailed nature of the Nottingham proceedings, it would have appeared straightforward to announce the same team. But there was a feeling abroad that the balance of the side was not quite right which probably explained why their discussions lasted for three hours. Somehow room had to be found for another bowler.

Root, the season's surprise packet, had demanded a further go by taking 11-51 for Worcestershire against Leicestershire the previous weekend. If there were niggling doubts about the venerable batting order, Patsy Hendren allayed them with a splendid double hundred in the Yorkshire match. Warner's assessment would seem to brook no argument from the rest of the panel: 'Seldom in the history of Middlesex cricket has a finer innings been played on a good wicket than that by Hendren.' In the same match George Macaulay took 5-70 and 6-84, selector nudging if ever there was. Elsewhere, Frank Woolley kept his hand in with a couple of fifties before a typically blazing hundred at Trent Bridge in the Championship match before the Test. Only the amateurs Carr and Chapman were short of runs.

The deliberations produced two changes. Jack Hearne, struggling for fitness, was dropped, along with Andrew Sandham as 12th man. In came Harold Larwood and Percy Holmes, vying for the last spot. Carr fought hard for Larwood's inclusion in the party. He had been nurturing him for almost two years at Notts and nobody knew more about his pace or how best he might be used. Macaulay was also asked to be on the ground on the morning of the match, which suggested the selectors were hedging their bets. Most observers assumed Larwood would make his debut, and Neville Cardus in *The Guardian* explained what the selectors had to do. 'If we neglect our attack by playing too many batsmen who cannot bowl really well, Australia's batsmen will have a good chance of retrieving any difficult situation into which their side's dubious bowling may land them.' The essential truth of Cardus's words was that if six batsmen could not do the job, then seven were hardly going to do better. How prescient he was. Australia faced a similar conundrum. They fielded an unchanged team, continuing to ignore the claims of Clarrie Grimmett. It was felt that they were a bowler light if the intention was to try to win the match. The suspicion was growing that this was not, at this stage in the contest, their primary objective.

Thousands queued all night outside the ground for the start of the match. A few were there by 8pm on Friday, by midnight there were 200 (not all of them reporters) and before the gates opened soon after 9am the line had grown to two miles. They played cards or dominoes by candlelight or bicycle lamp, sang blissfully inappropriate songs to the night air. Some read books. Among them doubtless was the new best-seller, *The Murder of Roger Ackroyd* by Agatha Christie, which featured her detective hero Hercule Poirot and produced a devastating plot twist which cemented her reputation. Christie mysteriously disappeared for 11 days later in the year, provoking fervid theories in the newspapers, and the book's sales rocketed.

When play began on a sun-kissed morning there were at least 30,000 inside the ground and at least 15,000 locked out. Its like had never been seen, especially since, as many reports pointed out, barely able to contain their surprise, there were also several thousand women spectators. The match contained a plethora of runs and a dearth of wickets. There were four hundreds, two each for either side. The youngest of the centurion quartet was Patsy Hendren at 37 years and 141 days, a mere stripling compared to Charlie Macartney at 40 years, 2 days, Jack Hobbs at 43 years, 194 days and Warren Bardsley at 43 years, 201 days. The innings, like the men who played them, were of contrasting nature, the main parts of an engrossing match which, despite a sensation midway through, often promised more than it eventually delivered. The overwhelming sense, however, was of relief that the game was being played, that this series, already much cherished, had at long last properly begun.

First Day

To popular acclaim, Bardsley dominated the proceedings after Collins won the toss. On a perfect pitch for batting, he was the only Australian who took full advantage. There were plenty who flattered to deceive but only Bardsley, the oldest man in the match, dug in and prospered. Larwood, as expected, was included in England's eleven, intended to lend them a cutting edge they had been lacking. The trio of Tate, Root and Larwood formed a multi-purpose seam attack, with Kilner providing left-arm spin, which it was hoped would offer England some prospect of conquering the surface.

The early signs at least were promising. To the first ball of Root's second over, the fourth of the match, Collins shouldered arms, expecting the ball to swing safely across his stumps. It went straight on, brushed the back of his pads and the leg stump was uprooted. Shortly afterwards, Bardsley, on six, cut a ball from Tate off the bottom edge and was put down by Bert Strudwick, up to the wicket. It was a fiendishly difficult chance if it was a chance at all, for the ball was going down as Strudwick was coming up, but another wicket then might have changed matters.

Macartney batted sublimely for more than an hour, the ball never far from the middle of the bat, the footwork gracefully assured. Larwood had his first spell from the Pavilion End and erred too often in length. Carr removed him from the attack after four overs but sensed his protégé might benefit from a change of view. Coming on at the Nursery End, Larwood produced a fast ball whose bounce from a length surprised Macartney and the resultant edge from the shoulder of the bat flew gently enough to first slip. At lunch, Australia were 112-2. King George arrived 20 minutes into the afternoon session.

Bardsley was imperturbable. He rode his luck against Tate at the start, edging several times through the slips, never entered the realms of flamboyance but took singles easily when the bowlers erred from off stump. Carr changed his bowlers astutely, his own fielding at point and short leg was magnificent and it rubbed off on his men. England were rewarded for this application to duty with regular wickets. Tommy Andrews, finding form elusive, gave Roy Kilner two bites of the cherry. In two minds about a straight drive, he offered a return catch which Kilner put down. Next ball he repeated the stroke, but to Kilner's left hand, and was not so fortunate.

Carr straightaway took Kilner off and re-introduced Larwood who immediately bowled Jack Gregory with a quick ball that tore through the batsman's defences. It was a piece of intuitive captaincy. Bardsley reached his painstaking hundred without alarm, but with the total at 208-6 Australia were in some trouble. Only another three had been added when Strudwick put down Bardsley, on 112, off Tate. The ball rose quickly but Strudwick was continuing to be chosen for the side because he was the best wicketkeeper in England, a wicketkeeper moreover who could not bat. At that moment, on the east coast at Southend, George Brown, Hampshire's man of many parts, was busy against Essex making his fourth hundred of the season. Strudwick's lapse allowed the tourists to go in at tea without further loss, 249-6. The King was still in attendance.

Two more wickets fell in the evening session. Australia were in no hurry. Kilner, in a long spell of 15 overs that included six maidens, bowled the vigilant Arthur Richardson with one that turned. Richardson faced 105 balls for his 35 and Jack Ryder, who followed, was barely less stoic with 28 from 83. On the stroke of the close, he edged Tate, and Strudwick atoned for his earlier errors with a reflex catch. The King had left midway through the session.

Close: Australia 338 for 8 (Bardsley 173)

With a rest day following, the Australians went to the theatre on Saturday night. They watched the musical *Mercenary Mary* at the London Hippodrome, which was vying with *No, No Nanette* to be the hit of the season. The show is long forgotten (and the Hippodrome is now a casino) but some of its songs, such as *Honey, I'm In Love With You* and *I'm a Little Bit Fonder of You,* are still given the occasional outing. It had two of the day's brightest stars, Peggy O'Neil and Sonnie Hale. O'Neil's enduring claim to fame is probably that she was the first person to be interviewed on television, at the Ideal Home Exhibition in 1930, but the last years of her life were bleak and she died in poverty. Hale was a big revue name for a few years, but nothing he did on stage or film eclipsed the scandal that ensued after he left his wife, the acclaimed actress Evelyn Laye, for the biggest star in the British firmament, Jessie Matthews. The cricketers, about whom such a fuss was being made everywhere else, went unnoticed and unbothered in the three private boxes they occupied.

Reporting for work again on Monday morning they found Lord's in a state of uproar. Once more, thousands queued all night outside the ground, snaking down Wellington Road past St John's Wood underground station. Among them was a young actress Audrey Cameron, who arrived shortly before midnight and reclined sleepily in a deckchair. Miss Cameron appeared in several West End productions in 1926, understudying five different roles in *The Unseemly Adventure* and co-starring with John Gielgud in a two-reel short, *Through A Window,* written and directed by Frank Wells, son of HG. Like so much of the country she wanted to be part of the cricket.

When at last they gained admission, it was to chaotic scenes. At 4am the Lord's groundsman, Harry White, had awoken mysteriously perturbed that all was not well ('telepathically disturbed in his sleep,' according to one report). He left his bed and went to inspect the turf he had so lovingly prepared, to find a hosepipe running. Water had flooded an area 10 yards or so from the pitch and leaked onto the business area itself about midway down. Consternation abounded. Who could have done such a dastardly deed?

Briefly, Harry White was the hero of the hour. Had he not been so vigilant, the entire ground might have been affected and play impossible. One headline was typical:

ATTEMPT TO FLOOD LORD'S PITCH
FOILED BY HEAD GROUNDSMAN

White had his own theories about what happened. He told reporters that in his opinion someone who knew the ground's layout had climbed the wall, found the hidden hydrant, linked up the hosepipe lying on the ground ready for use and turned on the tap. 'Never have I had such a shock,' White said. 'Imagine my horror when this morning I saw the hosepipe stretched across the ground and a steady stream of water flowing from it on to the turf about 20 yards by ten absolutely soaked with water, which had run down to the centre of the pitch and made that part very damp as well. Had the blackguard placed the end of the hosepipe nearer the pitch the turf for batting purposes today would have been ruined and England would have had a sticky wicket.' Agatha Christie herself might have been hard-pressed to conjure such a plot. As it was there were frantic conversations between the captains in the middle and an army of volunteers laid down sawdust on the offending area, except that on the wicket.

Unfortunately for Harry White, his story did not cut the mustard with the MCC Committee after it concluded its own investigation a few days later. There was, it seemed, no wall-climbing blackguard. The committee found that 'the cause had been traced to neglect and carelessness on the part of the groundstaff. H. White, ground superintendent, was held responsible.' White was severely reprimanded and told that he would continue to hold his post only on probation. He was saved from the sack only by the intervention of the long-serving MCC secretary Francis Lacey who said White had rendered admirable service. Lacey was perhaps prone to being well-disposed having been knighted a few days earlier in the King's Birthday Honours List, an honour which marked his retirement as MCC secretary after 26 years.

The errant hosepipe was not quite the disaster it might have been. Play was delayed for a mere 10 minutes, though it seemed bizarre to have a large pile of sawdust covering a side of the ground as the sun blazed down.

Second Day

England were held up for 40 minutes by the stubbornness of Bardsley and Bert Oldfield. There was a further delay when Bardsley was hit on the hand by Larwood, but he eventually continued. The pair put on 41 for the 9th wicket before Roy Kilner bowled a head-high full toss at Oldfield (deliberately if the field changes before it were a guide) which he miscued to Sutcliffe at fine leg. It was Arthur Mailey's job to stay with Bardsley while he reached 200 but he was swiftly lbw to Kilner and his partner was left unbeaten on 193, the second Australian to carry his bat after John Barrett, also at Lord's, in 1890. Bardsley's innings was the highest at Lord's in matches between England and Australia. Plum Warner considered Kilner, who took 4-70 to be England's best bowler, clever and persistent, and was full of admiration for his captain: 'I have never seen any man field better throughout a long day than the England captain. No praise is too high for Carr for the fine example which he set, an example which inspired the whole side.' Beware the praise of Plum.

It was 12.20pm when England began their innings. Hobbs and Sutcliffe played with real purpose and 50 came in 35 minutes, 74 in the 70 minutes to lunch from 28 overs. In the afternoon Arthur Richardson bowled a leg theory line with a packed field and runs were much harder come by. There was a feeling that England did not do enough to push on. Hobbs, masterly in the early stages, seemed to tire and was subject to unaccustomed criticism when he laboured to reach his hundred. On 83 he became the first player to score 4,000 Test runs, but the passing of that landmark seemed to slow him down rather than give him impetus. He faced another 93 balls to acquire the 17 runs he needed. Hobbs was the greatest batsman in the world by common consent and his deserved status as a national hero was untouched, but equally this seemed unfathomable. Some were willing to give him the benefit of the doubt, but others talked of timorous tactics which played into Australia's hands. Alf Noble said he must have been seeing the ball as big as a hayrick 'and it really seemed that getting a century was uppermost in his mind.' Certainly, England needed to get on with it if they were to have any chance of forcing a victory.

Hobbs was clearly stung by the reaction to his methods and responded with uncharacteristic asperity in his *Weekly Dispatch* column. 'I am seldom greatly concerned to defend myself personally against Press attacks,' he wrote. 'I play my game to suit my side and my captain to the best of my ability. If it pleases, well and good, if it does not please, also well and good. I have been told that I should have scored faster last Monday afternoon. There is an implied compliment here that I could if I would. At the risk of losing something in prestige I must confess that I scored just as fast as I was able. The fact was that Arthur Richardson bowled remarkably well not only on Monday afternoon but throughout the match ... Probably an unorthodox batsman such as Mr Jessop might have forced the pace with success. I am not an unorthodox batsman. I would not go in at No. 1 or No. 2 for England if I were.' Ghosted the column might have been but the censorious note sounded about his strategy obviously rankled. Nor did he quickly forget it. In his book *Playing for England*, five years later, Hobbs said: 'The critics took the attitude that I ought to have taken the risks. A characteristic British trait is it not that in order to be fair to others we cause our own to suffer!'

Sutcliffe, who had played with more gusto as he got into his work, was bowled by a Richardson off-break, this one unusually pitching outside the off stump, with the partnership at 182 in the 79th over. The openers must have taken the view that it was up to them because the others were not to be entirely trusted. It was the fifth time in 10 innings against Australia that this first wicket collaboration had exceeded three figures. Two overs later Hobbs finally reached his hundred. Early in the evening session, trying to break the shackles, he was caught off Macartney by Richardson running full tilt at third man.

For the next 90 minutes, Hendren and Woolley batted pretty much as they liked. Hendren showed more gumption, and though Woolley unfurled a couple of languid drives there was a lack of urgency. Ardour was not yet dampened. Hundreds of those not at the ground stood outside the windows of London's department stores where the score was being changed on boards every few minutes. Complete strangers engaged in animated conversation about England's chances. They finished 86 runs behind. Queues again formed early.

Close: Australia 383 all out; England 297-2 (Woolley 50, Hendren 42)

A few minutes after close of play, three miles across London, a women's rally was taking place in support of the miners whose lock-out had passed its 50th day. Kingsway Hall, home to the Methodist Mission, was packed to its rafters. Five miners' wives gave harrowing accounts of their poverty-stricken lives and the working conditions endured by their husbands. To try to end the impasse and press home its victory in the General Strike, the Government was about to introduce the Eight Hours Act, which would mean miners working eight hours a day underground – for wages yet to be determined but probably less than they were already receiving – instead of the seven which had been in force for 18 years.

Galvanising as these speeches were, bringing into sharp focus the harsh reality of lives in pit communities which was too easily overlooked in the endless political dialogue, none was as rapturously received as Sybil Thorndike. The actress was at the peak of her career, a summit on which she continued standing for most of the next 40 years. She also remained a committed socialist and humanitarian and in the Kingsway Hall that evening, on her way to the Ambassadors' Theatre where she was performing, she delivered a stirring endorsement of the miners' cause. It was a privilege, she said, to express public sympathy for the miners upon whose work the prosperity of the country depended. As one working woman to another she saluted the women who had come from the coalfields where conditions were beyond a joke. Thorndike launched a campaign on behalf of the Women's Committee for the Relief of Miners' Wives and Children. 'I appeal to every Christian, every impartial citizen, every person of goodwill, no matter what his or her political or economic views, to see that these women and children do not in the ensuing weeks fall into the hell of starvation.'

It is a pleasant thought to entertain that some in the Kingsway Hall audience went on to Lord's to join the queue for the final day's play. Such was the grip of the cricket on the country, its ability, apart from anything else, to allow people briefly to forget, it is also wholly plausible.

Third Day
With due respect to the others, the best batting of the match, in both defensive and attacking mode, was seen on the final day, witnessed by another bumper attendance. But it was still too little and too late. Hendren, Woolley and Chapman rattled along but not quickly enough to repair the damage done by the ponderous pace of the previous day. Later in the afternoon, Collins provided a magnificent example of stonewalling and Macartney played with the deceptively casual authority that marked his summer.

Hendren's innings saved his Test career. There had been mutterings everywhere that he might not have the right stuff for the truly big occasion

– in 13 Tests against Australia his average was 25. He took a little too long to get going with a scoreless first half hour but afterwards he did what he had done so often for Middlesex, banging the ball through point and covers with his powerful wrists and, occasionally, cheekily backing away to leg to do so. When he reached his first Ashes hundred the joy could be felt around Lord's. He was an attractive personality in a team full of likeable men and his accomplishments should not be overlooked. Only two men, Hobbs and Frank Woolley, have scored more runs, only Hobbs has more centuries than Patsy Hendren. Only four have played more than his 833 first-class matches but none of them also played 435 matches in the Football League.

Woolley was equally vibrant, caressing seven fours in that entrancing way of his before he walked in front of one from Jack Ryder and was lbw. In the 90 minutes before lunch, Hendren and Chapman added 112 in 33 overs. The pitch was still wonderful for batting. Richardson bowled intelligently, carefully, accurately, as all had come to expect, Gregory, once the colossus, was clearly struggling, his pace reducing as the overs increased, and he went at more than four runs an over in an innings when the overall rate was 2.8. England were utterly dominant. Ten times previously, in 109 matches, they had made more runs against Australia but on each of those occasions they had been bowled out, here they lost only three wickets in 168 overs.

Carr declared at lunch with a lead of 92. It was the only way England could win even if that would take a miracle on a benign pitch. The decision was entirely correct but it was also the start of the end for Carr. He was giving Australia the chance to have a further look at his bowlers in favourable circumstances and he was denying himself and the rest of England's order the chance to bat. The report in the *Wisden Almanack* took this critical line. 'What idea the England captain entertained was difficult to discover.' But Arthur Gilligan took another view: 'The advantages of Carr's declaration completely counterbalanced any imagined disadvantages. There was no earthly chance of a victory of any description had England gone on batting.'

The start of Australia's second innings suggested fleetingly that the miracle might happen. In the absence of Bardsley, Gregory opened with Collins. To the fifth ball of Root's third over the stand-in was caught by Sutcliffe at first slip, the second time in the match Root had made the breakthrough with the new ball. Collins then did what Collins did best.

He dug in to repel all boarders. Macartney at the other end adopted a different approach. Gilligan again: 'The Macartney innings is an event. It is more than that – it does people good.'

After Gregory's exit, Collins and Macartney put on 123 from 345 balls of which Collins' share was 24 from 197 balls. He was on 14 for 64 balls. Only two players have faced as many balls in an innings and gone more slowly, Collins himself in 1921 and Hashim Amla in a futile rearguard action for South Africa at Delhi in 2015. Plum Warner said that he played 'a most stubborn game of infinite value to his side,' though LD Brownlee, Clem Hill's sidekick in the *Daily Mirror*, thought it 'a dreadful business.' Macartney had slightly less of the bowling but was captivating. In all of England, only the dancer Fred Astaire, with his sister Adele packing them in at the Empire for the musical *Lady Be Good,* might have had more dazzling footwork. After Collins gave his wicket away in a rare show of intent Australia lost three more wickets in the evening, but the outcome had long been a foregone conclusion. The match had yielded 1,052 runs and 18 wickets. The batting had been simply too good for the bowling.

Close: England 475 for 3 dec; Australia 194 for 5 Match drawn

There was an immediate outcry that three days was simply insufficient for a Test match, an argument that was not to subside for the next two months. Opinions were canvassed as soon as the match finished and the players were unanimous.

> BERT STRUDWICK: 'The draw was very disappointing and it does seem to me a waste of time.'

> FRED ROOT: 'Why not play to a finish in our conditions as the Australians play to a finish in theirs?'

> MAURICE TATE: 'I am in favour of four days for the Tests.'

> ROY KILNER: 'Play to a finish! From the English spectators' view I think that if they saw one played to a finish they wouldn't want to see any other.'

There were cautionary voices from expected quarters.

> SHRIMP LEVESON GOWER, MCC committee member: 'It is not for you or me to say but for the counties. It is obvious that three days are not sufficient. Would four days be long enough? If not ... the County Championship would

have to be sacrificed to the Tests. Would the counties be sufficiently recompensed by their share of the Test profits to balance their losses on their county games? That is the problem which faces the counties and the decision rests with them.'

FRED TOONE, Yorkshire secretary: 'Playing to a finish would mean too great an interference with county cricket.'

Essentially, it was an argument about the balance between international and domestic cricket. Who would have thought that it might never be resolved?

The furore about playing time seems to have completely overlooked the overs bowled within it. In the three days at Lord's, 410 overs were bowled in 17 hours 48 minutes of play, a rate of slightly more than 23 overs an hour. It is unthinkable in the 21st century that such a rate should be reached – an innings in Twenty20, the breeziest international format of the game, is allotted 75 minutes - but looking at film clips of Tests at the time it did not seem as if the players were particularly rushing between overs or balls. They appeared to have the attitude that they were there to play, so that is what they did. But perhaps they played it far too much with safety in mind.

Of the 16 previous Lord's Tests with fewer overs, 11 produced a winner. Up to 2023, 115 of the 145 Test matches at Lord's contained fewer overs and 81 yielded positive results. This is all to say that they might have played a lot of cricket in the time available but they were not exactly in a hurry. They were being deliberately cagey. For instance, in the Lord's Ashes Test of 2023, play lasted for five days, contained only 360.2 overs, 50 fewer than in 1926, a batsman in Ben Stokes with feet like Astaire and Macartney, and produced a breathtaking win for Australia. The point about match duration might have been valid, but in retrospect it was not as significant as it seemed at the time. Still, it was quickly to lead to a lively debate about the direction the game was heading, led by no less a personage than Lord Harris, the old buffers' old buffer himself, who proposed revolutionary changes. It was almost as though he were a Bolshevik.

Roy Kilner

England

Left-hand bat, slow left-arm bowler

Born: 17.10.1890 Wombwell, Yorkshire
Age on 1.5.26: **35**
County: Yorkshire

Record at start of 1926

Tests: 5, debut 1924
188 runs @ 31.33, HS 74
17 wickets @ 26.94, BB 4-51

F/c matches: 336, debut 1911
12,267 runs @ 29.41, HS 206*
776 wickets @ 16.83, BB 8-26

Roy Kilner was one of the most popular cricketers who ever lived. When he returned from England's tour of Australia in April 1925 a civic banquet was held in his honour in Wombwell, the South Yorkshire mining town close to Barnsley where he was born and still lived. Kilner himself described the place as one-eyed in his speech to more than 200 guests who packed into the Reform Club. But it was a one-eyed place, he said, to which those who left often returned. Its prosperity, if it had any, came from coal mining. Two pits lay within the boundaries of the village which, like many other rural northern settlements, had been transformed by them. Wombwell Main and Mitchell Main collieries employed more than 3,000 men, the vast majority working underground. In the summer of 1926 they were all locked out as the bitter dispute between miners and owners continued. Kilner lived right among these men; his father was a former miner.

The dinner was an occasion fit for a king. Messages of approbation came from far and wide. It served as a precursor to Kilner's benefit, awarded him by Yorkshire that season and which raised a record £4,016, beating the £3,701 donated to the legendary George Hirst 22 years earlier. It equates to around £200,000 a century later, but even that adjustment for inflation is misleading since it would have been enough to buy six houses.

Part, perhaps most, of the reason that Kilner became so admired lay not in his all-round ability as a forcing left-handed batsman and left-arm slow bowler – though these were impressively persuasive calling cards – but in his being the antithesis of the typical Yorkshire cricketer of the day. Generally, the team was seen as hard-nosed, bloody-minded and perpetually dogged. If Kilner possessed some of these attributes he conveyed them somewhat differently. He batted and bowled with a smile on his face and was always ready to engage with spectators. In the England team he had something in common in that regard with Patsy Hendren. In the Yorkshire team he was probably an anomaly.

Kilner's father Seth went to Wombwell seeking work down the pit. Roy was lucky – he did not have to follow him there, thanks to his talent at cricket. He was in the Mitchell Main colliery team at the age of 14, and after some initial blips the county came calling when he was 20. In the three years before the First World War he established his place in the county side, almost solely as a batsman. During the war he saw action with the Leeds Pals Battalion. On the first day of the Battle of the Somme, Kilner was injured by shrapnel while moving explosives in the trenches. A few hours later his friend, Yorkshire team-mate and fellow soldier Major Booth, who had been his best man, was killed along with more than 19,000 others on that bloody day. Kilner spent the rest of the war as a mechanic in Preston, but he never forgot his old friend, naming his second son Major.

When cricket resumed Yorkshire found themselves short of bowlers, so Kilner honed his bowling skills in the back yard of the Wombwell pub where his father Seth was now the landlord. In 1921 he took 61 wickets and in each of the following four seasons passed 100, doing the double in three. For Yorkshire he was usually called on to bowl before Wilfred Rhodes. Kilner's engaging perspective shone through his conversations with the great cricket writer Neville Cardus, one of whose favourites he was.

For instance, he summed up Roses contests thus: 'Ay, it's a reet match. Tha knows, t'two teams turn up and we meets in t'dressing room and we all say "Good Mornin'" to one another and then we never speaks again for three days unless to say howzat!' Cardus once asked Kilner about the general state of the game and received the following reply: 'T'game's all right. It's crowd that's wrong – it wants educating up to t'game. When I were a young lad I goes up to London and there I sees a Shakespeare play. And by gum it did make me tired and weary wi' yawning. When I gets home I says to mi father, "No more Shakespeare for me." But mi father, he says, "Now look here, Roy, lad, that's just talking folly. Shakespeare's good enough for me and 'e's good enough for thee. Tha wants educating up to him, that's what tha wants." And it's the same wi't crowd and county cricket. They wants educatin' up to it.' Whether Cardus was embellishing the conversation and Kilner's neat drollery – not many Wombwell lads went to the London theatre in the early years of the 20th century – is beside the point. It captures the essence of the man.

Kilner proved his quality as an international player on England's 1924/25 tour. Omitted from the first two Tests as Australia were again rampant, he was included in the next three and took 17 wickets at 23.47 runs each, also scoring a crucial 74 in England's solitary victory. There was no question of leaving him out when the series began in 1926. But the weather and a discernible decline in Kilner's bowling potency affected his influence. He had his moments, but the selectors were desperate. They dropped Kilner for Rhodes for the last match. Kilner was never to play another Test, and 18 months later tragedy would befall him.

Arthur Richardson

PLAYER'S CIGARETTES

MR. A. J. RICHARDSON.
SOUTH AUSTRALIA

Australia

Right-hand bat, off-spin bowler

Born: 24.7.1888 Sevenhill, South Australia
Age on 1.5.26: **37**
State: South Australia

Record at start of 1926

Tests: 4, debut 1924/25
248 runs @ 31.00, HS 98
8 wickets @ 31.00, BB 2-20

F/c matches: 48, debut 1918/19
3,618 runs @ 42.56, HS 280
129 wickets @ 36.95, BB 6-76

Arthur Richardson was unmistakeable on a cricket pitch. Whether batting, bowling or fielding he wore a cap and round-rimmed spectacles. The combination made him look deceptively unathletic – though a lack of mobility in the field, in stark contrast to some of his extraordinarily nimble colleagues, merely emphasised the perception.

If batting was his stronger suit, he came to England as an authentic, if not high calibre, all-rounder in a team bursting with all-rounders. He first came to the notice of the English on the tour of 1920/21 when he scored 111 for South Australia. Two years later, on MCC's non-Test trip, he made 150 in the first match against the tourists and 280 in the second when he also became the first batsman in Australia to score a hundred before lunch. In the home season before the 1926 tour, he confirmed his place by being the leading run-scorer, with only the specialist spinners, Grimmett and Mailey, taking more wickets.

The highlight of his tour was undoubtedly his century at Leeds, his only score of three figures in Tests. He had his moments as a bowler, most notably against Oxford University when he took 11 wickets (6-28 and 5-36), but Australia were absurdly over-reliant on his fast off-spin – only Mailey and Grimmett bowled more overs both in Tests and in the arduous first-class programme. Aimed at a packed on-side field, often containing four short legs, Richardson's bowling never really took off in the Tests – especially at the most vital time of all – despite an impressive economy rate.

Richardson was one of two South Australians in the touring party, dominated as always by New South Welshmen and Victorians, and the other, Grimmett, was from Adelaide via Dunedin, Wellington, Sydney and Melbourne. Arthur and his namesake, Victor Richardson, carried their state's batting in the early 1920s, and their partnership in the 31 innings they batted together averaged above 50.

Back home, Arthur and Vic propelled South Australia to a rare Sheffield Shield title, their first for 13 years. Arthur scored 607 runs at 67.44, took a few expensive wickets and moved to Western Australia as player-coach. He scored a century for Western Australia against MCC; six of his 13 career centuries were against the English. But he was not done with England by any stretch and gained an undeserved notoriety when it was announced that he would be joining the Lancashire League club Bacup as a professional. The widely-speculated fee for his services – though he denied it – was £600, at least twice what most county professionals were earning at the time.

For a little while, Richardson was a *cause celebre*. In the same edition that recorded the exploits of the 1926 Australian tourists, the *Wisden Almanack* rose to its full height and puffed out its chest as far as it would go. 'There is to most of us something objectionable,' wrote the editor, C. Stewart Caine, 'in the idea of a man battling for Australia in the Test matches one season and a year later figuring as a paid player for an English local club. Did the matter end with the fact of a man accepting a situation, there would – much as one might regret the occurrence – be nothing more to be said on the subject.'

But Caine and others were concerned that Richardson was using his time with Bacup as a ruse to qualify for Lancashire, citing the precedent of his compatriot Ted McDonald, who had rampaged through England with Australia in 1921 and promptly joined the league club Nelson and then Lancashire. Richardson might well do the same and 'against such a development there would, I feel confident, be a very general and very proper outcry.'

Richardson did no such thing, and for the next few years played in Lancashire in the summer, breaking scoring records ('one of the greatest all rounders who has ever played in the Lancashire League'), and in Perth. He played all year round for six successive years, 12 summers in all, home and away, said to be unprecedented.

Richardson also took up appointments in South Africa and West Indies. He stood as umpire in two Tests on England's tour of the Caribbean in 1935, perhaps the first neutral umpire in international cricket. There was an element of controversy in the first match when both sides began bowling leg theory against a diktat recently announced by MCC in the wake of Bodyline. Richardson issued warnings to both Learie Constantine of West Indies and Jim Smith of England, and both were temporarily removed from the attack.

Richardson had been away from Australia for five years when he returned home in 1936. He lost his life savings when a share-broking firm collapsed but was restored to solvency when the game rallied round him. A coaching contract helped, as did a testimonial match which happened to be Don Bradman's final first-class appearance.

Maurice Tate

England

Fast-medium bowler, right-hand bat

Born: 30.5.1895 Brighton, Sussex
Age on 1.5.26: **30**
County: Sussex

Record at start of 1926

Tests: 10, debut 1924
253 runs @ 21.08, HS 50
65 wickets @ 20.07, BB 6-42

F/c matches: 253, debut 1912
9,237 runs @ 24.11, HS 203
1,059 wickets @ 16.98, BB 8-18

Of all the matches Maurice Tate might have nominated it appears an odd choice. 'The Third Test match of 1926 was the most sensational in which I have played,' he said. Since it finished as a draw after three days in which only 23 wickets fell and the runs trickled at 2.75 runs an over, the verdict seems a touch extravagant. Here was a player, do not forget, whose maiden Test match two years earlier, had seen South Africa bowled out for 30 in 74 balls, the briefest completed Test innings of all, and in which Tate took a wicket with his first ball.

But Tate was in the heat of the battle. He should know, and he was insistent on the matter, recalling it seven years later in his memoirs when his Test career was all but done, 'with a vivid memory of excitement in others both before and since.' In Tate's mind the Headingley match 'combined so many incidents and happenings to raise it from its fellows.' By 1926 Tate was considered the greatest bowler in the world and a sporting celebrity before they properly existed.

He wrote newspaper columns, appeared in department stores to promote cricket equipment and endorsed products from cigarettes ('After a hard day in the field I find nothing more restful than a few minutes with a Waverley') to chocolate ('I have found in Caley's Marching Chocolate a real provider of energy. It is wonderfully sustaining').

The story of Maurice Tate remains one of the most remarkable and uplifting in sport. It can never be told without reference also to his father. Fred Tate was an off-spin bowler whose sole Test appearance remains one of the most (unfairly) infamous in the game. In the 1902 Test at Old Trafford, with the Ashes still at stake, Fred dropped a catch at a crucial moment and was then the last man out with England needing four runs to win. (Fred's fielding lapse compares in the category of Ashes notoriety with Arthur Carr's off Maurice at Headingley in 1926.) It is said, probably apocryphally, but it is now part of the legend, that on the train home from Manchester, a still distraught Fred vouchsafed to his travelling companion, team-mate Len Braund, 'I've got a little kid at home who'll make up for it for me.' Fred never played another Test. That match had an enormous influence on Maurice. As John Arlott put it in his charming appreciation in the early 1950s: 'Never, possibly, has any cricketer's life been so affected by a match at which he was not even present as was Maurice Tate's by the fourth Test of 1902. In fact, but for this Test, Maurice Tate, as the son of Fred, must, for better or worse, have been a different man and a different cricketer.'

Son eventually followed father into the Sussex team and for six seasons either side of the First World War he, too, was no more than a journeyman professional. A much better batsman than Fred, who was a born number 11, Maurice was a blazing hitter who sometimes opened the Sussex batting. But he bowled a similar fast-ish off-spin. In all, there was nothing special about him as a cricketer. He batted a bit and he bowled a bit.

Accounts vary about what happened next, but the influence of the new Sussex captain, Arthur Gilligan, and an incident in a match at Eastbourne on 26 July 1922 had huge ramifications for English cricket. Phil Mead, the prolific Hampshire left-hander, was digging in for the day when Tate bowled him a faster ball which swung away and then cut viciously back to hit leg stump. Gilligan knew that Tate was on to something. He urged him to change his style.

A cricketer was transformed, a legendary bowler was born. Until then none had quite harnessed swing through the air allied to movement off the pitch as Tate seemingly did at will, all off eight paces with the wicketkeeper standing up. He was persistently accurate, and the movement from the pitch seemed also to be accompanied by the ball increasing in pace – defying the laws of physics, of course, but batsmen were not to be influenced by science. They saw what they saw and felt what they felt. In his new guise Tate was utterly confident in what he was doing. And he could bowl for hours on end without flagging in energy or precision.

Tate took 100 wickets in the season for the first time in 1922, the following summer he took 200, and the year after that he established himself in the England side. His international renown was secured on the Ashes tour of 1924/25. England were hammered again, a little unluckily, losing the series 4-1, but Tate took 38 wickets. No visiting bowler has taken as many in a series in Australia. When he returned, Tate was a national hero.

The air of congeniality enhanced his standing. This in turn seemed to be emphasised by his tendency to mangle words. He would refer to his long spells as examples of his 'stannima' and if someone was being critical, he would say that they were being 'opprolobus'.

In 1926 when a combination of the weather and the pitches made life difficult for all bowlers, he was still England's leading wicket-taker and bowled comfortably more overs than anyone else. Maurice Tate was a truly great performer.

Bill Woodfull

Australia

Right-hand bat

Born: 22.8.1897 Maldon, Victoria
Age on 1.5.26: **28**
State: Victoria

Record at start of 1926

Tests: 0

F/c matches: 33, debut 1921/22
3,163 runs @ 75.30, HS 236

W. M. WOODFULL
VICTORIA

When the bulk of the Australian party for the 1926 tour was chosen Bill Woodfull was omitted. Seven other batsmen were preferred in the 12 names, and most of the debate about those excluded centred on Charlie Kelleway. Woodfull barely rated a mention. It was not an oversight which the selectors would repeat. With three places still left to fill, he had only four first-class innings to persuade them of their error. He made 97, 236, 15 and 126, and late in January, when matters were finalised, he was picked as one of the four additional players.

Woodfull's style was immediately suited to English pitches. His bat was determinedly straight, his back lift discernible only under microscope, he had powerful arms and if his footwork was not in the realms of dainty it was positive and assured which can be almost as effective. His impact was immediate. In his first first-class innings in England he made 201, in his second 118. Considering rain and fog had wiped out the first day of the match at Leyton against Essex, that there remained a biting cold wind to contend with on the second and that the tourists' journey there had been fiendishly complicated by the lack of transport caused by the General Strike, it was a formidable start. At The Oval against Surrey, the strike still in full swing, Woodfull, going in at 98-3, once more rose above the confusion which must have pervaded the Australians' ranks, staying with grim tenacity for three hours and 40 minutes, his only four his last scoring stroke.

It emphasised his other main attribute, a fierce concentration which could blank out any external noise. In this and a general willingness to protect his wicket rather than be expansive for its own sake he could be easily compared with his English counterpart as an opening batsman, Herbert Sutcliffe. Those opening innings set the tone for Woodfull's tour and guaranteed that he would be in the Test side, Australia's only debutant of a summer in which he was never out of form. His two Test hundreds, at Leeds and Manchester, were overshadowed by Charlie Macartney also reaching three figures in both of those matches and doing so in a more eye-catching manner. But they were scored after he was elevated to open the innings and could not have been more necessary in partially disguising the general malaise in Australia's middle order.

After making 13 and 0 in his first two Test innings at Lord's, Woodfull was in a state of some apprehension for the next match at Leeds. This only grew when Warren Bardsley was out to the first ball of the match with Woodfull at the other end. What happened next – even before Macartney was dropped off the fifth ball – stayed with Woodfull for the rest of his life and may have helped to shape his career.

As he put it: 'The young and inexperienced cricketer may need just the touch which only a man of understanding can supply, and which can make all the difference. While I was disconsolately waiting for Charlie Macartney to put in an appearance, Jack Hobbs walked across from the covers and had a word with me. Perhaps his mind travelled back to the days of his early Test matches; of that I am not sure, nor do I remember just what was said, but this I do know, that it helped me to go on and make a success of the job.' Woodfull made 141, he and Macartney put on 235, then the highest second-wicket partnership for Australia in an Ashes Test and surpassed only six times since.

His vigilant defence led to his being called 'The Unbowlable'. This was more in the perception than the execution since he was actually bowled in 30 per cent of his Test innings (compared to Sutcliffe's 19). Nonetheless, it sums up the general mood of bowlers when they were confronted with Woodfull. On the first of his three England tours Woodfull scored 1,672 runs, at 57.65, the first Australian to average above 50 on his first tour, and scored eight hundreds. It was the most solid of platforms for the career which followed. As captain of Australia in 25 Tests, he was a reliable man of integrity who won two Ashes series in England, both victories being confirmed on his birthday. He had some improbable notoriety bestowed for his part in the 1932/33 Bodyline tour when, in terse conversation at Adelaide with the England manager Plum Warner, he issued what has become one of the game's most legendary quotations: 'There are two teams out there. One of them is trying to play cricket, the other is not.'

Like his team-mate Johnny Taylor, Woodfull was the son of a Methodist minister. By the time he came to England for the first time, he was 28 and established in his own chosen career as schoolmaster. He would flourish in that as in cricket. He became principal of the school he attended and was awarded an OBE not for his cricketing exploits but for his achievements in education. If the 1926 tour showed his capabilities it really was only the start for Bill Woodfull.

George Macaulay

England

Medium pace bowler, right-hand bat

Born: 7.12.1897 Thirsk, Yorkshire
Age on 1.5.26: **28**
County: Yorkshire

Record at start of 1926

Tests: 5, debut 1922/23
27 runs @ 6.75, HS 19
18 wickets @ 22.72, BB 5-64

F/c matches: 184, debut 1920
2,605 runs @ 17.84, HS 125*
854 wickets @ 15.00, BB 7-13

Without George Macaulay it is entirely probable that England might well have messed up their chances of regaining the Ashes in 1926. He was not included in the side until the Third Test at his home ground of Leeds when informed observers, such as Maurice Tate, fully expected him to be chosen from the start after his exploits the previous summer when he had taken 211 wickets.

This line of thought was disturbed by Fred Root and Harold Larwood who themselves made unexpected breakthroughs, and only at Headingley was it deemed opportune for Macaulay to play for the first time against Australia. For some reason, his rhythm departed him with the ball and, although he dismissed Charlie Macartney, the batsman had made 151 sublime runs by then and the bowler was going at almost four runs an over in a series which was mostly yielding fewer than three. But with the bat he played the innings of his life, scoring 76 at number 10 in an effort which was delightfully composed. It was not enough to save his place in the side, and he did not play another Test match for seven years.

Macaulay was a rarity among Yorkshire cricketers in being born in the North Riding, in the market town of Thirsk, and he went as a boarder to Barnard Castle School in County Durham where he first learned the game. He emerged quickly after attracting Yorkshire's attention when he was 22, first as a fast bowler who then reduced his pace following guidance from Wilfred Rhodes. Macaulay found himself admonished by a magistrate in 1923 for leaving a motorcar on the highway when he and team-mate Abe Waddington had gone to play for Yorkshire in the south for a few weeks. It was an early example of bringing down to size sportsmen who become stars. Mr Beaumont Morice told them that they should not be so obsessed with their own work and importance that they should ignore everyday matters and that if a person's head were in the clouds his feet should be on Mother Earth.

Ernest Tyldesley

England

Right-hand bat

Born: 5.2.1889 Worsley, Lancashire
Age on 1.5.26: **37**
County: Lancashire

Record at start of 1926

Tests: 4, debut 1921
139 runs @ 34.75, HS 78*

F/c matches: 325, debut 1909
17,250 runs @ 38.07, HS 244
6 wickets @ 45.83, BB 3-33

If ever there were form to nudge the selectors, Ernest Tyldesley provided it in 1926. Having played four largely undistinguished Test matches – he had been part of the mayhem in 1921 when Australia were rampant – he was probably fading from selectors' thoughts at the age of 37. However, he assembled such a prodigious run of scores that they had little option but to consider yet another veteran batsman who had started his career well before the First World War. Starting in late June, Tyldesley, Jud to his team-mates, went on a scintillating run which saw him compile hundreds in seven successive matches, a feat never achieved before.

'A CRICKET MARVEL,' said the *Daily News*. Reluctant to omit any of the vaunted quartet at the top of the order though the selectors were, the pressure of runs meant that by the time of the Fourth Test match at Old Trafford, there really was no option but to play him. His sequence of scores for Lancashire and the Players (it was probably his runs against the Gentlemen which clinched it) was: 144, 69, 144, 226, 51, 131, 131, 106, 126.

In the Test he went in at number three when England needed to stabilise their innings and shared in a partnership of 192 with Jack Hobbs, the stand-in skipper, suffering nothing by comparison after a nervous, uncomfortable settling-in period. Tyldesley's 81 was his tenth consecutive score above 50, making him also the first player to manage that – only two have done it since. It made him England's top scorer and although the chairman of selectors, Plum Warner, said that while fortune was on his side 'his batting was good and his innings attractive being full of excellent strokes.' It was not enough to preserve his place. Tyldesley was a home-town pick.

Tommy Andrews

Australia

Leg-break bowler, right-hand bat

Born: 26.8.1890 Sydney, New South Wales
Age on 1.5.26: **35**
State: New South Wales

Record at start of 1926

Tests: 11, debut 1921
543 runs @ 33.93, HS 94
1 wicket @ 67.00

F/c matches: 104, debut 1912/13
5,590 runs @ 36.94, HS 247*
73 wickets @ 27.41, BB 5-41

Rarely can a fielder have reached such heights as Tommy Andrews did in a superb fielding side. At silly point and short extra cover he frequently took the breath away. His hands were safe, his reflexes quick, his anticipation uncanny, his daring peerless. 'Never been equalled,' was the judgement of Alf Noble. Unfortunately, Andrews' batting in the Tests was dismal, and fortune deserted him utterly. There seemed regularly to be an England player ready to do something extraordinary – Roy Kilner's low catch off his own bowling at Lord's, Percy Chapman's stunning running effort as substitute at Old Trafford – and though he retained his place throughout he finished with a top score of 15 in six innings. Outside the Test matches he performed well, one of the four tourists to make 1,000 runs.

It was his second tour of England, and he performed with much more success in the Tests on the first in 1921. He scored 92 in the Headingley Test and went two better at The Oval. Perhaps his finest hour for Australia came at Adelaide in 1924/25 when Australia were in dire straits at 119-6 and facing a significant deficit which might enable to England to stay in the series. Andrews counter-attacked, scoring 72 in a century stand with Jack Ryder, and Australia went on to win by 11 runs. He also made 80 in Australia's crushing win in the final Test. Of his 16 Tests only three were at home.

Johnny Taylor

Australia

Right-hand bat

Born: 10.10.1895 Stanmore, New South Wales
Age on 1.5.26: **30**
State: New South Wales

Record at start of 1926

Tests: 17, debut 1920/21
984 runs @ 37.84, HS 108
1 wicket @ 45.00, BB 1-25

F/c matches: 106, debut 1913/14
5,846 runs @ 36.09, HS 180
1 wicket @ 53.00, BB 1-25

Much was expected of Johnny Taylor's batting on the tour. He seemed to have unlocked the code on how to compile Test innings in the Ashes series of 1924/25 when he was Australia's leading scorer with 541 runs which included a hundred and four fifties. He played only occasionally in the Australian season preceding the tour, but when he played he did well. Yet he never managed to get going in England, affected by the infernal cold and rain which blighted the first six weeks of the visit.

His right knee was almost certainly giving him problems. He had been shot during the Allies' spring offensive at Amiens in early 1918, and while he recovered after months in hospital and was part of the great Australian Imperial Forces team which took England by storm in 1919 it affected him for the rest of his life. In the field Taylor was a match for Tommy Andrews, and in the deep he was relentless. His throw and his pace set him apart from others, and the England selector and former captain, Arthur Gilligan, adjudged him the best outfielder in the game and added: 'I would back his throw at the wicket from 90 yards to beat for speed that of any of the other recognised outfield now playing.'

Taylor was the first of Australia's dual internationals. In 1922 he played two rugby union matches against the New Zealand All Blacks. He appeared in the first three Test matches in 1926 before being omitted.

8

DRAMA AT LEEDS

*After I had had a strike at the nets I inspected the wicket myself
for my own satisfaction. In my opinion it was without doubt a
batsman's wicket.*

Charlie Macartney
(offering his verdict on the Leeds pitch
on which Australia were asked to bat)

*There is not a Cabinet minister who dare stand up and face an
audience in the mining areas. I'm not suggesting that Mr Baldwin
or his colleagues would suffer violence if they accepted the challenge
but that, hard-faced though they may be, they cannot defend their
conduct to the people they are fighting.*

Arthur Cook
(speaking to miners in Notttingham during the Test)

The time had come to enter the heart of the storm: the North. It
might as well have been another country, the faraway place where the
catastrophic effects of the continuing industrial turbulence were at their
most extreme. Between them, the counties of Yorkshire, Durham and
Northumberland contained almost 300,000 miners, all of them locked
out as their bitter dispute over hours and pay showed no sign of ending,
all of them struggling to survive.

Yet cricket still cast its spell. As at Lord's, the queues started
forming on the evening before the Third Test at Leeds was due to
start – shortly before a torrential downpour flooded the ground. But
this time there was not an ingenue in a reclining deckchair in sight.
Somehow, it was fitting that among the first arrivals were three miners
from Newcastle. They had cycled the 100 miles from home, starting
the previous afternoon and spending the night sleeping in a field. They
were sanguine as they bedded down in a wet shop doorway, and as one
of them said: 'We've got some snap if we're hungry and coats if it's
cold.' Waiting for the cricket to start was the easy life. And what a game

they would witness, one that had a turbulence of its own: a last minute change of pitch, a controversial team selection, a brave, or foolhardy, decision at the toss, swiftly followed by a first-ball wicket and one of the most notorious dropped catches in all of Test cricket which permitted one of its greatest innings.

Miners' pay had been gradually reduced as the decade wore on. The district rates of pay applying at the time (much to the miners' anger) make it difficult to calculate precisely how much they were taking home in different areas, but official figures quoted in *Hansard*, the record of Parliamentary proceedings, show that the average pay across the industry in 1921 was 89 shillings 8 pence a week, working out at £232.96 a year when converted to decimal coinage, and that by the first quarter of 1926 it had declined to 53 shillings 4 pence a week or £138.84 a year. It was barely enough to feed their families and pay the rent to the colliery owners who also owned their homes. Nor should it be forgotten that some men who were working less profitable seams received much less.

Professional cricketers were not considered to be generously rewarded, but by comparison they were kings. The average senior professional in 1926 earned around £300 for the season – with the hope of a winter job – and the real stars such as Jack Hobbs, playing for Surrey, the richest county, made more. From that sum they had to pay their transport to matches and accommodation when there. For Tests that summer players were paid £33 a match plus their hotel costs and a third-class train fare. It was why the award of a benefit match was so important, as was the fight not to pay income tax on the proceeds.

Australia's cricketers were deemed to be amateurs, though this was not strictly the case. Each of them received £400 for the 1926 trip plus a share of the tour profits. In official scorecards they were all accorded their initials while English professionals were not. Most newspapers simply referred to all players by their surnames but it seems odd, and an impediment to the flow of the report, to read *The Times*, which was determined to adhere to what it considered to be form. Thus, all Australian players whose deeds they reported had the prefix Mr to denote status, while Hobbs, for instance, one of the most revered figures in all of England, was simply Hobbs, which denoted his.

After their struggles to take wickets at Lord's, the tourists restored their equilbrium with three successive wins, against Northamptonshire,

Nottinghamshire and Worcestershire. Warren Bardsley, continuing his glorious Lord's form, made 112 in the first, 87 in the second and was top scorer in both innings of the third with 35 and 55. In these matches, the Australians encountered three of the possible England Test team, Arthur Carr and Harold Larwood for Notts and Fred Root for Worcestershire. Larwood took three wickets in the county's innings defeat, including one with the new ball, and he was reported to have 'bowled well but with no great fortune.' Carr, finding runs ever harder to come by, failed in both innings. Root did not have quite the mesmerising effect on Australia that he had had for the North a month earlier, but he still managed to remove Charlie Macartney without scoring.

A trio of victories, however, did not quite amount to unhindered preparation for the Headingley match. Australia's misfortune with injuries and illness was now a serious concern. Herbie Collins, their captain, was in a London nursing home suffering from neuritis in the shoulder. Neuritis is the inflammation of a nerve which causes severe pain and when it occurs in the shoulder it runs down the upper arm. Collins hardly slept for three nights. There was no chance of him recovering to play in the Leeds Test. Warren Bardsley would captain Australia. In addition, Bill Ponsford was still feeling the long-term debilitating effects of tonsillitis, while Jack Ryder had sprained an ankle.

The former colossus Jack Gregory was in a struggle for fitness which he never truly won and, though this rugged hero bowled through the pain of shin splints, his effectiveness was severely impeded. The upside was that Clarrie Grimmett would have to be included. Perhaps he should never have been omitted. In his only previous Test appearance, in the final match of the 1924/25 Ashes series, he had run through England, and in the Australian season before the party left for this tour he had taken 59 wickets, 17 more than the next man on the list. There were also suggestions that Australia should call up Charlie Kelleway, who was in England reporting the series for *the Daily Express* (and might have taken up the appointment for precisely this possibility), or Ted McDonald, sensation of the 1921 tour who was now playing for Lancashire.

If Australia had troubles, England were in the happy position of having the upper hand. They picked their squad for the Third Test eight days before the match. There was only one change: Charlie Parker, the Gloucestershire left-arm spinner replaced Percy Holmes, the Yorkshire opening batsman. The inference was clear. The selectors felt that Lord's showed they had the batting to cope but that they needed more bowling. This was further emphasised three days before the match when George Geary, the Leicestershire fast medium bowler, was added to the party, bringing its number to 14. 'None can say that the present selection committee are not wide awake,' said one report. Since Geary had, within a few days of the original selection, taken 12-110 for his county against Gloucestershire and 5-52 in the first innings for Players v Gentlemen at The Oval they would have all needed to be comatose not to notice that he was in form.

As the more determined spectators began gathering outside and the Northumberland miners sought refuge in a shop doorway the mood inside the ground was suddenly despondent. Ted Leyland, the Headingley head groundsman and father of the rapidly rising Yorkshire batsman Maurice, had been working towards this moment for six weeks. He said in an interview on the afternoon before the match: 'That wicket will last until the Australians come again.' Hardly had he uttered the last word than the heavens opened. Within half an hour Headingley was a lake, and Leyland knew that all his efforts might be in ruins. 'Half an hour ago I promised that it would be as good on Tuesday night as it would be tomorrow morning. Now I can't say. It will be funny. It's nearly heartbreaking.' That evening one thought was uppermost, at any rate in pundits' minds: if play began – and it might well not – then Charlie Parker was a certainty on the team sheet.

First Day
After the deluge. Day broke around 5am and the sun shone immediately. It kept on shining for six hours. The combination of sun on a damp surface meant a sticky wicket was in prospect with potential to make batting hazardous. Ted Leyland's lovingly prepared pitch never had a prayer of being used, the storm having made it unplayable at one end. The strip nearby which had been intended for the Championship match a month earlier between Yorkshire and Nottinghamshire, abandoned without a ball bowled, was pressed into service.

Various members of the England coterie descended on the middle in the hour before the match was due to start. Arthur Carr was joined initially by Herbert Sutcliffe, who would have known what might be expected on his home turf, and there soon followed the selectors, Plum Warner, Arthur Gilligan and Jack Hobbs. Gilligan the only bowler in sight. The England captain was not short of advice. Two matters were certainly up for discussion – what to do if the toss was won and what the team should be – though Carr's involvement meant that a chat about dinner arrangements could not be entirely ruled out. As the England captain – and there had been 13 of them – had won the toss in 31 of the previous 63 Tests to have been played in England and had chosen to bat on 31 occasions it was pretty evident what Carr might choose to do. Australia had inserted England in 1909 and won but the other seven occasions in the Ashes when one of the teams had chosen to field had all been in Australia. In any event, the possibility of a capricious, drying wicket on which the sun was shining was a clear indication that Charlie Parker, probably the best sticky wicket operator in England and easily the season's leading wicket-taker, was about to double his number of Test caps. Neither of these things happened.

Ten minutes before play was due to begin at 11.30am England won the toss in front of the Headingley pavilion. Carr had another conflab with his confreres. Although he would have needed to reveal his team before he went out to toss, as was then the convention, the eleven, without Parker, was not publicly known until after he had gone to let Bardsley know that England would field. The two decisions were both in the realms of the sensational, and the feeling was that Carr had not acted entirely alone.

But the spectators now packing Headingley had seen nothing yet. From the team that played at Lord's England replaced Larwood and Root with Macaulay, on his home ground, and the bang in-form Geary. It seemed as though England were putting eggs of a similar kind in their basket: three right-arm fast-medium bowlers to lead the attack.

Parker's omission still seems a startling piece of cloth-headed thinking. If he was in the reckoning because he was in excellent form, there seemed to be a high chance that the conditions would also favour him. Form and conditions – a wonderful, oft elusive combination for a bowler. He was not everyone's pal, that is certain, because he had forceful opinions and his politics were distinctly radical and anti-establishment. There was no doubt where Parker's sympathies lay in the current industrial upheaval. The selectors would have it that by this stage it was up to Carr to nominate the eleven he wanted, but still it is difficult to suppress the thought that Warner and his chums had some say in both matters, guidance if not instruction. Carr said that fielding was a tremendously difficult decision and also bizarrely suggested that he was not quite old enough at 33 'for all the responsibilities and worries a Test captain has to face.'

As the teams walked out shortly afterwards the sun went in for the first time that day. It never reappeared. Although that was to matter a great deal it seemed singularly unimportant when the match started. Maurice Tate bowled the first ball to Bardsley, unbeaten hero of Lord's. It nipped away slightly, caught the edge and Sutcliffe at first slip took a smart catch by his toes.

Macartney came in, surprised to do so and not only because of the immediate fall of the wicket. 'After I had had a strike at the nets I inspected the wicket myself for my own satisfaction. In my opinion, it was without doubt a batsman's wicket. When Bardsley came in and said we were batting I told him I was glad that he had won the toss.' He played his first two balls defensively and then got off the mark with two behind point where Percy Chapman might have done better to intercept. To his fourth ball, the fifth of the over, Macartney nibbled outside the off stump. Carr, who had quietly shifted from gully to third slip, moved to his left to take the catch two-handed. But as his right hand came round, it dislodged the ball which fell to the ground.

Views differed on the level of difficulty of the catch. Plum Warner conceded it was not straightforward but said Carr would have held it four times out of five. Frank Mitchell said it was not difficult, Alf Noble difficult but not uncatchable. A consensus was that he would have been better advised to go with one hand instead of two. The two protagonists also had differing views. Carr said: 'Macartney slipped me a catch that I could have caught ninety-nine times in a hundred and I put it on the floor.' Macartney thought otherwise: 'I gave a difficult chance to Carr in the slips. In fact, I was surprised that he got his hands to it.'

What was in no doubt was that Macartney, thus reprieved, proceeded to play one of the greatest innings in all Tests. (Carr's mind might have drifted back five years. At Trent Bridge in 1921 the Australians were a wicket down quickly against Notts after Bardsley was out to his first ball. Macartney replaced him that day as well and was soon dropped at slip, though he had nine runs on that occasion and the errant fieldsman was George Gunn, Carr's partner in the cordon. He went on to make 345.) Once more, Macartney made the most of his escape against a side led by Carr. His timing was effortless, his placement precise, his stroke selection nonchalantly audacious.

The pitch, rather than containing demons, played angelically, and Macartney matched its qualities. The bowlers were rendered equally innocuous before a dashingly confident exhibition, combining, as it did, flowing movement and grace. Macaulay and Kilner, on their home ground, might as well have been playing on Mars. Macartney made 112 before lunch from 151 balls and with Bill Woodfull put on 235 for the second wicket, a Test record. When Macartney was out for 151, playing only his second false stroke of the innings, caught at deep mid-off, Woodfull had scored 80. Although Tommy Andrews was soon leg before to Kilner, Australia swiftly reasserted their authority. Woodfull reached his stoic hundred, Arthur Richardson was similarly entrenched but badly dropped by Geary at slip on 23.

There was no doubt whose day it was and equally no doubt whose fault it was. Arthur Carr went in at lunch, when the damage had been but partially inflicted, and was met with stony silence.

'The whole memory of that missed catch is almost more than I can bear,' he said in his memoirs. 'I think I spent the most dreadful luncheon interval in all my experience of cricket. Every blessed thing had gone wrong for me ... To add to my miseries PF Warner sat at the table a few places away with a face like nothing on earth.'

There were three big issues arising from the day. Was Carr right to field? If so, why was Parker omitted? And precisely how wonderful was Macartney's innings?

There was widespread sympathy for Carr's decision in the circumstances. EHD Sewell, whose reputation was built on forceful opinions, said it was the 'maddest of blunders' while sharing the apportionment of blame. Others were much more understanding. Several former Engand captains had opinions.

STANLEY JACKSON: 'If the sun had come out I think he would have been proved right.'

JOHNNY DOUGLAS: 'Whatever Mr Carr did he did for his side and according to his judgement. His judgement may be perfectly right for all we know.'

SHRIMP LEVESON GOWER: 'It is a bold course but Carr is a courageous captain and on that account deserves every credit.'

ARTHUR GILLIGAN: 'When the captains walked out to toss it is not at all sure either very much wanted to win the spin.'

PLUM WARNER: 'I had to walk most of the four miles back to my hotel and when I got to bed I dreamed that I was captain of a team in Australia, that I put Australia into bat and Trumper and Duff had made 400 without either of them losing their wickets.'

But none was as contentious on the subject as Archie MacLaren, a man never averse to controversy. In the *News of the World*, MacLaren wrote: 'On Warren Bardsley being caught first ball, the chairman of the selection committee remarked "We arranged to put them in last night."' The chairman and his selection committee were incandescent at such a slur. They eventually issued a statement to say that MacLaren's comments were completely without foundation. To which MacLaren responded: 'I withdraw not one word that I have written in regard to the putting in of Australia at Leeds.' It was sufficient to leave a scintilla of doubt about what actually took place.

Right or wrong, no England captain put Australia in to bat again for more than 50 Tests spanning nearly 30 years until Len Hutton chose to field at Brisbane in 1954/55. On that occasion, Australia made 601-8 declared and won easily. The next time it happened in England was in 1964 at Lord's when the first two days were washed out and a draw was all but inevitable. It was not until 1985 that England opted to field and won – by an innings and 118 runs at Edgbaston when the Kent swing bowler Richard Ellison enjoyed a remarkable match by taking ten wickets. But in 1926 the decision to put Australia in, allied to that of leaving out Parker, still seems inexplicable.

No hyperbole was too expansive, no praise too grand for Macartney's batting. The chairmen of selectors were in unison. Clem Hill, in the *Daily Mirror*, said: 'I have never seen a more beautiful innings. It was a cricket classic. I have seen little Mac play fine knocks but this was his masterpiece.'

This was prosaic stuff compared to Hill's opposite number Warner in the *Morning Post:* 'When he left the whole ground stood up and applauded as one man and applauded him as no batsman has ever been applauded and he deserved every cheer for this was one of the great innings in the history of the game. No Grace, no Ranji, no Trumper, no Hobbs could have surpassed this cricket.'

You probably get the picture, but there was yet more where all that came from. 'This innings opened for him the door where the immortals of cricket dwell.' 'His batting gleamed with the exquisite beauty of Greek art.' For the three hours he was at the crease at Headingley that day Charlie Macartney was batting *in excelsis*.

Rain stopped play for the day at 5.20, or Australia on this featherbed of a pitch might easily have added another 120 runs. As it was, they could not lose.

Close: Australia 366-3 (Woodfull 134, Richardson 70)

Both teams spent the evening in Roundhay Park, Leeds, watching the military tattoo as guests of Lt-Gen Sir Charles Harington, commander of the British Army in the North. The tattoo was the highlight of the city's tercentenary celebrations and attracted 120,000 people. With an estimated 30,000 having attended the Test match, it was said to be the busiest weekend in Leeds' history.

The Roundhay event enshrined most of the facets of British military might, and if it was designed to remind people that their discordant country still occupied a significant place in the world it hit the spot. One report suggested that in it 'we saw the spiritual presence of Britain herself.' The massed multitudes ended the evening by singing *Land of Hope and Glory* and *Abide With Me* and did not disperse until 3am.

A few miles down the road in the next county, Nottinghamshire, the miners' leader Arthur Cook addressed an audience of around 50,000 in Bulwell Forest. 'There is not a Cabinet minister who dare stand up and face an audience in the mining areas,' he thundered. 'I'm not suggesting that Mr Baldwin or his colleagues would suffer violence if they accepted the challenge but that, hard-faced though they may be, they cannot defend their conduct to the people they are fighting.'

Their conduct at that moment was readying for the implementation of the Eight Hours Bill on Monday morning. It was intended that mines would re-open with workers expected to work eight hours a day instead of the previous seven (plus an hour's winding time) with what was now decided should be a ten per cent reduction in wages. This was the 77th day of the dispute, and it put into perspective the slogan with which Cook had marshalled the workforce since its first: 'Not an hour on the day, not a penny off the pay.' His audience greeted the end of his rousing speech by singing *Pack Up Your Troubles* and *The Red Flag*. Sentiments in the songs apart, perhaps they were not much different from their fellow Englishmen who were packed into Roundhay Park.

The cricket reports in the Sunday papers were accompanied by a display advertisement taken out by businessmen claiming not to be involved directly or indirectly in coal production. They simply wanted the coal miners to have the facts. The advert duly pointed out that in the last three months of 1925 almost three quarters of coal from British mines were produced at a loss (which totalled around £3.8 million, equivalent to almost £2 billion in the 21st century). The Eight Hours Bill, it said, gave mines and miners the chance to turn a loss of one shilling, five pence a ton into a profit of six pence a ton. What the advert did not say was that royalties were still being paid to the owners on whose land the collieries stood and that the colliery owners had pocketed more than £60m in profits in the post-war boom years, none of which had gone into modernising the mines.

Second Day

In its way, this was the day that confirmed the direction the series was taking. Had Australia shown more gumption in the morning session they might have created a winning position. For a long while in the afternoon, England seemed determined to help them do it. As it was, they were content to dawdle and the suspicion grew that they were staking everything on a play-to-a-finish contest at The Oval – assuming that could be definitively agreed.

Arthur Richardson symbolised their approach. He had reached a dogged 70 on the first day from 125 balls but now faced another 109 to make the 30 runs he needed to reach what would be his only Test hundred. England, especially Tate, bowled with more zest than they had on the first day, but there was a lack of purpose about their opponents.

The tourists lost their remaining seven wickets in the morning session, bowled out five minutes before lunch having added 128. Woodfull was bowled by Tate, one of the few balls he missed in his entire innings, and poor Johnny Taylor, of whom so much had been expected, continued a lean trot by neatly leg-glancing George Geary only to find himself caught by the nimble Bert Strudwick, returning at last to form. It was the end of Taylor's international career.

Richardson was run out by a smart piece of work from Macaulay who intercepted a hard drive to his right off his own bowling, saw that the batsman had advanced and threw down the stumps with a direct throw.

Tate bowled 15 consecutive overs at the start of the day for only 22 runs and then returned to finish off the innings with something of his familiar pep.

He was a real student of bowling by now. He thought about each and every delivery, and he was aware both how good he was and how hard bowling was (and is). Tate was quite willing to try to explain what it was he was trying to do. 'A ball of my own that gets many wickets,' he said, 'is one that swings away from the batsman, then nips off the pitch to take off stump. The swing through the air and the way the ball comes back is what baffles the man at the wicket. Of course, a first-class batsman could undoubtedly guard against these evils if only he could tell by my hand what ball I intend to deliver. Many batsmen have watched me, however, and many say that it is impossible to guess that this ball is coming from any movement of mine. Perhaps the only peculiarity of this ball is the low trajectory and the flick of the wrist at the moment of delivery. Yet I do not doubt that if another player went through exactly the same action from first to last, he would not secure the same delivery. The plain truth about bowling is that every man must develop his own swing and break for himself.' Easy for him to say, you might suppose.

England's reply was based on survival, a decision they might have come to rue. Hobbs and Sutcliffe were in no trouble for long enough, but then they invited none. They pootled along at two runs an over before Sutcliffe, essaying adventure for the first time, popped back a return catch to Clarrie Grimmett, the leg-spinner's first wicket in a Test in England. Hobbs, on 49, attempted to push a single to the leg side off Arthur Mailey to bring up his half century but the ball turned, took the outside edge and ended up with Andrews at silly point.

From 104-1 England went to 182-8 as Australia's three spinners all had success on a pitch which was probably wearing more quickly than expected. In his first innings of the series Carr hung around for three quarters of an hour before getting his pad in front of a straight one. A brief entertaining interlude was provided by Roy Kilner who four times in an over pulled Mailey to the square-leg boundary – where he was eventually caught athletically. It was a cameo which showed Kilner's all-round value to England.

His star still seemed to be in the ascendant. The Roy Kilner Bat was much sought after, perhaps oddly considering the presence of Hobbs,

Sutcliffe, Woolley, Hendren. Advertisements trumpeted its qualities as the series gripped the nation. 'Every member, except one, of the Australian XI in the last series of Test matches against England, used a Roy Kilner bat and Jack Ryder's record Test score of 201 not out was compiled with the Roy Kilner bat.' Since Kilner was one of those who bowled at Ryder in that innings at Adelaide, sending down 54 overs, it must have been constantly perplexing to look at his own bat being used quite so proficiently.

Geary and Macaulay, both of them disappointing with the ball, saw out nine overs till the close without mishap. But England were still in a heap of trouble and needed another 142 runs to avoid the follow-on.

Close: Australia 494 all out; England 203-8 (Geary 6, Macaulay 18)

The crowd, estimated at more than 35,000, was greater on the second day than the first, despite it being a Monday. Several shops and businesses closed having 'anticipated the avalanche of grandmothers' funerals.' The attendances everywhere – at the Test, the Tattoo and the Miners' Rally – were doubtless fuelled by the country being in the middle of a heatwave at last.

Parliamentary business went on as normal. There was a brouhaha about government contracts being awarded to a company run by the family of the health minister Neville Chamberlain in which he held a significant shareholding. An opposition motion for a select committee inquiry was defeated after an intervention from Prime Minister Stanley Baldwin. 'When any person is asked to join a government, is he to sell out his interests at once or wait? What is he to invest in? Railways are dangerous, there might be a strike. A future Prime Minister when making up his government will have to advertise: "Wanted, foundlings with no relations and penniless."'

Any assessment or analysis of Baldwin should include mention of the remarkable gesture he made in 1919 when he was Financial Secretary to the Treasury in the Coalition Government. He had already given away around £40,000 to various charities in Worcestershire before and during the war when he wrote an anonymous letter to *The Times*. Signing it FST, which might have given the game away, he spoke of the crisis through which the country had passed, the challenges it still faced and the responsibilties of the wealthy classes. Perhaps embarrassed by the vast profits the Baldwin ironworks had made during the war, he proposed donating a fifth of his personal fortune to the Treasury to help pay off the Government's war loan and reduce interest rates. It amounted to £120,000 (around £9.1 million in 2024). It made a considerable dent in his future finances, but his hope that others with great financial resources would follow his lead and help to raise £1 billion towards paying off the country's debt fell on deaf ears. Only another £500,000 was forthcoming.

Third Day

Somehow, England needed to stave off defeat, a proposition made slightly easier by the opposition's reluctance to demonstrate that they were actually seeking to win. The task was achieved in relative comfort, though not before England were forced to follow on.

The pitch had returned to a state of blamelessness despite the doom-laden prognostications, and Geary and Macaulay batted with unexpected skill. Macaulay was the more eye-catching of the pair, but Geary ensured that nothing passed his bat. They took their ninth wicket partnership to 108 when Macaulay gave Grimmett a return catch. It was his only false stroke in an innings that contained ten fours and a fleetness of movement against spin hitherto largely concealed. Geary was left unbeaten when Studwick was held at mid-on in Grimmett's next over, and when he carried out his bat 'he had it crooked for the first time,' said Philip Trevor.

With the follow-on in mind and a long afternoon ahead, Bardsley conserved his bowlers' energies, using them largely in short spells and making nine changes in the 41 overs bowled before the innings ended. In its way, this was an ideal circumstance for Hobbs and Sutcliffe. All (all!) they had to do to ensure that England escaped with a draw and thus avoid the monumental task of having to win the last two Tests, was not to get out. Yet they faced a deficit of 200 and any mis-step might lead to danger. It is a measure of their mastery that nobody expected them to fail. They duly obliged, confronted with a labouring Gregory and a variety of spin.

By the time Hobbs was bowled for 88 by Grimmett at 4.10pm he had passed Clem Hill's total of 2,673 runs in Ashes Tests and he and Sutcliffe had shared their eighth century opening partnership (as well as another four above 50) in 18 innings. Sutcliffe, too, was denied a hundred, bowled by Richardson with the end in sight, which left time for Chapman to indulge himself gleefully by smiting 42 from 32 balls in 24 minutes, including the match's only six. If it were to be Chapman's last and only meaningful contribution of the series, it left the 12,000 spectators at Headingley with a smile on their faces.

Close: England 294 all out and 254-3 (following on) Match drawn

The inquest was predictable. The policy of three-day Test matches must be abandoned for the good of the game. Aubrey Faulkner, casting an old performer's knowing eye on the affair, had a notion of where the fault lay. 'I might be misjudging the Australians but never once throughout the match have I ever had the impression that they have played other than to secure a draw. It seems they were content to rest on their laurels until the Fifth Test comes to be played. They are in possession of the mythical Ashes and are apparently not in the least bothering as to what actually happens as long as they are not actually beaten.'

If blame were to be attached it might be at the door of bowling being generally too innocuous to dislodge batting which was too often unambitious (the pre-lunch first-day batting of Charlie Macartney being a glorious exception). But that is to look at it from the perspective of a century later. The number of hours and days played, by which everyone – players, officials, journalists, the paying public – was so exercised, seems less pertinent, as at Lord's, than the number of overs bowled and the runs scored and wickets taken in them. The Headingley match of 1926 comprised 379 overs featuring 1,042 runs and 23 wickets – a scoring rate of 45.82 runs per 100 balls and a wicket rate of one almost every 100 balls, neither of which would be nearly enough to effect a result other than the draw in any but a timeless match. Seventeen Ashes Tests at the ground, before and since, have contained fewer overs but only three of them have been draws. But the three-day Test had had its day. None other than Lord Harris entered the fray – with a vigour that belied both his 75 years and his reputation for defending the status quo, not only as an MCC mandarin but also as the Life President of the Stick In The Mud Club. In a speech to the Cricketers' Fund Friendly Society he said that the Laws of the game must be changed to make run scoring more difficult. His Lordship told an astonished audience that too many runs were being scored on wickets that were too easy because of their preparation using marl.

'I have been all my life a resolute opponent of any such alterations in the Laws of Cricket as would affect either the implements used or the law of leg before but I have at last come round to the view that something has got to be done to help the bowler.'

Such was the consternation created that *The Times* carried columns of letters for days afterwards. Not many of them cared or dared to disagree with Lord Harris, though CF Corbould-Harris wrote from Founders' Hall to suggest that Test matches should be played on a Sunday to take up the slack. 'If it is a matter of ecclesiastical sin to play a cricket match on Sundays,' he asked, 'why so is receiving a cup of tea from an overfed and underworked butler in a deanery garden? Why should we be balked of enjoyment on the best and most carefree day of the week?'

If this seemed heresy, John Gibb, a former Berkshire captain, invoked cricket's greater, almost mystical value. 'The effect of change affects first-class and village cricket all over the world. The prospects of the professional cricketer have to be considered. Our morals, our ethics are the very atmosphere of the game. It is one of the finest influences in the formation of character in which snobbery and conceit have no place. It would seem therefore that any change must be in the best interest of the game and not merely to satisfy a commercial tendency.'

The Bowlers' Union spoke as one. Maurice Tate said he found it difficult to get any life out of pitches and 'something ought to be done.' Fred Root warned that the surfaces were too perfect which meant the bowler had little chance and also worried that the batsman was always given the benefit of the doubt, while George Geary pointed out that the dressing used meant that 'even on a wet wicket the bowler's chances were not greater.'

As Lord Harris was involved, there was bound to be some sort of response. The following summer the ball was made smaller by three-sixteenths of an inch. But it was not until 1931 that the height of the wicket was raised by an inch and 1935 that the lbw law was changed in favour of the bowler. So great has the dominance of the bat become a century later that there might be a case for starting a new campaign on behalf of the bowler. Percy Chapman might have stood alone in striking the only six in the Headingley Test of 1926 from the 1,042 runs scored but in the Ashes match at the ground in 2023, though the art of defence seemed to have been mislaid, the total of 978 runs contained 18 sixes. Lord Harris would definitely have delivered a speech.

ENGLAND
v.
AUSTRALIA.

ANOTHER
DRAW.

THE TEST QUESTION.

Disgusted Miner. "WHY DON'T THEY WORK LONGER HOURS?"

Frank Woolley

England

Left-hand bat, slow left-arm bowler

Born: 27.5.1887 Tonbridge, Kent
Age on 1.5.26: **38**
County: Kent

Record at start of 1926

Tests: 47, debut 1909
2,325 runs @ 34.70, HS 134*
64 wickets @ 36.25, BB 5-20

F/c matches: 515, debut 1906
30.503 runs @ 39.00, HS 305*
1,792 wickets @ 18.82, BB 8-22

In a Test team full of stars few shone as brightly as Frank Woolley. His special relationship with those who followed the game was built simply on his style: everything he did as a cricketer exuded grace and elegance. When Woolley batted, or bowled, or fielded, it was always high summer. Using a heavy bat, standing tall at the crease, he hit the ball crushingly hard to all corners, but it seemed as though he were caressing it with a wand.

By the time the 1926 series began, Woolley had played in 47 consecutive Test matches, beginning with his debut in 1909, the longest run by far of any England player. Only Wilfred Rhodes had played more overall. His figures with both bat and ball, which did not much change, were not especially outstanding (though his 57 catches as a fielder were far more than anyone else). Yet from the moment he played for England, three years after making his Kent debut, there was never any serious proposal to leave him out.

Woolley was born to play the game. The family home was in Tonbridge, barely 100 yards from the famous Kent nursery, which had been established at the Angel Ground in 1897 when he was ten and was to pay handsome dividends. The youngest of four brothers, they played every day in the summer in the courtyard of their home in the town's High Street where their father had established the Medway Motor Company. Years later Frank would recall: 'My sixth birthday. What a wonderful present! For the first time my brothers allowed me to bat. It made me feel like a man.'

It all happened pretty quickly. At 10 he was first paid for playing when the Tonbridge club's opposition turned up a man short; the watching Woolley was recruited and later rewarded with half a crown. When he was 12 he was standing one day by a tree behind the Angel Ground watching a left-arm spinner bowl. The bowler noticed the boy and, on being told that he too bowled left-arm, invited him to take part. It was 20-year-old Colin Blythe, one of the first graduates of the Angel Nursery who was on the verge of making his Kent debut. A friendship – and a bowling action – was sealed. He was already 6ft 3ins tall when at 14 Frank's father placed him on the waiting list for Tonbridge School, but Kent offered him a place at the nursery. There, young men effectively served apprenticeships in cricket while also receiving an education. 'As usual Father wisely left the decision to me. "Was it school or was it cricket?" And of course there was only one answer. At that time, and nearly forever after, nothing else seemed to matter.'

At 18 he was called up to Kent's first eleven when Blythe was injured. He had a horrendous start – out for a duck and dropping Johnny Tyldesley three times before he had made 20, only to watch despairingly as he went onto 295 not out – but it was swiftly forgotten. In his third match Woolley scored 72 and 23 and took 3-27 and 5-82 in a thrilling Kent victory against Surrey, and in his fourth he scored his maiden century. He was 19. The *Athletics Weekly* reported: 'The man of the moment is indubitably Frank Woolley, the tall, reedy Kent cricketer. Everybody knows this boy now. The debutant of a few days ago, he is counted among the towering personalities of the great, exacting profession he has embraced. This Woolley has clutched and hangs on to a sensationally high rung of the ladder of his particular life in one dramatic bound.'

He never really let go. After the First World War, in which his dear friend Blythe was killed, Woolley was still in his prime. England, ravaged by the conflict, needed him for all manner of reasons. In 1921, when they selected 30 players in a futile Ashes campaign, he was one of only two to be retained for all five matches. At Lord's in that year, he scored 95 in the first innings and 93 in the second, supreme examples of glorious batting in adversity. With Ted McDonald and Jack Gregory rampant, Woolley not only resisted but counter-attacked. 'Very great innings,' said *The Times*. Woolley himself said they were his two finest innings. 'I don't think I ever worked harder at any match in my career to get runs as I did then.'

Woolley's long legs were said to be matched by his deep pockets. Virtually a teetotaller, he occasionally had the odd drink but seems not to have been keen to buy one for the other lads. His relationship with fans was based on the divine nature of his play rather than any claims to being a character. But like so many other professional cricketers of his generation, he was always immaculately turned out, a habit he was never to lose.

The Frank Woolley cricket shirt, marketed throughout the 1926 series, was an example of this trait. 'The Famous Frank Woolley sports shirt, made especially to the requirements and as a result of the expert experience of the world-famed All-England and Kent cricketer,' ran the tag line on the adverts. There was the impression that England felt they were fortunate to have someone like Woolley, a man who transcended mere facts and figures.

Clarrie Grimmett

Australia

Leg-break bowler

Born: 25.12.1891 Dunedin, Otago
Age on 1.5.26: **34**
State: South Australia

Record at start of 1926

Tests: 1, debut 1924/25
12 runs @ 12.00, HS 12*
11 wickets @ 7.45, BB 6-37

F/c matches: 33, debut 1911/12
931 runs @ 19.00, HS 57
158 wickets @ 26.74, BB 8-86

In the final match of the 1924/25 Ashes series, Clarrie Grimmett burst into Test cricket. He was 33, he had already played for Wellington, Victoria and South Australia and he took 11 England wickets, 5-42 and 6-37, beginning his mutually profitable collaboration with Bert Oldfield. It was a debut performance without precedent, and it would be unsurpassed for almost half a century. But when he came to England 18 months later he was still a one-Test wonder. The presence of Arthur Mailey, the English pitches, the infernal weather, the balance of the side, conspired to make Australia reluctant to pick Grimmett for the Tests. When they arrived in Leeds, there was little option, for the tourists were riven by illness and injury. Grimmett continued, more or less, where he had begun. For the third Test innings in succession he had a five-wicket haul and finished with seven in the match.

He was described, like Mailey, as a leg-spin bowler, but there the comparison ended. They were altogether different bowlers with different personalities. Bowling bad balls was part of Mailey's schtick; it was almost as if he relied on them as part of his armoury. Mailey was also a true spin bowler in that he was a copious and delighted spinner of the ball, either when bowling conventional leg-spin or the googly. Grimmett turned the ball but not as much, and he had other ways to torture the batsman. He did not drop short, his length was usually pinpoint; he did not bowl many wrong 'uns because he was not one to give too much flight, but he had myriad variations up his sleeve. Grimmett was a serious cricketer and a serious man. That is not to say that he and Mailey and, later, he and Bill O'Reilly did not get along. They did, and Mailey and O'Reilly spoke fondly of their fellow leggie.

Mailey: 'This man thought a full toss was the worst form of cricket vandalism and a long hop a legacy from prehistoric days when barbarians rolled boulders towards the enemy. Collecting a wicket was a mere incident in the game for Clarrie.'

O'Reilly: 'Grimmett never insisted on spin as his chief means of destruction. To him it was no more than an important adjunct to unerring length and tantalising direction ... And Grimmett was the best and most active cricket thinker I ever met.'

He developed several types of ball, of which the crowning glory after the leg-break, googly and top-spinner was the flipper. He used it sparingly and even deceived batsmen while not bowling it. Hearing the snap of his fingers, those on the receiving end thought they had picked the flipper – but meantime Grimmett was snapping the fingers on his left hand and delivering a leg-break.

Grimmett was born in Dunedin on the southern edge of New Zealand, and shortly afterwards the family moved to Wellington where he first began the rigorous regime of practice which was to serve him so well in big cricket. After playing nine first-class matches for Wellington with modest returns, he emigrated almost by accident to Australia in his early 20s – 'a working holiday that lasted 66 years' – first to Sydney and then to Melbourne. There, in his backyard he continued to bowl and bowl, putting the finishing touches to a long, dedicated schooling in his chosen craft, assisted by a fox terrier who fetched the stray balls.

The sight of Grimmett was utterly deceptive. He was slight, almost frail in stature, he looked as though he should be off for an audition in Snow White. But he knew instinctively what was going on in batsmen's minds, and he was strong and ferociously determined. His citation for his induction into the Sport Australia Hall of Fame said he was 'one of the most remarkable men ever to play cricket for Australia'.

It was a combination of ambition and marriage that took him from New South Wales, where Mailey blocked the way, to Victoria where he was offered scant opportunity, and finally to South Australia where he began by taking nine wickets in his debut match against Victoria. Five matches later he was in the Test team.

No bowler properly thrived in England in 1926, but Grimmett should probably have been in the team from the start as specialist bowler and proven performer. It was no more than the start for him, and he played in the vast majority of Australia's Test matches for the next nine years. He was the first man to reach 200 Test wickets, and his last three Test matches in 1935, at the age of 43, yielded 10, 10 and 13 wickets, after which he was mysteriously dropped, much to his continued anger. He is the only bowler to have ten-wicket hauls in both his first and last Tests. It was said that he was too old; Clarrie thought he was at his peak.

Fred Root

England

Fast-medium bowler

Born: 16.4.1890 Somercotes, Derbyshire
Age on 1.5.26: **36**
County: Derbyshire, Worcestershire

Record at start of 1926

Tests: 0

F/c matches: 154, debut 1910
3,412 runs @ 13.75, HS 81
654 wickets @ 19.95, BB 9-40

It took 16 years for Fred Root to become an overnight sensation. The son of the Leicestershire groundsman, he formed an early ambition to be a professional cricketer and on doing so shuffled in for more than a decade, never pulling up any trees, rarely disturbing the branches. But Root was smart and he worked out a deep and meaningful hypothesis about bowling. In the early 1920s, having moved counties from Derbyshire to Worcestershire via the Lancashire League, he developed it to its full. It was leg theory, the early manifestation of the most notorious bowling method in cricket history, which came to be known as Bodyline. Root was the pioneer of bowling fast, late inswingers on a leg stump line with a packed onside field. He preferred the wicketkeeper to stand back because of the lateness of the swing which, while it might offer stumping opportunities, took the ball well down the leg side.

Like two others in the 1926 team – Patsy Hendren and Maurice Tate – Root was a late bloomer. In the nine seasons in which he played at first-class level between 1910 and 1922 he took a total of 112 wickets. As early as 1912 he had an idea that leg theory could be effective, but it took until 1923 to put his cunning plan into action. With the necessary support and collaboration of Maurice Foster, his county captain – 'Bowl how and what you like, Freddie, so long as you stop opposing teams getting 500 runs every time they bat against us' – he took 170 followed by 153 and then in 1925, his apotheosis, his victims totalled 219.

He was undoubtedly a character, usually a cheerful chap, aware that playing cricket for a pittance was still preferable to what he might be doing otherwise. Equally, he could be grumpy about the assessment of his own worth. Root told an engaging story, part self-deprecating, part self-righteous indignation, about an episode in 1925, when he was approaching his cricketing peak. A Worcestershire supporter offered Fred the present of a car if he took 200 wickets and scored 900 runs in the season. Having taken his 200 wickets, Fred arrived at Blackpool for a festival match needing 18 more runs. According to Root he threw away his wicket in the first innings for 12, was down to open in the second when an amateur pulled rank. With one final chance in the annual match between the Champion County and The Rest, Fred claimed he was again denied on the morning of the match when he was made 12th man. Thus was he deprived of a car. The trouble with the story is that Fred reached his 900 runs when he scored 33 for the South v the North in his second festival match at Blackpool. No doubt he related it to emphasise the lot of the professional cricketer but, as he himself said, averages were an abomination of real cricket.

England's desperation to retain the Ashes in 1926 suddenly made Root, despite coming from one of the most unsuccessful and least fashionable counties, a viable option for the Test team, and in early June he was picked for the North of England XI against Australia. According to Root's entertaining testimony in his memoir he was a late call-up for a bowler who dropped out at the last minute, but all reports at the time indicate he was chosen in the initial eleven, though not selected for either team in the England v Rest match which seems to suggest that he was not uppermost in the selectors' thoughts at the time. Whatever, the tourists had never seen anything like it – which was very much the point – and Root ran through them with figures of 7-42. He was billed as the mystery bowler, and eight days later he was in the Test team.

That it was too good to be true was, as it happens, like some of Root's yarns, only partially the case. After rain ruined his debut and the First Test, he bowled 55 overs in the run festival at Lord's, was mysteriously dropped at Leeds when Charlie Parker, equally mysteriously, was also overlooked, and then bowled a heroic 52 overs in Australia's innings at Old Trafford, including one spell of 21 overs, to finish with 4-84. Leg theory needed accuracy, but its essential companion was stamina. Root had plenty of both and nor was he short of chutzpah. He had been in the game long enough to know his own worth; he was a professional's professional. After four matches of which he had played in three, Root was England's best bowler in terms of average and runs conceded per over. He was given half a nod for the final crucial Test. But half a nod is only the opening of negotiations, it is never enough to confirm selection in a cricket team.

Jack Ryder

Australia

Right-hand bat, medium-pace bowler

Born: 8.8.1889 Melbourne, Victoria
Age on 1.5.26: **36**
State: Victoria

Record at start of 1926

Tests: 11, debut 1920/21
829 runs @ 55.26, HS 201*
11 wickets @ 38.27, BB 2-20

F/c matches: 92, debut 1912/13
5,578 runs @ 42.58, HS 242
184 wickets @ 28.94, BB 7-53

Jack Ryder had a moderate time of it in the series. He scored 73 runs in four innings, took one wicket and did little to allay the grievances of his critics at home. There were many who felt he was not worth his place in the party and that he owed it to having been appointed a selector. His great performance in the Third Test at Adelaide in 1924/25 stayed in the mind, however, and made him hard to overlook. After Australia fell to 119-6 in the first innings he made 201 not out and added 88 in the second – then the highest aggregate in a Test – as they sneaked home by 11 runs.

Ryder may have been a victim of his side's apparent policy not to lose at any cost. This meant adopting a cautious approach when his natural game was to force the pace and he suffered accordingly. Ryder started his Sheffield Shield career as a quick bowler of high promise with the new ball who also batted proficiently, but after the First World War it was the opposite and he became a batsman who bowled much slower and much less frequently.

With the series on the line, tough decisions had to be taken and the fact that Ryder stood out as a slow-coach in an otherwise outstanding fielding side made his omission easier to make. At the age of 37 that might well have been the end of his international career. Far from it.

He was unexpectedly appointed to be captain of Australia in 1928/29 in his 40th year, and although it was a salutary experience his individual performance was outstanding. He was long a part of Australian cricket at international level as a limited player who still averaged above 50 in 20 Tests, as a selector for nearly a quarter of a century and at grade level where he became known in Melbourne as the King of Collingwood. When the Centenary Test was played in Melbourne in 1977 he was the oldest former player present.

Bill Ponsford

Australia

Right-hand bat

Born: 19.10.1900 North Fitzroy, Victoria
Age on 1.5.26: **25**
State: Victoria

Record at start of 1926

Tests: 5, debut 1924/25
468 runs @ 46.80, HS 128

F/c matches: 28, debut 1920/21
3,207 runs @ 74.58, HS 429

By the time Bill Ponsford came to England for the first time in 1926 he had scored 13 hundreds, a rate of slightly under one every three innings. The second of them, in only his fourth visit to the crease, was a world record 429. A few months later he shared in an opening partnership of 456 which for 63 years was Australia's highest for any wicket. Ponsford also scored hundreds in both of his first two Test matches in late 1924, the first to do so.

There was a slight fuss about whether his highest individual score was truly first-class (it was made for Victoria's second team against Tasmania and not a single player had appeared in the Sheffield Shield match immediately before). Despite the reservations of many, including Archie MacLaren, the previous record holder whose 424 against Somerset in 1895 Ponsford's score surpassed, it was granted official designation. In any case MacLaren's doubts should be perhaps greeted with scepticism since his innings had been made against a county side that contained nine amateurs including a 17-year-old village bowler who was more of a rugby player. Whatever the criteria, Ponsford looked to be a run machine. The English climate did for him in 1926.

He seemed to be coming to terms with the bitterly cold and damp May when, on his first, appearance at Lord's, he made 110 not out against MCC – 'a truly admirable display,' said *Wisden*. A few days later in Bradford, just before a thunderstorm struck, he was laid low by tonsillitis and taken to hospital. He never properly recovered the whole season. Out of action for most of June he was in no sort of form for weeks afterwards, though there was little option but to pick him for the last two Tests matches. Finally, in late July and early August, he scored successive centuries against Glamorgan and Warwickshire. But his first experience of England was forgettable.

Greville Stevens

England

Leg-break bowler, right-hand bat

Born: 7.1.1901 Hampstead, Middlesex
Age on 1.5.26: **25**
County: Middlesex

Record at start of 1926

Tests: 1, debut 1922/23
13 runs @ 6.50, HS 11

F/c matches: 142, debut 1919
6,531 runs @ 30.95, HS 182
432 wickets @ 24.12, BB 8-38

When Greville Stevens was seven years old a full page was devoted to him in the fashionable weekly magazine *The Sketch*. A series of photographs showed him imitating, with some accuracy, the styles of some of the great cricketers of the day including Ranji, CB Fry and George Hirst. The photographic feature was itself copied in provincial newspapers throughout the country. When he was 18, Stevens scored 466 not out in a total of 548 after coming in at 0-2, for Beta House against Lamda House at University College School, London (and then took 13 wickets in an innings victory). Barely a fortnight later he made his first-class debut for Middlesex and took ten wickets in the match. A few weeks after that he followed WG Grace in being selected while still a schoolboy for the Gentlemen in their Lord's match against the Players. By any yardstick Stevens was a prodigy.

His career, as an opening bat and leg-break-and-googly bowler who made things happen, continued its rapid progress for a few years. In 1920, still a teenager, he played a key role in securing the County Championship title for Middlesex. He started the summer by playing for Oxford University and joined up with Middlesex in July when they were barely above mid-table in the Championship.

It was Plum Warner's last season as captain at the age of 47, 28 years older than the youngest member of his side. Middlesex went on an improbable sequence of victories when, apart from anything else, it was vital they held their nerve. None did so more than Stevens. At Bradford he took the last wicket in a four-run victory over Yorkshire, and in the final, crucial match at Lord's the opponents were fellow title contenders Surrey. Nothing less than a win – their eighth in succession – would do for Middlesex to be champions for the first time in 17 years. It was a tense affair, and Stevens played a full part. He made 53, batting at number eight, in a disappointing Middlesex first innings which averted disaster at 149-6 and then took 5-51 including the last wicket to fall as the county got home by 55 runs. Warner was chaired from the pitch at a full Lord's. He was not the type of man to forget how much his young protégé had contributed.

Stevens played in the Varsity match for four successive years, and opening the innings for the Gentlemen he scored hundreds in 1922 and 1925. He was 'a bit of a glamour boy and had a large female following but he also had a dry sense of humour.' He could only have been an amateur. Although he would appear in Gents v Players matches for nine years he said after the second: 'This match isn't what it was and I'm bored with it.'

In 1922 he was involved in an incident which, though inherently trivial, would probably have finished a professional cricketer. Playing for Oxford University against Somerset he was given out lbw and said: 'I hit it.' Stevens continued to walk off but was then invited to resume his innings by the county captain and returned to the crease, though the umpire had not overturned the decision. MCC's secretary Frederick Lacey wrote to Stevens: 'MCC cannot too strongly remonstrate against such a disregard of the Laws of Cricket.' Stevens defended himself by insisting he was told to continue his innings by the opposition, but the incident was a blot on his escutcheon.

His cricket was beginning to be limited by his new career as a stockbroker. But he had a good summer in 1925, his last when he had a proper run of matches, and made himself a viable contender for the Ashes by making an immediate impression in 1926. He played two valuable innings against the Australians, first for MCC and then for Middlesex when, opening the batting, he scored the first hundred of the season against the tourists. Although he did not play any cricket from the end of May until the end of June he had caught the selectors' eye which was much easier to do at Lord's than at Leicester. His amateur status probably helped, and the patronage of the chairman of selectors should not be underestimated. No doubt with 1920 in mind, with the hunch that here was a player with the right stuff when it mattered, Warner acted.

Stevens' batting was built on a determined defence with the occasional threat to break the shackles, hitting powerfully despite a disconcertingly short backlift. He bowled a lot of indifferent balls, but his good balls were wicket-taking ones with a top-spinner that was hard to tell apart from his wrong 'un. It was still a leap of faith to call him up for the Fourth Test, but he acquitted himself adequately. Apart from anything else, Stevens, like a few others in the England side, was a big-game player. And they needed those more than ever.

9

MONSOON IN MANCHESTER

*The task of captaincy made no difference to me. The accident of Mr
Carr's illness may have made history but as far as I am concerned
I simply went through the game in an ordinary way.*
Jack Hobbs
(explaining his underwhelming reaction to becoming
the first professional to assume the England captaincy)

I used to believe in forever, but forever's too good to be true.
Winnie-the-Pooh
(explaining his philosophy in Winnie-the-Pooh by AA Milne)

Cricket was a travelling circus. Another day, another town. Same cast, by
and large. There was neither time nor place for rest. As soon as the Third
Test in Leeds finished at 6pm on Tuesday, ten of the England team – eight
professionals and two amateurs – took the all-night train to London for the
Gentlemen v Players match at Lord's on Wednesday, starting at 11.30am.
The Gents, Arthur Carr and Percy Chapman, travelled first-class, courtesy
of MCC. And the players might have felt preposterously grateful that they
too were having a third-class fare reimbursed, which was not the case when
they travelled for county matches. It was costing MCC around £2 – 2s
(£168 today) for the first-class singles and £1 – 5s for the third.

This was the way it was then. You had to put up and shut up. Privately,
the players might have been disgruntled, but they never said as much. The
aims of the General Strike two months earlier had not trickled down that
far. Some of them were probably uncomfortable about playing during
those nine days back in May – when there were nine Championship and
two Tourist matches – but they played anyway.

As Carr and Chapman travelled to London, quaffing a drink or two *en
route*, they were blissfully ignorant of what fate had in store. Here were
two posh good-time Charlies together. At point in their lives they
probably thought they would live forever, if indeed they gave it a thought.
But a new literary hero, the honey-loving bear Winnie-the-Pooh, created

by AA Milne and quoted at the top of the chapter, knew something about that. Arthur and Percy seemed to like each other, indeed they were like each other in many ways, as men and batsmen. But one was captain of England after serving a long apprenticeship in county cricket which had begun as a 17-year-old, and the other seemed little more than a passing fancy who had played most of his cricket for Cambridge University, MCC, Berkshire, various invitation elevens and, when he made his Test debut in 1924, precisely no Championship matches. Within a month of that train journey both their lives were changed utterly and forever. It would start with a night out in Manchester during the Fourth Test, at which both were present and the details of which remain hazy. But that evening, following the events at Headingley, perversely hastened Carr's downfall and Chapman's spectacular rise.

Carr's Ashes captaincy was hinting at the surreal. At Leeds he surprisingly left out Charlie Parker, the bowler who might inflict most damage; asked Australia to bat; dropped their best batsman on two and watched them dominate. Then, at Manchester, he fell sick: his absence for two days, suffering from tonsillitis, caused a tremendous kerfuffle and eventually myriad theories about the nature of the illness. In the immediate aftermath, that was overshadowed by the elevation to the captaincy of Jack Hobbs. The promotion, albeit temporary, was greeted with dismay by all sides in a country where deference remained the preferred, and usually the mandatory, option. That much had been resoundingly demonstrated when the proletariat were put firmly in their place during the General Strike. A professional captaining the England side represented, if not quite revolution and a Bolshevik insurgence, then a significant departure from the norm. Fortunately, it was Hobbs. Hobbs was liked by all, the faithful old retainer if you like. Jack could be trusted.

All the miners and thousands of railwaymen continued to pay the price of defeat. The miners were still locked out, still trying to negotiate some kind of settlement that would offer long-term security to an industry losing money. Arthur Cook was re-elected as general secretary of the Miners' Federation and came up with a new slogan. Not quite as catchy as 'Not A Penny Off The Pay, Not An Hour On The Day,' he unveiled it at a rally in Burnhope, County Durham. It was 'To Work We Will Go On The Status Quo'. It probably needed a bit of work itself. But the North-East pitmen responded as one when asked if they wished to continue the struggle. The railworkers' plight was linked to the coal dispute. Their employers imposed swingeing restrictions on a return to work while insisting that any future industrial action was curtailed. More than a quarter of rail staff, around 45,000 workers, had still not been allowed to return.

The Churches became involved. Randall Davidson, the Archbishop of Canterbury, had already tried to intervene during the General Strike, and a panel formed by him now proposed a settlement. The Archbishops' Committee, comprising delegates from several churches and led by John Kempthorne, the Bishop of Lichfield, spoke to both sides and hatched a plan for the miners to resume work. He wrote to Baldwin: 'I know how extremely busy you are but the representatives of the Anglican and Free Churches who are acting with me desire me to ask you whether you would consent to receive a deputation from us in the very near future.'

Although the Prime Minister agreed to meet them – 'This is of course, a request I cannot refuse' – there was an insurmountable obstacle. The return to work depended on a continuation of government subsidy, amounting probably to as much as £10m (a little more than £500m in 2024 values). Baldwin said the government plainly could not assent to this and told Bishop Kempthorne bluntly: 'Apart from any other consideration the disastrous effect of this prolonged stoppage on the national finances has made any further subsidy in aid of wages quite out of the question.' The Churches, like everybody else in the sea of intransigence, had failed.

By comparison to the long train ride south for the England players, the Australians had the doddle of a trip to Liverpool for a match against Lancashire. But they had other problems: it was the 22nd match of their tour and several players were still out of action. Stork Hendry was down in Somerset still suffering the effects of scarlet fever, Gregory was dreadfully under par and, with the benefit of almost a century of hindsight, was clearly bowling with an injury when he desperately needed rest. Collins, the captain, was on the mend but still unfit to play after being released from his London nursing home. He spent several days in July attending race meetings with the celebrated Australian-born trainer Stanley Wootton, who had stables at Epsom for 40 years. By that time the Wootton family were already a fixture in English racing circles. They had emigrated in the early 1900s, and Stanley's brother Frank remains the youngest UK Champion Jockey. He was only 16 when he rode 129 winners in 1908.

Herbie liked Wootton's company; he felt at home in the world of racing. The pair were often also accompanied to the course by Eileen Carthew, who had a string of thoroughbreds in Wootton's stable. She was the daughter of Edward Shortt, Home Secretary in Lloyd George's Government, and had been involved in a scandalous divorce case in 1920. The marriage lasted only two months when her husband left home and Eileen had used her settlement to invest in bloodstock. For a week or two Collins was quite the man about town, partnered by these two faintly exotic creatures. But his frustration at being told he would have to miss the Fourth Test was real enough.

The Players were grateful that Hobbs, captain for the 12th time in this fixture, won the toss against the Gentlemen. It meant that they could put their feet up after the overnight journey. On a spiffing pitch, the day after saving the Test, Hobbs and Sutcliffe resumed normal service, putting on 263 for the first wicket. It was only the second time that the opening partnership had exceeded 200 in this fixture, and the other occasion 51 years previously had featured WG Grace. Ernest Tyldesley, in the form of his life, also scored a century, his fifth in successive matches, for the Players (and he was not finished yet). In reply, Chapman supplied a timely and characteristically rumbustious 108 for the Gentlemen. The match yielded 1,218 runs for the loss of 21 wickets, the second highest aggregate in the fixture's history. It was red meat to the Lord Harris faction demanding fairer pitches for bowlers. When George Geary went over on an ankle and had to be helped off the field, almost certainly forcing his exclusion from the Fourth Test, the selectors had more to ponder.

The Australians had by far the better of the exchange with Lancashire at Aigburth. Arthur Mailey took 9-86 in Lancashire's innings, exemplary figures but not his career best. He had taken 10-66 against Gloucestershire on the 1921 tour. The tourists then repaired to Scotland for three two-day matches, away from the din of the Ashes. At this stage it might have been welcome respite. There was no reduction in the cacophony surrounding the series.

England's party was announced the day after the Gents v Players match. Wilfred Rhodes was again absent from the meeting because his contract with Yorkshire seems to have taken precedence over selection duties and he was not in the Players' team, presumably because the county had already been required to release three of their players. Hobbs, who was playing in the match, was there. As was Arthur Gilligan, the other playing member of the panel, who was able to attend because Sussex defeated Worcestershire in two days – after he scored a century.

The squad named was a mite confusing. It comprised 13 names, but there was no place for Macaulay, one of the heroes of Headingley. Tyldesley was designated as reserve, meaning that if the selectors stuck to their plans, the final team would be picked from the other 12. Fred Root and Charlie Parker were again present, but the surprising inclusion was that of the 25-year-old Middlesex amateur all-rounder Greville Stevens. Towards the end of May, Stevens had become the first player of the season to score a hundred against the Australians but he had played precious little cricket since, prevented by his job as a fledgling stockbroker. It amounted to an invitation match against Oxford University and two appearances for the Gentlemen in matches against the Players at The Oval, when he impressed by taking 5-62 with his leg-spin in the first innings, and Lord's.

Stevens had played one previous Test in South Africa four years earlier when a seriously depleted England party went out to contest the series, but here and now was a game of altogether a different vintage and status. His call-up demonstrated three things: the dearth of spinners, the belief that England needed spin to win the Ashes and that it did no harm at all to be a favourite of Plum Warner. But if Stevens was something of a wild card, he could play all right. Stevens brought to three the number of amateurs in the cadre.

But there was also the prolific Parker to consider as a spin option. Bizarrely omitted for the Leeds Test when conditions appeared to be completely in his favour, he remained bang in form: in the match after the Test squad was announced he took ten wickets and by the time it was due to start he had already bowled more than 1,000 overs in the season and taken 123 wickets, 20 more than the next man on the list. How could he be left out again?

This then was what much of the population, rich and poor, far and wide, was talking about. Such was the attention on the Test series that a proclamation in Parliament which would have a greater and more enduring effect on people's lives – more so perhaps even than the outcome of the industrial unrest – was yet another news item to play second fiddle. Postmaster-General Sir William Mitchell-Thompson told the House of Commons as part of the Post Office annual statement that the British Broadcasting Company, until then a commercial organisation, would be replaced under Royal Charter by the British Broadcasting Corporation.

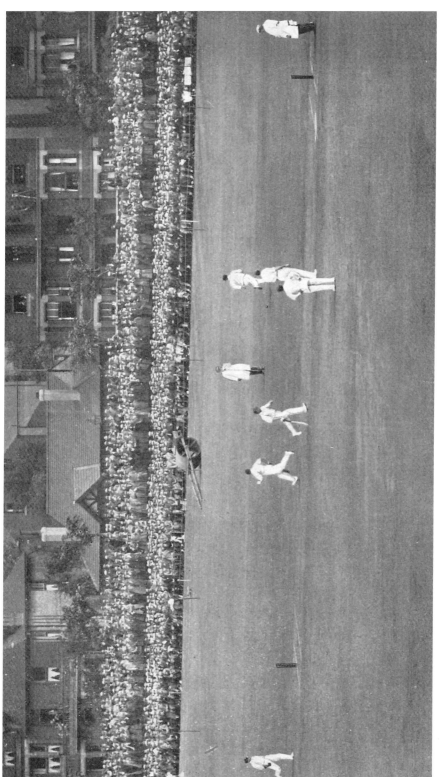

Jack Hobbs nudges a single to mid-wicket for the first run of the series from Jack Gregory's fourth ball.

Volunteers during the General Strike. Many of them were
undergraduates and officer cadets, wearing steel helmets, carrying
truncheons and ready to do their duty on behalf of the state.

Herbert Smith (second from right) and miners' delegates after another round of failed
negotiations during their long dispute. Smith's mantra was: 'We've nowt to give.'

Troops on London's streets as the General Strike takes hold. They were there to keep order and to ensure the peaceful transportation of food supplies.

Prime Minister Stanley Baldwin and his wife, Lucy, at Chequers. Both were passionate cricket followers and Mrs Baldwin was an accepted authority on the game who had played with distinction for the White Rose Ladies XI.

The mystery of the Lord's floods during a dry spell was later cleared up as a groundsman's error with a hosepipe. With the sun beating down, vast amounts of sawdust were necessary to ensure play went ahead with minimal delay. This shows Hobbs reaching his century.

England captain Arthur Carr moves to his left at third slip to try to catch Charlie Macartney off the fifth ball of the Leeds Test. He dropped the chance and Macartney went on to score one of the game's most perfect centuries.

Charlie Macartney acknowledges the crowd's awe-struck reaction as he leaves the field at lunch on the first day of the Third Test at Headingley. Having been dropped on two he went on to score an exquisite 112 before the break.

Jack Gregory, Australia's much-diminished titan, bowled through injury most of the summer. Here he is displaying his flowing, muscular action for the camera.

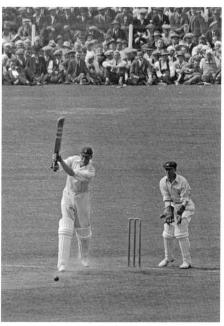

Frank Woolley drives through the covers in typically elegant style during the Third Test at Headingley but as so often in the series he flattered to deceive.

The captains toss in the Fifth Test at The Oval. By winning it, new captain Percy Chapman performed his first task correctly and answered the prayers of a nation.

Play on the third morning when Hobbs and Sutcliffe combined to save England with one of the greatest opening partnerships in all of Test history. Despite the sticky wicket, Hobbs penetrates a packed leg side with typical aplomb.

Hobbs and Sutcliffe on their way through the crowds as they leave the field at lunch on the third day at The Oval. Elation was mixed with relief at their epic deeds.

Tommy Andrews can only look in utter befuddlement as his off stump goes cartwheeling, undone by a rapid ball from Harold Larwood that broke back five inches and ensured England were on their way.

With the series grabbing attention everywhere, pupils from Eton College inspect bats outside the sports shop in the town High Street run by the school professional Mat Wright.

Small boys playing cricket in a London street watched by their mates.
It is what lads and lasses did then. Note the leg theory field.

With five men close to the bat, Herbie Collins, Australia's captain doggedly defends against Wilfred Rhodes, recalled at the age of 48, during the tourists' first innings at The Oval.

The crowd swarms on to the ground at The Oval immediately after England have regained the Ashes. Players in the background can be seen racing to reach the safety of the pavilion.

One of the great scenes in English cricket as Percy Chapman and his team gather on the Oval balcony to hear, see and feel the adulation of an adoring public.

England's victorious team shortly after the crowd had dispersed with the Ashes safely recovered. Note Chapman has changed out of his cricket boots.

The all-embracing hold of the wireless grew tighter. 'Even the present prosaic Postmaster-General,' said the *Westminster Gazette*, 'who is anxious to be as unromantic as possible could not divest himself of the character of a genie of the Arabian Nights. The magic carpet is out of date beside the modern wireless.' Mitchell-Thompson was nothing if not a survivor, however, and, as Baron Selsden, he wrote the White Paper which led to the BBC being given approval to develop television and indeed appeared on screen on the very first day of BBC television broadcasts in 1936. In 1926 they had only just left the foothills and were approaching base camp. The number of radio licences, said Sir William, had grown to 2,076,000 (in a population of almost 39 million). The licence fee was 10 shillings (50p) and would remain so under the new arrangements.

Cricket was already a regular part of the schedules. There was no live commentary, but in July alone there were programmes featuring Patsy Hendren, Fred Root (*The Mystery Bowler from Birmingham*), *Some Cricket Stories* from Mr WA Oldfield and a documentary from E Le Breton Martin, *Cradles of Cricket*. Edward Le Breton was a regular on the wireless in its early days. He was best known for his best-selling book *Boys of the Otter Patrol*, a ripping yarn about scouts which was later made into a popular silent film.

Another element to the BBC's role was also introduced by Mitchell-Thompson. In an effort to ensure uniformity of pronunciation an advisory committee was established to adjudicate on how words should be spoken by announcers. Led by the poet laureate Dr Robert Bridges and including the phonetician Professor Daniel Jones, who described it as 'received pronunciation', it was charged with reforming the accepted pronunciation of English so that all announcers sounded similar. There was protest and puzzlement from listeners in the north who were both annoyed and mystified by many cases: the long 'ah' being used to pronounce words such as 'task' and the 't' being omitted from those like 'often'.

Manchester was in a state of eagerness similar to that which had enveloped all three of the previous venues in the series. It was expected that there would be a repeat of the crowds which had descended on Trent Bridge, Lord's and Headingley, and the security operation was strengthened. To the 80 uniformed police officers due to be on duty inside the ground were added 20 detectives who would, said Lancashire Constabulary, 'protect the spectators from the usual gangs of pickpockets and tricksters who are always to be found on such occasions.'

Virtually on the eve of the Test there was news all of England had been hoping for. Their captain made some runs. In the final county match before Old Trafford, Arthur Carr hit a blazing 98 for Nottinghamshire at Lord's. Reporters could hardly contain their glee. True, he had made a fifty on the eve of the Third Test but that was a stodgy affair. This was Carr at his commanding peak. He whacked the bad ball in his usual dismissive fashion but he was watchful too, aware that he needed to find form by staying at the crease. It was a corner turned, and Aubrey Faulkner noted that it could not have come at a more opportune moment and should prove a fine tonic.

That evening, Carr was driving in Mitcham, Surrey and might have been over-excited by his return to form. He was stopped by a policeman for speeding – clocked at 22.5mph when the limit was 10mph. Carr told PC Williams, who stopped him, that he was hurrying to the Test match. This was being economical with the truth since his match against Middlesex was not due to finish until the following day. More likely, he was on his way home from Lord's to Walton-on-the-Hill where he and the family were living by then. Carr was fined 40 shillings (£2) on the speeding charge and 10s (50p) for having an out-of-date licence.

The Australians arrived at Manchester Station in a dishevelled state after travelling from Scotland where they had dominated all three of their matches (none first-class). Jack Ryder, who made a much-needed hundred in the third of them, told a porter as he was woken up by his team mates: 'This country isn't big enough for a sound sleep.' Bill Woodfull interrupted to say: 'I've had a terrible dream. I thought I had been bowled.' At least, they had a day to rest after the journey. One of the umpires, Sailor Young, arrived at his hotel in the early hours of Saturday after officiating in the Championship match between Warwickshire and Northants in Birmingham which went to the wire. Unable to rouse the landlord, he was forced to sleep outside.

As it turned out, there were not the multitudes outside Old Trafford that had descended on the other grounds. There was rain in the air, lots of it, and in any case a woman in the (short) overnight queue for her fireman husband who was on shift, had another theory: 'I expected thousands, I don't think Lancashire people are as interested in the game as Londoners and Yorkshire people.' Gradually the numbers increased and throughout the night, under gloomy skies and aware of the dire forecast, they sang the recent ukulele hit *It Ain't Gonna Rain No Mo'* by Wendell Hall with its terrific chorus: *'It ain't gonna rain no more, How in the heck can I wash around my neck if it ain't gonna rain no more.'*

There was no doubting the general fervour and the willingness of so many to be carried along by it. Unfortunately, it produced some insidious effects. Letters were being sent to players pointing out their perceived shortcomings – 'some very critical and even bordering on the abusive.' If nothing else it shows, sadly, that 21st century social media was not the original begetter of cranks and crackpots.

Arguments continued about what was needed to make the game fairer, and Lord Dartmouth, a former MCC president, entered the debate with a particularly novel idea, suggesting that pads should be abolished to discourage batsmen from getting their legs in the way. There appeared no end to an increasingly barmy discourse which could have been terminated by pitches being prepared differently, batsmen being less cautious and bowlers being, well, better. Dartmouth had a brief but singular first-class career – one match for MCC against Hampshire in 1877 when he was not out in both innings and therefore finished with an aggregate of 29 runs and an average of infinity. It was time for the Test to start and yet again there was to be disappointment.

First Day

More in optimism than expectation the crowd had reached 19,000 by 11am. It was raining then and did not relent until 2.30pm, allowing the toss – Bardsley called correctly – upon which it rained again. England prevaricated about their side, fearing that both the toss and the weather would be influential. From their 13 they omitted Chapman and Parker. If Tyldesley, originally nominated as reserve, was a home-town pick he also had the advantage of having scored centuries in seven successive matches and making what could be described as an unanswerable case. Chapman, having scored his thunderous hundred for the Gents, might have been slightly miffed. Parker's absence once more provoked some severe hand-wringing in the papers.

None were wrung so agonisingly as those belonging to BJT Bosanquet, inventor of the googly. 'He is presumably chosen to be present so that he can be played if there is any prospect of a wicket suited for him. What happens? He is present at Leeds, the wicket is such that before the team is chosen it is bad enough to put the other side in and it is then decided to leave him out. We come to Manchester. It has rained previous to the commencement and more rain is probable. Parker is again omitted, and this time after the other bowlers have shown their inadequacy on a slow wicket. One is tempted to ask under what special circumstances would he be played?' For Parker the circumstances were never again special enough for him to be chosen in a Test match. After he was left out at Leeds, perhaps it should have been no surprise. By this time in his life and career, Parker was his own man, an autodidact with strong feelings of right, wrong and about the imbalance in society. It could be easily concluded that he was not Plum Warner's cup of tea; Greville Stevens was, probably with a dash of milk and two sugars.

England's team remains their oldest to take the field in a home Test match at an average age of 36 years, 57 days. Their side was older in all four matches in the West Indies in 1929/30 but that was the winter of two tours (they also went to New Zealand and two of the Tests in each series overlapped), so it hardly counts. For this Fourth Test of 1926, two England players (Jack Hobbs and Bert Strudwick) were in their forties, four over 35 (Frank Woolley, Patsy Hendren, Roy Kilner and Ernest Tyldesley) and only one (Greville Stevens) in his twenties.

Australia introduced Bill Ponsford for his first Test match in England which enabled them to reduce their average age to 35 years 72 days. They dropped Johnny Taylor but retained Jack Ryder, who, of course had the advantage of being one of the selectors. Gregory was also playing. There was no way they could contemplate going into the field without him, but he had bowled a total of 10 overs in match play since the Headingley Test, never more than five in a spell.

As the England team sat in their dressing room, weary of waiting, irritated that the promise of this summer was being so frequently crushed, their spirits were lifted. Their old pal Cec Parkin, the cheeky chappy himself, poked his head round the dressing-room door. By now Parkin had not only burned his bridges with the Test selectors but with Lancashire where he had severed ties a few weeks earlier after another disagreement. He looked round at the players and, eliciting immediate guffaws, asked: 'Am I playing or am I not?'

Play started at 2.42pm. As Bardsley walked out with Woodfull, he seemed to be heading for the striker's end but midway through the pair's advance to the wicket he swapped over, perhaps suddenly recalling the first-ball dismissal at Leeds. He had good cause. Woodfull faced the first ball from Tate, and as it lifted menacingly off the pitch he could only edge it high off the bat. (Tate's father Fred had sent a touching letter to Lancashire earlier in the week hoping that Maurice could redeem the mistake Fred had made at Old Trafford in 1902 – nearly a quarter of a century previously but nobody had forgotten – when he dropped a crucial catch).

The ball flew between Sutcliffe and Hendren in the slips. Some lamented the paucity of modern slip fielding although they were probably being harsh and as *The Times* reported in splendidly euphemistic fashion 'the fielders turned to one another and appeared to make the appropriate remark simultaneously.' It was generally felt not to be as difficult as the catch put down by Carr at Leeds. Woodfull took a single off the third ball and Bardsley was beaten by the fourth and struck on the pad. Tate appealed loudly but it was adjudged to be just missing.

Maurice was one of the more dynamic appealers in the game and, although he accepted the decision in his Sunday newspaper column, Alf Noble was characteristically trenchant. Tate might have been one of the most popular men in England, but Noble was having none of it. 'If when Tate is bowling the ball goes near the wicket or is edged away Tate signifies his surprise by raising both arms and twisting his body as a gesture of disappointment. Although this mannerism has always in some degree been a feature of his bowling it has lately become more pronounced and it is frequently observable when it has not been a close shave. It should be restrained as it conveys at times a wrong impression of the actual value of some deliveries.'

Root bowled four balls, one of which beat Woodfull all ends up and almost bowled him. The heavens opened again and they did not close for the rest of the day. As one headline put it, the spectators, given that between them they paid £2,000 for the privilege, had coughed up £333 per run.

Close: Australia 6-0 (Woodfull 5, Bardsley 0)

The teams spent Saturday evening at a banquet in the Midland Hotel hosted by the cotton magnate, Sir Edwin Stockton. The seven courses included *saumon d'ecosse au court bouillon, pommes vapeur, sce. Collins, Seraphin d'Agneau Kangaroo, Salade de Carr, Panier Macartney* and *Café aux Ashes*. Seventy of the 300 diners travelled from London and the guest list, apart from the cricketers, was eclectic. Among those invited were the main speaker Sir John Simon, the eminent lawyer who was the first man to hold the offices of Home Secretary, Foreign Secretary and Chancellor of the Exchequer, and the former secretary of the Miners' Federation,

Frank Hodges. Sir Edwin was a devoted cricket fan who in his brief career as a Conservative MP opened the batting, in the annual House of Commons v House of Lords match, with the future Labour prime minister, Clement Attlee. In welcoming his guests Sir Edwin said that it was a remarkable gathering representative of the last government, the present government and possibly the future government. It was suggested that it was not 'beyond the bounds of possibility that such an assembly of influential men of all parties, exchanging views in an atmosphere of sociability and goodwill may have some ultimate effect in the settlement of the coal situation.'

Since Sir John, at the height of the General Strike, had caused convulsions by declaring in an impromptu speech in Parliament that the stoppage was illegal and that workers could be sued in the County Court for damages, he might have had trouble establishing a rapport with Hodges, who, though a conciliator, had been a Cabinet member in the first Labour government two years previously. Simon's cricket had been largely confined to keeping wicket for Wadham College during his time at Oxford University when CB Fry was also in the eleven. Plum Warner loved the banquet, recalling that bishops mingled with umpires, MPs with cricketers, railway magnates with racing men, famous lawyers with captains of industry.

Carr spoke briefly at the end of proceedings and was already looking forward to the next match. They might have to play for a week at The Oval, he observed, and then they would know what six-day cricket meant. 'To think much and say little is a captain's virtue,' wrote the man from *The Times*. Carr was in good spirits, as he was the next afternoon, Sunday, when Sir Edwin's hospitality, as had become customary during Old Trafford Tests, extended to a tour on the Manchester Ship Canal. What happened after this happy trip has become the subject of some conjecture. It was the catalyst for changing the lives of both Carr and Chapman.

That evening Carr and his wife Ivy again dined at the Midland, with Chapman, the journalist and *bon viveur* Sir Home Gordon, and Colonel Gilbert Hamilton, an officer in the Grenadier Guards. According to Gordon, Carr had one glass of champagne. 'Hints that he had exceeded were heard not only in the pavilion but suggested in some sections of the Press.' Carr himself claimed that he was in bed by 10pm and thought then that his throat felt 'a bit funny'. Waking up the next morning with the match due to resume in a few hours, Carr was running a temperature and unable to speak. He phoned the selector Peter Perrin – it was telling that he did not contact Warner, the chairman – to say that he was likely to be unfit.

Dr William Garden was summoned to the Queen's Hotel from his surgery in Cross Street and immediately declared that Carr was too ill to play. The doubts and insinuations about Carr's illness and what caused it were never substantiated in any meaningful fashion although Noble – him again – wrote that he was up past 11.30pm. Carr's fondness for a drink was well known even then, but the fact that his wife was with him indicates that he may well have departed when Gordon said he did. And Dr Garden was in no doubt about the severity of what was afflicting him. Garden was a well-known GP around town who earlier in his career had been assistant medical officer at county asylums and was a neurological and medical specialist for the Lancashire Federation of Master Cotton Spinners. The doctor issued a statement in which he said that Carr was feverish with a temperature above 100, could swallow only with extreme difficulty, had severe pains in the neck, could only drink fluids and was strongly advised not to play again in the Test. 'It is a bit of bad luck for everybody and Mr Carr feels it very keenly,' Garden said. It meant England had to find a new captain in pretty short order. Naturally, given the proprieties to be observed, it was not a straightforward decision.

Second Day

The man who led out England was perhaps the country's most respected citizen, Jack Hobbs. At his side as he stepped on to the Old Trafford turf, as if to emphasise what a big deal this was, walked Greville Stevens, the only amateur left in the team. Stevens was 25, playing in his first Test in England and, under the unwritten regulations governing the English game, should have been captain of the side. Everyone but everyone recited the words of Lord Hawke from a mere 18 months previously: 'Pray God, no professional will ever captain England.' But Stevens was overlooked. Even then, however, the selectors were prepared to make a mess of it. By Warner's own account, Strudwick, as the senior man, was offered the job but declined. This was a remarkable move, for it was Hobbs, not Strudwick, who was regularly captain of the Players in their matches against the Gentlemen – he and Rhodes all but shared it for several years. Good old Struddy deferred to his best friend.

When the spectators – and despite the virtual certainty that it would be a draw there were 34,000 of them – got over their shock, Hobbs duly acquitted himself as might have been expected. In Carr's absence, England had to find a substitute fielder and that was the 12th man Chapman. It was the last thing he wanted, for Percy, unlike Arthur, had not gone to bed early, having no wife present to keep him in check. Indeed, according to Carr's account in his memoirs, 'the always-ready-to-be-matey-and-social Percy had – thinking himself unwanted at cricket – sat up a bit late on Sunday night. When he was roused and told to get up at once and go and do a bit of fielding he got a pretty nice jar; in fact he afterwards told me that the sudden summons to get out of bed that morning was among the awful experiences of his young life and that he will never forget it.' Albeit nine years after the event that still seems, another 90 or so years on, a case of being dobbed in by your mate.

Hobbs naturally went about his business unfussily. He brought on Stevens before too long after Tate and Root found nothing doing on a slow pitch. The leg-spinner's second ball was short but it was also his quicker one, on to Bardsley faster than the batsman would have wished, forcing him to mistime his intended hook to short-leg where, to local joy, Tyldesley held the catch. Macartney played forward to the next ball, was beaten and there was a huge lbw shout. The suspicion that it had pitched outside leg stump saved the Governor-General. That was the extent of England's success for the next two hours as Macartney and Woodfull, with increasing ease, put on 192 for the second wicket. Root bowled leg theory with seven men on the on-side and skilfully contained the pair. Woodfull faced by far the greater proportion of the strike, and Macartney, though not quite reaching the heights of his performance at Leeds, was still sublime in movement and execution. He was the first batsman to score hundreds in three successive Test innings, and none of the four others who have subsequently surpassed the feat, not even Everton Weekes and Rahul Dravid, can have done so with quite such elan. Woodfull, scoring his second century in a row, once more provided a demonstration of thou shalt not pass.

Australia drifted when they ought to have been forcing the pace. Once more, they wanted to prevent defeat rather than plot victory. It was to the credit of England and Hobbs that they then made short work of the Australian middle order. After Macartney, essaying something extravagant, was bowled by the persevering Root, Woodfull was out on the stroke of tea, nudging Root to short leg. Five more wickets fell in the final session. Chapman, seemingly having recovered from his previous evening's revelries, ran in 20 yards from deep square-leg and held a catch close to the ground to remove the hapless Andrews. Anything seemed possible for Chapman then. Richardson was caught at slip to give Stevens his third wicket and Ryder held at the wicket off Root. Ponsford and Gregory briefly promised a revival before the former drove Kilner and saw the bowler take a sharp return catch to his left while the latter became Root's fourth victim when he hoisted him to deep mid-on. As Warner reported, Root's persevering and accurate bowling was one of the features of the day's cricket. This Test might have been going nowhere, but it had seemingly clinched for him a place in the decider.

Close: Australia 322-8 (Oldfield 2, Grimmett 4)

As if the Government did not have enough to worry about, it decided to make trouble for itself that Monday evening. It banned the broadcasting of playwright George Bernard Shaw's 70th birthday speech. After its overt interference in the coverage during the General Strike this was an early example of the willingness to try to influence what was heard on the BBC.

Given the turbulence in the country at large, the Cabinet was concerned that Shaw, a renowned socialist, would use the occasion of his celebration dinner to tell them where they were going wrong. The event in his honour was organised by the Labour Party, and its leader Ramsay MacDonald was asked by the government to guarantee that Shaw would not be controversial on public topics. MacDonald could not agree and pointed out that nothing could be better designed to ensure that the old man of letters would be controversial on public topics.

The dinner proceeded on Monday night, and Shaw duly delivered his verdict on the row. Government heads, he said, had been turned rather violently by Miss Bondfield. Five days earlier Margaret Bondfield, a veteran Labour Party campaigner and Trades Unionist (who was the first woman to chair the TUC and later the first female Cabinet Minister), had been returned to Parliament for the second time with a landslide by-election victory. Shaw said: 'They have got the glorious idea of cutting off ideas in this country by damning me. Of course, that is very funny but the laugh will go a little further than this room. I would dearly like to believe that this move was levelled at me personally, that I am the one person who can terrify the British Government into putting a muzzle on me. But it is impossible to believe this is really the truth. There is no objection to me except that I am a supporter of His Majesty's Opposition.' Thus were Baldwin and his party, hands full elsewhere, made to look faintly foolish by becoming involved in a minor matter. With the match in Manchester heading the way of its predecessors, Shaw's birthday was welcome light relief.

Though there was always Lord Hawke in that regard too. As the man who said that no professional should ever captain England it was natural that his opinion should be sought now that one had. He duly sent a telegram as his response to the *Daily News* reporter who asked: 'I have no wish to add to the worries of the Selection Committee and you would be well advised not to open your columns to unimportant opinions. My advice is "Leave the Selection Committee alone."' It was difficult to tell what the old boy thought, but it was not quite a ringing endorsement of dear Jack Hobbs.

Third Day

The luckless Tate finally earned some due reward. He took the last two wickets to fall and Australia's innings was done and dusted in 18 minutes. The tourists' last nine wickets had gone for 114, another indictment of their unwanted dependence on a few heavy run-getters. Whereas Macartney had three centuries, Woodfull two and Bardsley and Richardson one each, Ryder, Taylor, Andrews and now Ponsford had between them contributed 140 runs in 11 innings with a top score of 42. Australia's batting line-up, vaunted and expected to be formidable, was being dismantled under brooding skies and before mass gatherings whose collective will was urging England towards their Holy Grail.

Hobbs and Sutcliffe were circumspect for more than an hour. Grimmett and Mailey rarely bowled in tandem, but one of them was bowling at one end throughout the innings. Life was never easy for the batsmen and although it was surprising that Sutcliffe, at his most obdurate and strokeless, edged Mailey behind in the 30th over the outcome of the match was clear by then. The dismissal at least allowed the Manchester crowd to see their favourite son and Tyldesley did not let them down in making 81 from 218 balls in 160 minutes. It was not a seamless innings, for he offered chances at 35 and 45 and might have been stumped when he was 80. Nonetheless, around those lapses, it was the innings of a man in supreme form. No doubt it helped that his partner while he settled in was Hobbs. For the first and only time in his Test career Hobbs had the opportunity to play a captain's innings, and he took it. Never rash, he still played shots when the ball was there for a shot to be played, his square-cut being especially effective. By the time he was deceived in the flight by Grimmett he had ensured his side were safe from defeat. These were ideal circumstances for Woolley with nothing to lose and he was at his most alluring for an hour and a half. Tyldesley was caught by Oldfield playing back in Macartney's first over (strangely the 93rd of the innings, since he had shared the new ball in the three previous Tests); and Woolley, having caressed rather than walloped Mailey for his second six, was out next ball. Hendren and Kilner were in relaxed mode and at 6pm after Australia had bowled 125 overs at England in five hours, 22 minutes the umpires drew stumps.

Close: England 305-5 (Hendren 32, Kilner 9) Match drawn

Hobbs was Hobbs when he was asked about being England captain, at long last, in his 49th Test and 18th season of international cricket. 'The task of captaincy made no difference to me,' he told reporters after play. 'The accident of Mr Carr's illness may have made history but as far as I am concerned I simply went through the game in an ordinary way.' He expanded a little in his *Weekly Dispatch* column, again, like his captain's innings, not being rash but playing a shot or two. There was no reason, he said, why a paid player should not captain England at home as long as he had a captain's ability. Revolutionary words indeed but quickly tempered. 'The only place I find it really advisable for an amateur to be captain is abroad and even then his cricketing credentials should be beyond question. On a tour a captain is obliged to represent his team at all sorts of functions and make speeches and so on; duties for which most professionals have little aptitude.' Hedging a bit, measured, but with that lingering sense of deferment to Lord Hawke and his cronies.

Tate was much less equivocal in his Sunday paper column. 'In years to come when the question of the captaincy of England comes up for discussion we shall not say: who is the most capable amateur for the job but rather shall we say who is the most capable man. And that, as I think you will agree, is the question that should always be asked."

It was heading to The Oval. After three months of the tour and four inconclusive Tests that had in equal measure enraptured and frustrated the nation (it was a wonder that the series had still managed to do the former considering the latter), that was probably the proper way of deciding the contest. All that had to be worked out were the terms of engagement and who would be involved – much like the settlement to the mining dispute. From the Prime Minister down, in both cases, the answers were anxiously awaited.

George Geary

England

Fast-medium bowler, right-hand bat

Born: 9.7.1893 Barwell, Leicestershire
Age on 1.5.26: **32**
County: Leicestershire

Record at start of 1926

Tests: 1, debut 1924
Did not bat, 0 wickets

F/c matches: 178, debut 1912
4,027 runs @ 16.43, HS 122
751 wickets @ 19.92, BB 7-24

In five Championship matches between 19 June and 5 July 1926 George Geary took 51 wickets. In seven of the 10 innings in which he bowled for Leicestershire during those 17 days he had five or more, with a best of 9-33. There could hardly have been a more persuasive plea to the selectors had a Bill been introduced in Parliament compelling Geary's inclusion in the Test team. His bowling did the talking, however.

There is plenty of anecdotal – not to say apocryphal – evidence that players from the smaller counties struggle to win England caps. Plenty have left clubs in search of greener pastures. But in 1926 two of the five faster bowlers chosen by Plum Warner and his panel were from counties who perennially finished towards the bottom of the Championship and whose fortunes they frequently seemed to be carrying on their shoulders: Worcestershire (Fred Root) and Leicestershire (Geary). It probably shows the influence of the two professionals, Jack Hobbs and Wilfred Rhodes, and that as a whole they were prepared to do anything it took to win back the Ashes after so long. The other faster bowlers were from Yorkshire (George Macaulay), Nottinghamshire (Harold Larwood) and Sussex (Maurice Tate), a county not quite of the first rank, but partly because of their proximity to London, partly because they so frequently contained great outstanding individual players, one which never had too much difficulty attracting selectorial attention.

Geary played in the Third Test at Leeds when England found themselves up a gum tree after asking Australia to bat. He pointed out later that the biggest mistake made by the captain, Arthur Carr, was in taking out batsmen with him to look at the pitch and not bowlers. Geary (41-5-130-2) did not exactly disappoint with the ball in the match, but it was with the bat that he made a crucial contribution with the side facing a huge first-innings deficit. By this time, this long, lean man with a permanent suntan, knew his game inside out.

He began with Leicestershire in 1912, established himself in 1913 with 79 wickets, and in 1914, when he went on to take 117 wickets, was chosen for his first representative match, the Lord's Centenary fixture: MCC's South Africa XI (from the previous winter) v The Rest. The 20-year-old Geary arrived at the ground to find that the veteran Sydney Barnes, great bowler and a man well aware of his own worth, was agitating that they not play unless they received more money. It would have given Geary his only opportunity of watching Barnes perform. Barnes withdrew from the match, citing a muscle strain.

Geary, like some of the others in the series, could count himself lucky to be playing cricket at all. He had joined the newly-formed Royal Flying Corps at the outbreak of the war, and early on he was severely injured by the propellor blade of a Sopwith Camel which cut into his left upper thigh and shoulder. Another few seconds and he would have lost both lower and upper limbs. It took Geary a long while to recover from this near-catastrophe, and when cricket resumed he was still not ready for the daily grind of the County game, instead signing to play in the Lancashire League (where his pay may very well have been similar). In 1922 he was fit enough to play again for his home county, and it was not long before he showed the pre-war form that had seen him take 100 wickets in 1914 when still only 21. In 1924 he was chosen for a Test match, at Old Trafford, when the captain, Arthur Gilligan, was injured but did not take a wicket. Another man making his debut in that match was Jack MacBryan, who never played again and remains the only Test cricketer not to have batted, bowled or dismissed anyone in the field.

There was also something else Geary had in common with many of his fellows in the 1926 series. He was simply a nice bloke, good to be around, happy to chat. He was the eldest of 16 children of a bootmaker from the Leicestershire village of Barwell, was in the village team at 12, joined the county ground staff at 14 and cycled the 15 miles there and back each day. When he was not rolling the ground, he was bowling in the nets, and he perfected an easy action – fast-medium with a stock ball that moved into the right-hander and a leg-cutter which demanded a change of grip and became much feared. And there was yet another quirk he shared with some of the Test bowlers of 1926. He bowled while wearing a cap, as also did Roy Kilner and Wilfred Rhodes for England and Arthur Richardson for Australia.

At the age of 33 Geary was very near his peak in 1926, a bowler from the top drawer and he was by no means finished. But it was as a batsman and magnificent fielder that he made his enduring contributions to the series.

Wilfred Rhodes

England

Slow left-arm bowler, right-hand bat

Born: 29.10.1877 Kirkheaton, Yorkshire
Age on 1.5.26: **48**
County: Yorkshire

Record at start of 1926

Tests: 53, debut 1899
2,232 runs @ 30.57, HS 179
111 wickets @ 26.06, BB 8-68

F/c matches: 943, debut 1898
36,444 runs @ 31.33, HS 267*
3,674 wickets @ 16.42, BB 9-24

The clamour began early for Wilfred Rhodes to be in the side to regain the Ashes. Barely had the First Test stuttered into life than BJT Bosanquet wrote in the *Weekly Dispatch*: 'I am a little fearful of the bowling ... I should have liked to send a telegram to Leeds yesterday morning and fetched Wilfred Rhodes along.' A fortnight later Robin Baily in the *Daily Herald* said: 'Doubtless like everyone else interested in the game, I feel that the committee's chosen XI could be improved upon. Why not Wilfred Rhodes?'

In mid-July, the *Daily Mirror* assembled what it described as an expert panel to 'find an England side capable of winning the next Test match.' Not only did this collection of the great and the good (the *Mirror* did not identify them) include Rhodes in their team, they also designated him as captain: 'Wilfred Rhodes has a knowledge of the game second to none.' Facing this sort of cacophony, the selectors probably had no choice but to pick Rhodes for the final, decisive Test.

He was leading the national bowling averages, England had bowled out Australia at least once in three successive Tests, but it had never taken fewer than 150 overs. Implored by his fellow selectors, the old warhorse reluctantly agreed to play at The Oval. The truly astonishing aspect of it was that nobody considered that recalling a 48-year-old five years after he had been dropped amidst the carnage of 1921 was in any way a gamble.

Rhodes was considered to have the wisest cricketing brain in the country. He had taken over as senior pro at Yorkshire and whoever was captain (Cecil Burton, Geoffrey Wilson and Arthur Lupton in the early 1920s) nobody doubted that Rhodes was pulling the strings. By his own reckoning his bowling had regressed. 'I was nothing like the bowler I had been. I had lost my flight and much of my spin and had to rely on my length and experience.' Indeed, in 1925 there were suspicions that he might be rapidly nearing the finish. He took only 57 wickets, the first time since cricket resumed that he had not reached 100 wickets. 'In the nature of things,' said *Wisden*, sounding a note of doom, 'Rhodes, approaching the completion of his 48th year, could not be expected to prove very deadly in a dry summer.'

But in 1926 something clicked once more. He began it by scoring the season's first century on the opening day in Yorkshire's match against Essex when the county were in a spot of trouble at 45-4. It must have impressed his fellow selector, Percy Perrin, who was captain of the opposition. Before long, he was suddenly again taking plenty of wickets cheaply. In late May, he took nine against Warwickshire; in early June, 14 against Somerset. The rumblings for his Test recall began.

Rhodes had been in the game 29 years by then. His first wicket for Yorkshire was Alberto Trott, then still at his peak, in 1898. Having won his place, he took 13 wickets in his second match and never looked back. He took 154 wickets in his first full season, he played his first Test in 1899, and by the time he was 24 he had taken 1,000 wickets. His action was a model of economy: four paces to the crease, right arm held rigidly outwards and the left-arm travelling quickly through a full circle. 'Seldom if ever has cricket known an action which combined such beauty of rhythm and economy of effort,' wrote Rhodes' biographer, Sydney Rogerson. 'He looked as if he could bowl all day and not infrequently did.'

Although from the West Riding, heart of Yorkshire's industries and particularly its mills, Rhodes was from farming stock, part of the few who had managed to cling on to the rural past. Born in the village of Kirkheaton, he and his family moved not long after to a farm a few miles away. Young Wilf, at first a medium-pace bowler, did much of his early spin practice on a pitch he set up in a barn and then on another strip he fashioned against a hayrick. After a couple of seasons as a teenage professional in Scotland between jobs on the land and the railways, he was 18 when given his chance by Yorkshire, who were looking for a replacement for Bobby Peel, sacked by Lord Hawke for drinking. Rhodes liked an occasional beer, but he was never likely to cause them problems on that front.

For a few years he also managed to fashion himself into a world-class batsman and formed an improbable opening partnership for England with Jack Hobbs. Their exploits on the 1911/12 tour included a partnership of 323 at Melbourne when the Ashes were regained, and it remains the highest for the first wicket for England against Australia.

He never said much when he was playing either on the field or off it. He never felt the need. According to historical rankings Rhodes was the leading cricketer in the world in 1909, the number four batsman and number five bowler in 1913. There was nothing else left for him to achieve. Was there?

Arthur Mailey

Australia

Leg-break bowler

Born: 3.1.1886 Sydney, New South Wales
Age on 1.5.26: **40**
State: New South Wales

Record at start of 1926

Tests: 16, debut 1920/21
213 runs @ 13.31, HS 46
85 wickets @ 32.54, BB 9-121

F/c matches: 120, debut 1912/13
1,294 runs @ 14.06, HS 66
605 wickets @ 23.43, BB 10-66

PLAYER'S CIGARETTES.

Mr. A. A. MAILEY.
NEW SOUTH WALES.

It could be said of Arthur Mailey that he pioneered it all. He started the long, if not quite unbroken, line of superlative Australian leg-break-and-googly bowlers. Warwick Armstrong preceded him as a purveyor of leg spin, but he was many things more besides. Mailey made an immediate impression when in December 1920 he was called up for his first Test series a few days away from his 35th birthday and took a record haul of 36 wickets. This included, in his fourth match, an innings analysis of 9-121 which remains the best for Australia. It was truly the start of something, and the path was cleared for myriad successors. Leg-spin has been at the heart and soul of the country's cricket as much as fast bowling.

In all, Mailey teased and tormented England in four Ashes rubbers: in the 1920/21 5-0 clean sweep of victories; in 1921 when it was a mere 3-0 and he was not needed quite so much, such was the potency of the speed pairing of Jack Gregory and Ted McDonald; in 1924/25 when it was 4-1; and even, if to a lesser extent, in 1926 when at long last the gap between the sides had been narrowed. In a series when only 96 of the 200 available wickets fell, Mailey took 14 of them after managing nine in the final match.

In his 21 Tests, 18 against England, Mailey provided slow bowling which invariably turned a long way and a wrong 'un that he had practised throughout his teenage years and that was never easy to spot. There was always plenty of air to his deliveries, his mission to turn the ball as much as possible. 'A mixture of spin, flight and sheer fun,' someone said. He bowled plenty of dross, and his length was never uniform. It mattered not, for his style and personality meant he was prepared to buy a wicket: the bad balls were bad but the good balls were better. His preoccupation throughout was the taking of wickets and hang the runs that he conceded.

Mailey had several extraordinary bowling figures. In his third Test he had his first match return of ten wickets, in the next came the nine in an innings and on the 1921 tour of England he returned the analysis that stayed with him for the rest of his life and would give him the title of his biography – 10-66 against Gloucestershire at Cheltenham, including the 18-year-old Wally Hammond for a duck. The book was called *10 for 66 and All That*. (His top score as a batsman in first-class cricket happened also to be 66.) And there was his 9-86 against Lancashire in 1926. Contrast that with the return he had later in the year back at home – 4-362 from 64 eight-ball overs without a maiden as Victoria amassed a total of 1,107 all out. They were the most expensive figures of all time, in a match New South Wales lost by an innings and 656 runs.

Mailey had another significant talent. He was a hugely engaging cartoonist and caricaturist, with the elusive gift of capturing a moment and a person's foibles in a single drawing. He was hired by the *Bystander* magazine at £1,000 a year when Australia toured England in 1921 – compared with the £400 he received for playing cricket on the trip – and drew for *The Graphic* on the following tour. Almost all his work featured cricket in some capacity or other. His 1926 strip of a player dashing to the match, encountering all manner of obstacles and arriving in the nick of time only to be told that the wicket will not suit him and he is 12th man, was especially typical of his dry delivery.

All this was at odds with his formative years. By his own description, he was born in a Sydney slum and the family lived in near poverty. He left school at 13 and began his working life with a job pressing trouser seams, moving on at 16 to glass blowing which helped to increase his lung capacity and, he said, played a part in his having a successful bowling career. By his late twenties he was a labourer for the Water Board. His was a long apprenticeship in Sydney grade cricket, and he was almost 28 when he first played in the Sheffield Shield. But he had made a mark by then. Touchingly he told of how he dismissed his hero, Victor Trumper, with a perfect wrong 'un. Trumper was beaten and stumped by yards. 'I felt like a boy killing a dove,' said Mailey. But he was to play alongside Trumper briefly for New South Wales before having his greatest triumphs between the ages of 35 and 40. He had already decided to retire from international cricket after the 1926 series.

My only picture was a pin-up of Vic Trumper

Arthur Mailey's cartoon memory of his childhood bedroom: 'When the wind blew, Vic appeared to go through his whole repertoire of strokes.'

Percy Chapman

England

Left-hand bat

Born: 3.9.1900 Reading, Berkshire
Age on 1.5.26: **25**
County: Kent

Record at start of 1926

Tests: 6, debut 1924
193 runs @ 27.57, HS 58

F/c matches: 105, debut 1920
5,757 runs @ 37.87, HS 183
17 wickets @ 36.35, BB 5-40

During four days in August 1926 Percy Chapman became a national hero. It was a stratospheric, bewildering rise, prompted by a historic England victory which he was instrumental in winning. Barely a fortnight earlier, he had been appointed as captain, extraordinarily entrusted with leading the team to the promised land where the Ashes would be found. The politest reactions could be summarised as suggesting the selectors had finally lost their marbles.

Chapman had played for England before, though not much and not well, with a top score of 58 from eight attempts. His appearance in the first three Tests of the summer's Ashes series amounted to little – in common with most of the rest of the England middle order he blew hot and cold. He was dropped for the fourth, probably the victim of a (wholly justified) home-town selection. Ernest Tydlesley, in the form of his life, of most people's lives, had been picked instead of Chapman and scored 81 at Old Trafford.

And then with the Ashes on the line, Tyldesley, the diffident Lancastrian, was out again, and Chapman was in. And not only in but captain to boot as the selectors discarded Arthur Carr who had been captain for the first four matches. Both Carr and Chapman were amateur cricketers which was the cardinal qualification for the role. But there was a substantial difference between them: Carr had vast experience of captaincy with Nottinghamshire, the county he had led for eight years, and Chapman had virtually none since being skipper of the Uppingham School team in 1919. Chapman was without question a cordial cove, always ready for a drink and a chat, and he exuded *bonhomie*. Whether that was enough to win the greatest prize in sport was another matter, and few thought that it was.

But Chapman pulled it off. He was beholden to a few outstanding individual performances – which winning captain isn't? – but he impressed from the moment he won the toss. If he was offered help from time to time by the team's senior professionals who knew much, much more, then his acceptance of it was a sign of strength, not weakness. The attention that came his way immediately afterwards was inescapable, and on reflection it might have been pre-ordained. When he walked down the street people gathered round him, he was a sought-after guest at the best bashes in town.

As a boy Chapman carved out his gilded path with a rare talent allied to a pleasing personality. He was not from an especially well-off background. His father was a sports-obsessed school headmaster, himself the son of a parson. It must have been a stretch to send the lad to Uppingham School where he was indifferent academically. Sport, mainly cricket, and his agreeable nature made him popular. It is said that when he was thumping sixes for fun at school he would apologise to the bowler: 'Perfectly good ball, just got lucky.' For the first 19 or so years of his life he was known by his first name of Arthur. Somehow that was dropped when he went up to Cambridge University and became Percy.

Life seemed to be a doddle because Chapman made it so uncomplicated. His approach to cricket reflected this. He had manifold batting gifts. He could hook, cut and square-drive mercilessly and had a front foot straight drive whose power came from strong wrists. But he was never too concerned about improving a defensive method which clearly made him fallible. The start of his first-class career was typical of the way things so often turned out for him in his golden years. He had a pretty dreadful time of it in the two trial matches for the University team – he fielded well but his batting in a good line-up was much too loose. Percy was omitted from the team for the first fixture of the 1920 season against Essex. On the morning of the match Geoffrey Brooke-Taylor dropped out. Chapman was called for, and he went out and made 118 against an attack led by the England captain Johnny Douglas. If he looked uncomfortable at times his off-driving was irreproachable.

He could not be left out from then on, was virtually ever-present in the next three years and appeared in the Varsity game in each of them. It was not until 1922 that he sprang to greater prominence – and this was characteristic of his style – by scoring hundreds in two successive matches at Lord's. In the Varsity match he made 102. 'Last season Mr Chapman failed to make the advance in judgemement and pertinacity which was to be expected ... Yesterday, unless we are mistaken, he established himself.' Ten days later Chapman went one better. He scored 160 for the Gentlemen against the Players, sharing a fourth-wicket partnership of 140 with Arthur Carr who made 88 as both blazed merrily away.

'During the long and severe partnership between Mr Carr and Mr Chapman the elderliness of the older professionals was thoroughly exposed. Mr Chapman was, of course, the outstanding figure. He played one of the great innings in the history of the game.' That verdict by the special correspondent of *The Times* might have been a slight exaggeration, but there was no doubt that Chapman dominated an experienced professional attack that included Cec Parkin, Alex Kennedy, George Macaulay and Frank Woolley. He was still only 21 years old.

The rest of Chapman's cricket in the early 1920s was for Berkshire. Born in Reading, the strict regulations meant that he was ineligible for any other county until he became qualified by residence (this also delayed, for instance, Wally Hammond's career with Gloucestershire). Apart from the University fixtures and games for MCC and the Gentlemen, most of Chapman's cricket was distinctly low key. Before the world of work intruded he was able to go on MCC's 'A' tour of Australia and New Zealand in 1922/23, and there he both cemented his reputation as a batsman of glittering potential and also announced his engagement.

His batting was more consistent than it had been since his time at Uppingham. From the start in November to the end in March he was in superb form, making four hundreds and nine fifties, and averaging 57. The crowds warmed to him – 'he has become the idol of the Australian cricketing public who want to see more of him' – and he responded with equal joviality. Eighteen months earlier at a Cambridge May Ball he had met Beet Lowry, sister of his team-mate in the university side, the New Zealander Tom Lowry. During the tour the couple were reunited at her home in Okawa Station, a sprawling sheep station near Hawke's Bay, and made marriage plans.

Chapman could do no wrong, and the editor of *Wisden* was gushing in his notes for the 1923 edition. 'Our great hope at the moment is APF Chapman,' wrote Sydney Pardon. 'By right of his batting and his glorious fielding he is the most attractive personality in the new generation of players. He has the genius of the game in him and as he is happily going on with his cricket no limit can be placed on what he may do in the next few years.'

What he did for the next two years was play little because his new job with a brewery company precluded it. But such was the impression he had made that he was picked for the Test team against South Africa in 1924 and for the Ashes tour which followed. His 1924 summer was interrupted by a motorcycle accident. He was thrown off the machine when his raincoat was caught up in the rear wheel and was found unconscious in the road several minutes later by friends following in a car.

As part of a losing side on the 1924/25 tour he did not properly establish himself as a player of international class. At the end of the tour he went down to New Zealand where he and Beet were married. At last in 1925 he played his first cricket in the County Championship but in all managed only five matches. Otherwise he was playing club cricket. The idea that he would shortly be the captain of England was definitely one for the fairies.

He forced himself into the team, however, with some sparkling displays early in the 1926 season. Two innings against the Australians of 51 for MCC and a scintillating 87, which contained 11 fours and two sixes, for The South, in what was effectively a Test trial, bracketed 159 for Kent against Hampshire. The century garnered publicity for other reasons and showed Chapman's endlessly boyish character. GL Mackeson, formerly a director of the company where Percy worked, made a wager on Percy's score in the first Championship innings of the season, two bottles of port against each fifty, with an additional bet of 50 cigars that he would not reach 100. Not long after the innings Mackeson received a telegram: 'Six Cockburn 1896. Large Coronas. Percy.'

There was another incident in June with which Chapman was not directly involved but which showed his status. It also had a dreadful poignancy, considering how things were to turn out. A man called George Charles Brandon Collier was sentenced to three months' imprisonment with hard labour for obtaining money under false pretences by claiming he was Percy Chapman. Collier, an old boy of Dulwich College, had fallen on hard times because of his fondness for whisky. In a Tunbridge Wells pub he had been elated to be mistaken for Chapman. Outside he beckoned to a passer-by and asked: 'Do you know who I am? I'm APF Chapman, the cricketer, I'm on the rocks' and flourished a stick in an attempt to show he knew how to use a bat. Strangely, this trick fooled one passer-by who handed over seven shillings and sixpence. Collier was later arrested and identified by his fingerprints.

No sooner had Chapman won the Ashes than thousands would have wished to be mistaken for him. Percy revelled in it all and was only too willing to enter into the spirit of the whole thing. *The People* sent him a rag doll mascot called Desmond which was lost in the commotion after the match. The paper was delighted when it received a telegram from the man of the moment. 'Many thanks your dog. Stolen in pandemonium last night. Very much appreciated gift. Can you possibly get duplicate for wife.' The editor duly dispatched Desmond's double, and Chapman arrived home with it the day after. These were the days of wine and roses, and there and then it seemed they could go on forever.

10

THE LAST ACT

If it were not that Wilfred Rhodes happened to be taking the field in this match I would be genuinely alarmed at the thought that A.P.F. Chapman has been given charge of the most important match of the series.

G. Aubrey Faulkner
(Westminster Gazette before the Fifth Test)

Do you realise, I wonder, that we are living in amazing times? For the last three months the staple industry of this country, coal mining, has been at a standstill because of the strike. Millions upon millions have been lost to individuals in wages and royalties, and to the State in taxation. And yet there has not been so brilliant and so crowded Cowes Week as this year since the war.
Review in the society magazine, The Bystander, in early August

London had plenty of other things to occupy itself. Or so it might have liked to think. The final Test was not quite a distraction, but it was simply another element of summer's social whirl. Indeed, much of the well-heeled section of the metropolis was leaving – for the continent, for the yachting week at Cowes and for the Yorkshire and Scottish moors to mark the Glorious Twelfth, the start of the grouse shooting season in August, two days before the start of the finale of the Ashes series.

As Bertram Wooster put it in a short story by PG Wodehouse, *The Great Sermon Handicap*, which featured Bertie and his manservant Jeeves: 'I'm not much of a lad for the birds and the trees and the great open spaces as a rule but there's no doubt that London's not at its best in August and rather tends to give me the pip and make me think of popping down into the country until things have bucked up a trifle.' Wodehouse was the other Pelham, also, like Warner, known as Plum.

The capital remained vibrant. More than anywhere else in the country, it had adopted, during the General Strike, an approach of all being in it together, with hundreds of middle-class volunteers ensuring – if after a fashion – that essential services were kept going. *Sangfroid* was the order of the moment. In the long weeks since those bizarre nine days, London, hundreds of miles from the coal fields, had insulated itself against the chilling effects of the lock-out. There was the usual constant stream of stars, then, as now, designed to depict another world, where they might live but to which the *hoi-polloi*, if only in their imaginations, were invited to escape. Noel Coward was one of the biggest, acting in some plays, writing others and, in between, composing songs. His play *Easy Virtue* was coming towards the end of its run in August, *The Queen Was in the Parlour* and *Rat Trap* were about to start, while the author was rehearsing for the starring role in *The Constant Nymph*. The previous year, Coward had four plays running simultaneously in the West End. He was not a cricket fan, though he referred to the game in his song *The Stately Homes of England*, reflecting on the educational limitations of the aristocracy: 'We know how Caesar conquered Gaul / And how to whack a cricket ball.' And Coward had something in common with Hobbs: they were both known in their respective fields as The Master. There, the similarities probably ended. Coward was a willing habitué of the gossip columns, but the gossip columns also reserved the right to bring him down. *The Queen Was in the Parlour* was indifferently received: 'What a pea from the Coward machine gun,' was one critic's verdict.

Anita Loos came to town early in August and was immediately the centre of attention. She had already established herself as the first female screenwriter in Hollywood and was now riding on the crest of the wave created by her best-selling book *Gentlemen Prefer Blondes*. The showbiz writers queued up to see her, and she liked to be seen, ready and willing to talk about the book's heroine Lorelei Lee. Briefly, Loos became part of London's social scene, mixing at parties with the likes of Coward and the rising young actor John Gielgud. She was in town to oversee the production of her play *The Whole Town's Talking*, and she revelled in the fact that the whole town seemed to be talking about her.

Two other women commanded the stage. Suzanne Lenglen, the incomparable French tennis player, renounced her amateur status and turned professional. It was an unprecedented act. Winner of six Wimbledon singles titles, she had abandoned the tournament in July after being late for a match which Queen Mary was due to watch. It was hardly done to keep a monarch waiting, but even then some might have wondered who the actual royal personage was. In accepting the offer of a $50,000 contract (a little more than £500,000 today) for a four-month tour of the United States to play a series of what were effectively exhibition matches she offered her reasoning.

'In the 12 years I have been champion I have earned literally millions of francs for tennis. And in my whole lifetime I have not earned $5,000 – not one cent of that by my speciality, my life study – tennis. I am 27 and not wealthy – should I embark on any other career and leave the one for which I have what people call genius? Or should I smile at the prospect of actual poverty and continue to earn a fortune – for who? Under these absurd and antiquated rulings, only a wealthy person can compete and the fact of the matter is that only wealthy people do compete. Is that fair? Does it advance the sport?' Those words still have resonance and stand as a rebuff to those who question the apparently unseemly rewards of 21st century sports stars.

Lenglen's tour was a huge success, and her cut of the take ended up at $100,000. It was more than Babe Ruth, the baseball legend, earned that year with the New York Yankees. Naturally it dwarfed the salary of the professional cricketer. Lenglen was an exception, of course, but the notion of female excellence at professional sport was also embodied by Gertrude Ederle, an 18-year-old New Yorker and Olympic champion, who on August 7 became the first woman to swim the English Channel. If that were not notable enough, her time of 14hrs 30mins was nearly two hours faster than the quickest of the five men who had previously made the swim.

As Ederle came ashore, Parliament went into recess, with the coal dispute and the general dislocation unresolved. It was not due to sit again until November. Stanley Baldwin was on the verge of nervous collapse. As one snippet had it when the House of Commons term ended: 'I hear the Prime Minister at the close of a strenuous session, in which much of his time has been spent in thinking coal, reading coal and dreaming coal is badly in need of a long rest. After a few engagements in his constituency, he is off to Aix, his favourite resort.' But Baldwin did not depart immediately for Aix-les-Bains in the French Alps upon completing his duties in Worcestershire. He also had a Test match to watch.

And despite these myriad other diversions, that Test match still intruded into most conversations. If there was nothing to say about preparations for the match – and there was usually much to say – the papers threw in corny one-liners.

Brown: By the way, my grandson works at your office.
Smith: Yes, I remember he went to your funeral during the first Test match.

There were 18 days between the end of the Old Trafford match and the start of the Oval game on 14 August, a week longer than the gap between the previous Tests. It lent a kind of desperation to the anticipation. England had waited 14 long years for this moment of relief and now the country was being kept waiting, tantalised before the hour of truth arrived. Ostensibly, it provided opportunities for players to influence the selectors before their meeting on Sunday 8 August. Jack Hobbs received dozens of letters imploring him to put the case for this player or that player in the meeting and politely told them that the great majority would be disappointed. In truth there was probably not much scope to break into the side at this juncture. Given subsequent decisions, a few matches might have been deemed significant.

It was generally felt that England needed a cutting edge. Jack Mercer, the Glamorgan fast bowler, fleetingly found favour with many commentators when he took 5-74 against the Australians at Swansea, including Warren Bardsley and Bill Woodfull cheaply. But he was rather outshone by Harold Larwood's 6-60 and 6-67 at Hastings, which included the second-innings wicket of another selector, Arthur Gilligan whose defiant century at number 10 was brought to an end with what the *Westminster Gazette* called 'an almost unplayable ball which broke back the width of the wicket and knocked the leg stump down.' The 'almost' sounds superfluous because as the reporter added 'nobody could do anything to speak of with Larwood.' As auditions went it was compelling. Poor Jack Mercer enjoyed a fruitful career as player, coach and scorer, but he never did win a Test cap. Percy Chapman meanwhile made his typically swaggering contributions to Kent's win against Hampshire in the Canterbury Festival. It can be seen as perfect timing in every sense, but it was still a long, long way from being entrusted with the captaincy of an England side to win the Ashes.

The final seam bowling spot was between Geary, injured for the previous Test, and Root, early-season scourge of the Australians. Root was top of England's series averages, he had bowled a marathon stint of 52 overs at Old Trafford. Warner told Root's wife that her husband was an important man in English cricket and that she should look after him. He also advised Root to ensure his county captain used him sparingly in the period before the Test and to take brine baths at Droitwich. Root took 23 wickets for Worcestershire in seven innings before the selectors met without any notable easing in his workload. Geary took 16 wickets in six innings, which included a commendable effort against Yorkshire. Root thought he was in the team until the moment he was omitted. He could be considered unfortunate. But the issue might have been settled when Geary bowled Wilfred Rhodes, a selector, remember, who was playing for Yorkshire in the Championship match, with a ball that swung and took out the middle stump.

Perhaps the Championship performance which counted above all came in Yorkshire's previous fixture at Old Trafford against Lancashire, the two titans, first and second in the table. Although Lancashire had the best of things Rhodes took 7-116 from 42 overs in their only innings (Roy Kilner, his left-arm spinning companion who had played all four Tests so far in the summer, had 1-90 in 47). The movement for Rhodes' recall was given irresistible clout. In common with what had even then become convention, all the papers seemed to be claiming that it was their idea for the veteran Yorkshireman to be recalled.

If there had become about it an air of certainty, it took little account of how little bowling the old maestro had actually done in Test matches in the latter years of his international career as his batting became more significant. From 1899 when he made his Test debut until 1907/08, he bowled 727.2 overs, 21 per cent of England's total in the 22 matches he played, and took 83 wickets at 22.89 each, easily the most by an individual and 23 per cent of the total taken by the team. From 1909 until the first Test of the 1921 series, after which he was dropped, he played 31 of England's 32 matches, bowled 366.5 overs and took 28 wickets at 35.36, respectively 7.5 per cent and 5.3 per cent of the totals. Looked at it in that light these were unconvincing figures, but in his twilight years Rhodes had reinvented his bowling, imparting less spin but by more practice becoming a master of length and accuracy. In the four summers from 1921 to 1924 he took 503 wickets at 12.09 runs each, and although he was less successful in the batsman's summer of 1925, he was atop the national bowling averages throughout 1926. Averages were published at least once a week in all the papers then and the name of W. Rhodes (Yorks) constantly at the top of the list acted as a drip, drip, drip of persuasion on everyone's thoughts. Eventually the old boy himself succumbed.

Ernest Tyldesley whose record sequence of ten fifties had ended when he made only 44 at Leyton, returned to pristine form in the Roses match with 139. It was difficult to know what more Tyldesley could do, what anyone could do, to persuade the selectors to give him a place somewhere in the top four of the England team. But these were anxious times. How much should the boat be rocked, how might it be best balanced? Would the Ashes ever be won again?

Meanwhile, Carr, entirely in keeping with his approach to his fellow cricketers, travelled to The Oval to play in Hobbs' Benefit Match, only five days after he had been forced to miss two days of the Fourth Test. He was clearly not in peak health still, wore a bandana round his neck and could hardly speak. But he was determined, he said, to be there. He won the toss against Hobbs who had been given the honour of flipping the coin by county captain Percy Fender and within the hour had been bowled for a duck. There were eight days before the England team was selected, during which Carr had another three innings. He made 16, 15 and 20, scores that were neither one thing nor the other. But the point was that he was playing and was leading his county.

The repercussions of the team announcement six days before the match started were felt all week. Carr had his say and a bit a more after the initial pleasantries were seen to be a nonsense. Few of those directly involved had much, if anything, to add. Chapman issued his bland but credible statements of surprise; Peter Perrin, ambushed by reporters, told it like it was. Hobbs seemed to have been caught in some type of newspaper sting operation, quoted in the faraway *Liverpool Daily Post*, a distinguished provincial morning but hardly a redoubt of cricket coverage: 'I think one thing ought to be made clear. Carr has given the impression, accidentally I'm sure, that he was not present when the Selection Committee decided to accept his offer to resign. Not only was he present then but he was with us the whole time while we drafted the statement to the Press about his resignation being due to the fact that as of late he had not been in good health. And we spent nearly an hour on the job before we were satisfied with the wording.' Hardly had this statement appeared than Hobbs himself denied having made it: 'In my opinion Mr Carr's resignation is a matter far too delicate for me to talk about.' The *Post* stuck by its story.

As for Plum Warner, he said nowt. So did Rhodes, who said less than nowt. So did Herbert Smith, the miners' president, as his men, angry at the Eight Hours Bill, rejected the proposal by the Churches to end their dispute. But the pitmen, as it happened, were merely storing up trouble for themselves.

The ramifications of selection and the ensuing row were for a day supplanted as the major cricket story by what happened in Canterbury. Not Chapman's exploits, nor those of Jack Newman of Hampshire becoming the first player to achieve the Double for the season, but that Lord Harris fell ill and had to be rushed to hospital by ambulance, borne from the pavilion on a stretcher. Grave fears were expressed, but fortunately he quickly recovered. The Festival and Lord Harris remained huge components of the social season. Those of the upper classes who were not at Cowes, on the Continent or preparing to go up North to shoot grouse appeared to be at Canterbury.

All the leading correspondents had been blind-sided by the dropping of the captain and the choice of his replacement, most of them also dumbfounded. Aubrey Faulkner was both measured in his opinions and respected in the game, and his assertion that Rhodes, in effect, would be captain was impossible to dismiss lightly. It was hardly a surprise that the *Daily Herald*, the people's paper, continued to lay it on thickly. 'Can anyone sincerely suggest that the youth Chapman can be seriously expected to hold his own in the subtle and swift game of cricket tactics with an old hand like H.L. Collins?'

The Australians, left largely to their own devices, had much the better of a draw against Surrey; overwhelmed Glamorgan despite Mercer posing a little difficulty; had the advantage against Warwickshire in yet another match shortened by rain, but one in which Collins, out of action since the Lord's Test in late June, returned; and saw off Gloucestershire and probably Charlie Parker's chances of making the England team. They then went to Lord's for what amounted to a goodwill match against a Public Schools XV side and promptly found themselves at the centre of controversy. Collins must have pined for a return to the race courses which he had been frequenting for a month.

After winning the toss, Collins went out to open the innings and found that the Public Schools were fielding all 15 of their players. He had a word with their captain, Tom Killick, and four players left the field. Twenty minutes later a note was sent out to Collins from MCC secretary Sir Francis Lacey. It informed him that the custom in England, unlike in Australia, was for all the players to field in a side which contained more than the usual eleven. By this time Collins was being barracked by the crowd. Incensed, he immediately threw his wicket away when he 'cocked the ball up to mid-on.' Collins had settled down later when he was called on to explain his actions, terming it a simple misunderstanding since in Australia the convention in such matches was that 50 players could bat if they wished but only 11 could field. The palpable tension engendered by this was lessened when rain stopped play for the day after 80 minutes. It disappeared completely the following day when the Public Schools bowler, William May, took five wickets in as many overs to finish with 6-53. The *Daily Mirror*, quoting experts in the pavilion, prophesied a great career for May who had a disconcerting off-break. With that, the young man went off to a career in the Army and never appeared in another significant cricket match. Only two of the Public Schools multitude had anything like a notable career in the game. Killick, the captain, who scored a tenacious 30, went on to play for Cambridge University, Middlesex and England for whom he opened the batting with Herbert Sutcliffe in his two Tests. He was a clergyman, and he collapsed and died while playing cricket in a diocesan match in 1953. The other was WHV Levett, Hopper to everyone in the game, who played 175 first-class matches including once for England and became one of the game's great raconteurs.

As if this hullaballoo were not enough for Collins to deal with after his illness, he was under severe pressure for his place. Clem Hill, who had chaired the Australia selection panel that had nominated him as captain eight months earlier, now called for his omission. 'I consider he is in neither the condition nor the form to do himself or his side justice. If he is being included merely on the score of captaincy, I cannot see that Australia is gaining any particular advantage there and for the sake of Australia he should stand down.'

Attention turned to how the Test pitch might behave and what influence it would have on the length of the match. The papers were desperate for any information they could find, and although Jack Martin, the Oval groundsman, was happy and willing to give his opinion, some were not satisfied. The *Daily Chronicle* sent a reporter disguised as a plumber and found himself in a conspiracy of silence. 'Everyone pretended to know nothing about everything or was too busy to speak.'

It rained for most of Wednesday when the ground was covered in hailstones. Martin remained sanguine and even when it poured down again on Friday afternoon, he was confident of play the following morning. Soon after 4pm the queue began forming. Close to the front was John Deegan, a former Army staff sergeant who had lost his sight in action during the last days of the war. Accompanied by his wife and baby daughter he was eager for the match to start and assured interviewers he would know perfectly well what was going on. 'My wife tells me who goes in and who makes the big hits and I'll guarantee at the end of the game I'll be able to tell you more about it all than many a man on the ground with full use of his senses.'

There was a roaring trade in balcony spaces in the flats overlooking the ground. Some residents were charging as little as 10 shillings a person for the day, but the preferred option was for a block booking for 12 people costing anything from £40 to £70 for the match. By midnight the numbers queueing were estimated at 1,000.

So important was the match that there was a belated change in the nomination of umpires. Under the agreed procedure eight umpires had been chosen to stand in the series, the names to be drawn from a hat to decide who stood in a particular Test. This was done before the rubber started, but Sydney Smith, Australia's tour manager, insisted that the names not be made public until just before each fixture. Eight different umpires stood in the first four games. Just as the umpires were to be announced for The Oval, Smith intervened. He wanted a change to be made so that Frank Chester would stand 'simply because in our opinion he was the best umpire in England.' MCC readily agreed, especially as Chapman shared the opinion. So it was that Chester and Harding Young, known to one and all as Sailor, were the chosen umpires.

Chester was perhaps the first of the great umpires. He might have had a glittering playing career after starting it with Worcestershire when he was only 16. But he lost part of his right arm below the elbow during action at Salonika in the First World War and fairly soon afterwards turned to umpiring. He was only 27 when he first stood in 1922 and had already cemented his reputation four years later. Chester stood in 48 Tests.

Sailor Young was so called because the chairman of Essex, Charles Green, saw him batting in the nets while Young was in the Royal Navy. Green was so impressed that he bought him out of the service and Young had a successful career with the county, though it was blighted by rheumatism. He played two Test matches and umpired in three, the 1926 finale being his last.

Chapman prepared for the biggest match of his career by missing Kent's Championship match at Sussex and appearing instead in the Hythe Cricket Week. He made scores in the two matches against Oxford Harlequins and Free Foresters of 7, 15, 10 and 18 and, by way of seriously limbering up, was captain in the second. He travelled by train from Folkestone to Charing Cross on Friday evening. There was an appealing guilelessness about Chapman. No-one really knew if he had any clue about how to lead a cricket team, but he seemed like a nice enough chap. As he marched casually along the station platform the driver leaned out of the cab and shouted: 'I'd like to wish you good luck, sir.' Chapman went over, held out his hand and waited while driver and fireman wiped their oily hands on a cotton rag. Then he went on his way to a taxi, blushing and smiling, as a crowd gathered round him.

As the numbers in the line at the Oval swelled there was to be one more selectorial twist. A telegram was sent to Weston-super-Mare summoning Bert Strudwick to London upon completion of Surrey's match against Somerset. George Brown, his designated replacement, was in trouble after bruising a thumb while playing for Hampshire. The injury had occurred in the county's first match in Leicester earlier in the week, and the call for Strudwick seemed to be nothing more than an excess of caution. At Dean Park, Bournemouth, on the day before the Test, Brown made a vibrant hundred. It seemed odd, however, that England's wicketkeeper for the most crucial Test in years had not kept wicket for his county in the two Championship matches leading up to it. Brown travelled to London but had to submit to a doctor's examination on Saturday morning.

The moment was almost here but it seemed determined to arrive kicking and struggling.

First Day

Brown was told by a doctor that his bruised thumb rendered him unfit to play. He was bitterly disappointed. Strudwick was included for his 28th and final England cap at the age of 46 and remains the oldest to have kept wicket for any side in a Test match. Australia recalled Collins as captain and left out Jack Ryder, the vice-captain and fellow selector – presumably they worked out that there would be hell to pay if both played, given the doubtful fitness of one and the poor form of the other. Chapman, the youngest man to captain England in an Ashes match at home, did what all of England were praying for and won the toss, using a coin he had apparently found in a Christmas cake during the previous Australian tour. It took Plum Warner to point out that Pitt the Younger had been Prime Minister at 25 and that both he and Chapman were at Pembroke College, Cambridge.

Shortly before 11.30am Hobbs and Sutcliffe walked out. They did so cheered by considerably fewer spectators than envisaged. Such had been the constant publicity that this was the match to end all matches – that big money was changing hands for seats overlooking the ground, that it was imperative to claim a place in the overnight queue – that thousands, fearful that there would be no space, stayed away. There were perhaps 15,000 when 30,000 had been fully expected.

For an hour, the great pair essayed the scene. Hobbs was serene, Sutcliffe was beaten a time or two but did not mind that. They had reached 50 from 23 overs, and in the 24th Hobbs took two off Mailey whom he was finding to his liking when to general dismay he heaved across the line to a full toss and was bowled. None could believe what they were seeing. At silly point Tommy Andrews simply murmured: 'Oh what a turn up for the books!' Woolley batted well enough before being bowled by a googly from Mailey – a leg-break to a left-hander. On the stroke of lunch Hendren who had started confidently cut a ball from Gregory into his stumps. It was Gregory's first wicket in the series with his 488th ball. The scourge of England in 1921 had been muted, but nobody begrudged him this wicket on his 31st birthday, even though it left England in potential trouble.

After lunch Chapman dispelled the prospect of disaster by batting like a man with the world at his feet. Sutcliffe, mostly becalmed, reached his fifty with a fourth four, but Chapman, cheered on by a coterie of adoring female spectators in the pavilion seats, decided that watchfulness for its own sake would get England nowhere. He ran quick singles, hit with purpose to leg and was altogether exhilarating in a stand of 81 lasting 77 minutes. It enthused England, and when he was out a run short of his half century, deceived by Mailey and smartly stumped by Bert Oldfield, something went from England's day. He departed, still grinning, and as his admirers waved handkerchiefs he went into the wrong door on the way to the changing room. Stevens, too, was set on entertainment and needed only four scoring stokes to make his 17 before he was caught, hesitant in his shot, the ball after driving Mailey for six. Rhodes now came in to an ovation fit for an old champion, and although he narrowly evaded Collins at forward short leg before scoring, he then settled to the task. England's innings was changed irrevocably by the loss of Sutcliffe. Attempting to sweep Mailey, he edged the ball into his face. He took a few minutes to try to compose himself, but the imperturbable one was perturbed and next ball he was bowled through the gate for 76 from 252 balls. It was an innings deliberately without risk, and it was vital to England's cause. Chapman had shown what could be done, Sutcliffe demonstrated what needed to be done. Geary was run out, responding to Rhodes' call for a single to mid-off, Tate took his cue from his skipper and carved merrily away for 23 from 16 balls, which seemed to put it not only in the wrong series but in the wrong century. After Tate departed, bowled by a quicker one, Larwood poked one to silly point. It left time for Strudwick on his home ground to be given the second rapturous reception of the day before Rhodes gave Mailey his sixth wicket by edging him behind to the exemplary Oldfield who had offered a quiet masterclass in his craft. England were all out for 280 and, although there was some uneven bounce throughout the day, this was still about 100 runs short of their likely intended target.

The new ball was taken by Tate and Larwood who were quickly into their stride. Tate found swing, Larwood was very fast. Soon Bardsley, struggling with the pace, edged Larwood behind but this only brought in Macartney, scorer of three successive hundreds. For half an hour, no more, Australia looked in the mood to take the game away from England. Macartney was magisterial, Woodfull blocking to his heart's content. Not only did Woodfull have the patience of Job, he had the patience of Sutcliffe, which was an altogether different level of forbearance. Chapman changed the bowling, Stevens seemingly mysteriously coming on for Tate who had bowled eight overs for five runs. Macartney dismissively struck the wayward Stevens for two fours, but after the second came a match-turning moment. Attempting to hit another boundary with a sweep shot, Macartney dragged the ball onto his stumps. There were differing views of the Stevens delivery. Some saw it as a palpable long hop, others as a clever top-spinner which went on more quickly to Macartney than he bargained for. Six overs later with the close approaching, Ponsford was run out by Larwood, reacting sharply at short-leg as the batsman thought of a single and, too late, changed his mind. With two overs left in the day Larwood produced a wonderful ball which moved rapidly off the pitch, broke five or so inches and removed the luckless Andrews' off stump. In that second, England knew, if they had not known before, that she had found a fast bowler. Tate came off the pitch and said: 'It is many a year since I saw a lad send them down at such a speed. He bowled faster than I have ever seen him bowl, perhaps faster than I have seen any man bowl.'

Australia survived the ten balls remaining, Collins repeatedly glancing up at the clock, but the advantage for now was with the home side. Fourteen wickets had fallen in the day for 340 runs. It was all going to be over by Christmas after all.

England 280 all out; Australia 60 for 4 (Woodfull 22, Collins 1)

It was the first night of the Proms. They were in their 32nd year, and the large crowds attending the Queen's Hall to see Sir Henry Wood conduct meant that promenading, the original purpose of the concerts, was no longer possible. Indeed, the size of the audience exceeded expectations as much as the Oval crowd had fallen short of them. It was the final Proms not to be broadcast by the BBC.

The miners entered the 16th week of the lock-out, and delegates prepared to gather in London for a conference to discuss yet more new ways of engaging the owners. They were misguidedly optimistic that a settlement might be reached on their terms. The rail unions warned employers about mistreating workers who had been part of the General Strike and said the tide would turn. One union man told delegates at a mass gathering in Kent: 'No-one except railway officials could have conceived such dastardly, diabolical and underhand methods of victimisation as those which have been put into operation since the conclusion of the strike.' There was no end in sight to either dispute.

Second Day

The Oval was full to bursting on Monday morning. Whatever had kept people away on Saturday, they were determined to be there now that the match had taken shape. It was a work day in London, but it was being treated as a second Bank Holiday. The ground, with 31,000 inside, was closed before lunch. Collins and Woodfull added 24 in 14 overs before Chapman, at last, introduced Rhodes for the first time in the 46th over of the innings, his first bowl in Test cricket for more than five years. That morning Plum Warner received a letter from a Yorkshireman imploring him to remind Rhodes that in the match between Yorkshire and the Australians in Sheffield the bowler had caused Woodfull to play on to a ball that looked to have the left-hander's natural break but instead went on with the arm. Warner showed the letter to Chapman and Rhodes before play.

Rhodes bowled two maidens. The fifth ball of his third over went straight on with the arm. Woodfull chopped it on to his stumps, 'presumptive evidence that the old man schemed again for a similar downfall,' wrote Arthur Gilligan. Cunningly plotted or plain good fortune it left Australia at 90-5. It brought in Arthur Richardson to join Collins, who by then had scored 16 from 62 balls and was showing no inclination to go anywhere. Chapman immediately took Rhodes off and reintroduced Tate who was rendering the batsmen virtually scoreless but seemed to be posing no threat. After four overs from Tate, Rhodes was brought back again. There were virtually no runs being scored from the bowling at the Vauxhall End. After Larwood's early spell (12 from six overs) Rhodes and Tate virtually sealed it off. With Hendren moved from the outfield to silly mid-off, Richardson decided it was time for a change of tempo. He offered Rhodes a hard return catch which was declined but, refusing to be discouraged, he continued to leave his crease and again unleashed a fierce drive. Geary at mid-off took a splendid catch low to his right, and Australia were in deeper trouble still at 122-6. In the first 42 overs of the morning session they had added 62 runs.

Gregory now joined Collins and together these two luminaries of the old AIF team dragged Australia back into the match. Collins did not alter his approach: he stoutly defended most balls and when he scored it was usually a nudged or dabbed single. Gregory, a wounded gladiator all series, complemented him perfectly. He saw Rhodes out of the attack and never let any of England's bowlers, steady as most were, dictate terms to him. Occasionally, he lived dangerously, snicking the ferocious Larwood through the slips, offering a difficult chance to an otherwise impeccable Strudwick. By lunch Gregory had overtaken his captain. The morning session lasted 2hrs 30mins and brought 62 overs, 37 of them from the quick bowlers. The rate of scoring was 1.75 runs an over, and if that was woefully slow it could be excused by the position in which Australia found themselves.

For almost an hour after lunch the seventh wicket pair continued to defy England. Collins struck his first boundary from his 225th ball, Gregory continued to be the more assertive. The crowd, rapt as they were in this dauntless rearguard, were also becoming worried. The stand had reached 107 when Gregory, perhaps relieved not to be facing Larwood's cannonballs, gave Tate his overdue reward when he popped one up to short-leg. Two runs later Collins' vigil ended, his concentration perhaps broken, when after almost four hours he was well held in the gully by Stevens off Larwood. Had Stevens taken an equally tough catch off the same bowler at short-leg four hours earlier when the ball went agonisingly over his head, it might have spared England a good deal of anxiety. Collins was given a wonderful reception when he was dismissed for 61 from 286 balls because the spectators well understood that without him Australia would already have been dead and buried. Now, although they were still 49 adrift, the Ashes remained on the line.

It was the turn of Oldfield and Grimmett to ensure that these valiant efforts were not wasted. They put on an invaluable 67 for the ninth wicket in 78 minutes, almost jaunty in the context of what had gone before. Tate took the last two wickets to finish with 3-40 from 37.1 overs, remarkable figures in their way but the suspicion was that he might have done more. Generally, the duo resembling spring and autumn – their combined age of 69 hardly hinted at the disparity in ages – were adjudged the best of England's bowlers. 'Larwood, who with a possible exception of Rhodes, was England's best bowler,' hedged *The Times*.

After a delay of 15 minutes England had 70 minutes' batting left. When the openers went out, Hobbs remarked to Mailey: 'Now then, Arthur, play the game, no more full tosses.' And Mailey replied: 'All right, Jack.' The 25 overs were negotiated with enviable skill by England's great opening pair. Apart from three overs delivered by Gregory at the start they faced the spin of Grimmett, Mailey and Macartney; if the batsmen were not fluent, nor they did put a foot wrong. England reached the close 27 runs in front with – and the importance of this could not be overstated – all ten wickets intact. It had been a slow, gripping, intense day of Test cricket – 156.1 overs, 291 runs, six wickets – 'so keen and intense that the youngest individual will remember it when his hair is white with the snows of time.'

Close: Australia 302 all out; England 49-0 (Hobbs 28, Sutcliffe 20).
England lead by 27 runs

In the small hours it rained over south London. Actually, it pelted down and the thunder accompanying it could be heard for miles around. The exposed pitch at The Oval avoided the heaviest parts of the deluge, but that probably made the conditions for batting even worse. The surface was on the wet side of moist and at some point it would dry and the ball would misbehave. This was a sticky wicket to end all sticky wickets.

The sound as the crowds made their way once more to The Oval was no longer thunder, it was the collective sinking of English hearts. The advantage was now decidedly with Australia.

Third Day

Hobbs and Sutcliffe knew what to expect. They fully understood that they were about to receive a searching examination and that no matter how high their level of skill, how calm their temperament, they would probably fail. In an act of astounding self-awareness they conceded as much between themselves. 'Jolly bad luck that rain, it has cooked our chances,' said Hobbs to Sutcliffe not long after they had arrived in the middle, and Herbert readily nodded his agreement. So, too, did the umpire Sailor Young who overheard the exchange and muttered: 'Yes, it's hard luck.'

What unfolded in the next two hours utterly defied doomsayers. Given the circumstances – a diabolical pitch, the Ashes on the line, a nation hoping against hope for its weary soul to be rejuvenated – it was and remains the greatest of all first-wicket partnerships for England against Australia.

Grimmett, from the Pavilion End, and Macartney, from the Vauxhall End, were given first crack under overcast skies. Hobbs took a couple of leg-side fours from Grimmett, but otherwise dealt mostly in singles. Sutcliffe dealt only in defence. In that initial exchange he faced 45 balls of the 11 overs sent down by Macartney, who bowled his left-arm spin almost exclusively over the wicket, and scored from none of them, leaving it when he could, mainly offering a dead bat. He did not add to his overnight total until the 17th over of the morning when he had been in occupation for another 40 minutes and in a flurry of activity he took a two and a three off Grimmett.

The wicket was not yet at its most capricious, but with an hour or so gone the sun came out. Now there would be tricks. Arthur Richardson, glasses and cap in place, replaced Macartney, who had given up only two runs. Bowling over the wicket he was immediately clouted for two leg-side boundaries by Hobbs, the first of which brought up the England opener's fifty, his 35th for England for those who were counting and plenty probably were. For his third over, after speaking to Collins, Richardson changed to round the wicket. The leg side was immediately packed with seven men, a backward short-leg, four short-legs in a row like a chorus line at one of the West End revues, flanked by a long-leg, cover and mid-off. Shortly afterwards, Hobbs took a single to register the first wicket pair's ninth century partnership in their 18 innings together and their third in a series in which their lowest stand had been the unbroken 32 terminated by rain at Trent Bridge.

Richardson bowled 19 overs in succession; Hobbs, whether by accident or design, faced by far the larger proportion – 82 balls to Sutcliffe's 32. At one point Richardson bowled nine maidens in ten overs. It was turning and bouncing, and Hobbs was imperious, batting outside leg stump before moving into line and playing the ball down, never once misjudging. Sutcliffe repelled a combination of Mailey and Grimmett, both spinning the ball, at the other end. Collins resisted what must have been an overwhelming temptation to give Gregory a bash and was being criticised for not doing so even as Richardson laboured sternly away on his leg-stump line. But this was to forget Gregory's woebegone state for so much of the season.

A few minutes before lunch, after a little more than three hours, Sutcliffe went to his 50 with only his second four. They reached the interval together. England were 161-0, Hobbs was 97 and Sutcliffe 53, they had added 112 in the morning session in 56 overs. 'Well played, Herbert,' said Hobbs as they patted down the pitch before following their opponents into the pavilion. 'Well played, Jack,' said Sutcliffe. They were aware, of course, of what they had done but it needed no elaboration from them. At lunch, the Prince of Wales stood up from his place and walked over to Hobbs to shake his hand.

Hobbs achieved his hundred early in the afternoon, patting gently towards point and setting off for a bold single, typical of the sort he and Sutcliffe stole throughout their association. Collins moved from his place at backward short-leg to shake Hobbs' hand. Play was held up as the crowd cheered and kept on cheering. And just as it was about to resume 30,000 stood as one and gave three cheers to the man of the moment, of so many moments. This was his 13th Test century, and it was not merely a knee-jerk reaction to assess it as his very best. Around London and the rest of the country shopkeepers erected bulletin boards conveying the score, forcing the police to move crowds on in some places. The Strand was packed and stayed packed for the rest of the match. Train passengers murmured the scores to one another, and the men shutting the doors of London tube trains shouted the latest score as they did so.

At the ground one correspondent was again taken by the number of female spectators. 'This interest of women in cricket is one of the symptoms of the modern feminine movement, for in pre-war days the presence of a woman at The Oval, if not quite rare as a black swan, had still something of the air of an explorer in strange waters.' One of the foremost cricket experts in the country was Mrs Lucy Baldwin, wife of the Prime Minister and herself a skilful cricketer, who had left Collins astounded by her knowledge at the first lunch when the tour started. The point was that cricket and this particular match held the entire country in its embrace.

Suddenly, without warning, came the breakthrough Australia craved. Gregory, on at last, was as penetrating as he had been all summer and found some nip off the pitch. It was enough to account for Hobbs as the ball seared past his forward prop and trimmed the off bail. No praise seemed too great for the partnership or the contributions of both men on this gluepot of a surface. Hobbs, because of his exalted status and because he showed a little more attacking intent, received the greater plaudits. Still, it was as a pair that they were saluted.

> COL PHILIP TREVOR: 'I will say at once and without reservation of any kind that Hobbs and Sutcliffe together gave the best batting display on a difficult wicket I have ever seen given in a Test match.'

> PLUM WARNER: 'I assert without fear of contradiction that England never possessed a finer first wicket pair than Hobbs and Sutcliffe. August 17 will ever be a memorable day in the annals of English cricket. It showed our cricketers at their best, full of courage and grit and sand, as the Americans put it.'

> NEVILLE CARDUS: 'The wicket was difficult and Hobbs and Sutcliffe alone stood between England and defeat.'

> ARTHUR CROOME: 'Before they started their performance, if I had been given my choice of all the pairs who have ever gone in first for England, I should have selected Dr WG Grace and Shrewsbury to bat for my side in existing circumstances. Now I consider reincarnation unnecessary.'

> AUBREY FAULKNER: 'The manner with which Hobbs and Sutcliffe coped with the situation must rank as quite one of the finest things that have happened in English cricket.'

And on and on and on. Only Alf Noble spoiled the sense of magnificence, suggesting that Hobbs had deliberately made Richardson seem virtually unplayable to ensure that Collins kept him on. That did not really account for what thousands saw with their own eyes and was roundly rebuffed by Hobbs who insisted he was playing the bowling on its merits and could not get it away.

The two great batsmen delivered their considered verdicts a little later. Hobbs remembered how he felt at the start of the morning: 'I thought we had precious little chance. The Aussies had a wicked glint in their eye and they were on tip-toe. I guessed that the great crowd felt what I was feeling, for I heard the sigh of their relief at the end of every over.' By lunch, Hobbs could acknowledge the achievement. 'We felt we had pulled the game round, and so we had.'

Sutcliffe, as measured in his analysis of his batting as the batting itself, was less effusive. He was miffed that an impression was given in the morning papers that Hobbs had nursed him during Richardson's spell. He did not think the battle was quite as fierce as that which the pair faced three years later in Melbourne on another sticky – but then their brave resistance did not achieve quite so many runs and only Sutcliffe reached three figures. 'But it was trying enough, I was there for 40-odd minutes before I got a run and I can tell you I was the happiest man on the ground to know I was still there. We surmounted our difficulties, and I say that Hobbs' innings was a masterpiece model of determined and skilful batting.'

In his instruction manual, *Batting*, published in 1937, Sutcliffe offered an insight into batting on gluepots. 'We are not going to the wicket with an inferiority complex,' he said. 'There are so many batsmen who, when once they see a ball turn and pop, are prepared to have a foolish 'blind' – they are not prepared to fight. What a great mistake this is, for there is no wicket quite so interesting and thrilling to play on as a gluepot.'

Sutcliffe was prepared to fight all right and when he wrote those words his mind perforce must have drifted back to The Oval in 1926. He repeated the tenets he exhibited over an innings of seven and a half hours:

> The only safe scoring shots can be made from long hops, full tosses and the occasional foray into the covers when you can get bang on top of the ball.
>
> Do not hit against the break.
>
> Play all defensive strokes with a dead bat.
>
> Those players who have specialised in sticky wicket displays and who have been highly successful, are the ones who have been able to concentrate very deeply on the task of cutting out certain strokes, thereby reducing risks to a minimum. That is the secret of all successful sticky wicket play. The best method as

soon as one sees that popping, turning ball, is either to get clear of its course altogether or take the blow on the chest. It doesn't hurt much and a slight chest or rib tickler is much better than losing a wicket. That is one of the finer points of batsmanship.

He was, of course, describing Hobbs and Sutcliffe.

The scale of their accomplishment and what might have happened without it became all too clear as the hot afternoon wore on. England's batting virtually surrendered before an Australian side which was not giving up the Ashes lightly. Woolley invigorated Sutcliffe but flattered to deceive yet again. After unfurling a host of languid shots he was given lbw to Richardson, and although the verdict looked mistaken it was typical of Woolley in the series, getting in and getting out. Hendren was uncomfortable against the spin, and he failed several times to connect with his inside-out shot, backing away to leg and hitting to cover. He was there when Sutcliffe reached his hundred to more ecstatic cheering and was eventually out in a swirl of activity. He seemed to have been bowled as Oldfield caught the bails and the ball, but was clearly bewildered when umpire Frank Chester put up his finger at the bowler's end following several muted appeals. In the morning papers he was given out as bowled, but Chester then contacted the scorers to say that he had been caught, which would at least better explain the upraised digit. Whatever the mode of dismissal, Hendren had failed again, though Sutcliffe's growing assertiveness meant that England added 48 and 57 for the second and third wickets. Chapman, too, made it comfortably into double figures before being bowled by a quicker one from Richardson. Stevens stayed for nearly an hour and helped add another precious 57.

Sutcliffe was worn out. He told Mailey as much and that he would be glad when the last ball of the day was bowled. It was Mailey who bowled it. Three balls, three defensive shots, nothing to worry Sutcliffe. But he was tired and just a touch vulnerable. Mailey's fourth ball was a fast leg-break which pitched exactly where he wanted it. It turned, beat the shot and took off stump. After seven hours at the crease and facing 477 balls, then more than any England player had received in an innings at home, Sutcliffe was out for 161. England had a lead of 353. It seemed enough, but nothing was ever enough against Australia. They had never wilted in the field, they would have their say with the bat.

England 375-6 (Rhodes 0) lead by 353 runs

When Sutcliffe left the ground after play he was greeted by legions of admirers. Four mounted policemen and a host more on foot had to clear the way for him as he walked to his car. Hundreds of fans raced after him as he drove away and several had to be removed from the footboard. Hobbs, the day's other hero, dined at the Trocadero restaurant where the only talk was of the third day's exploits and what the morrow would bring.

Fourth Day

Opinions on the state of play from England's point of view varied from cautious optimism to weary pessimism. Essentially, despite the evidence of the scoreboard and their own eyes, nobody quite dared believe that the Ashes could be prised from Australia's grasp. Australia could scale Everest if necessary, and a lead of 353 with four wickets in hand was made to seem like a mere molehill in some quarters.

'On paper that reads a good position,' said Colonel Trevor in the *Telegraph*. 'I cannot think it is quite enough.'

'The pertinacity of the Australians was rewarded,' said the man from *The Times*. 'It may be that today and tomorrow they must tackle a heavy but not a hopeless task.'

'The interest increases and still the result is in doubt,' said Shrimp Leveson Gower.

'Fortune has given no real indication as to which side she will eventually favour ...,' wrote England's chairman of selectors, Plum Warner, 'the outcome no man can predict with any certainty.'

Only his Australian counterpart Clem Hill seemed to differ by insisting that 'England has never really lost the whip-hand and she stands in a stronger position than ever.'

What counted was whether the players believed. Did it help that three of them were young enough never to have tasted defeat in an Ashes rubber or that another three were old enough to have been part of series victories? First there was a lead to consolidate.

The crowd was again large. Soon to be among them, a simple measure of the effect of the event, was Prime Minister Baldwin. With the miners' dispute at yet another critical juncture, the men at odds with their leaders, he had postponed his much-needed holiday in France and returned to London. Rightly or wrongly, it was the cricket that demanded his attention.

Play, due to start at noon in accordance with the arcane regulations drawn up by who knows who but perhaps Lord Harris from his hospital bed, was delayed for 15 minutes by a shower. This gave police the opportunity to interview Geary about a theft of several notes from his wallet which he had found slit open. After telling all he knew, he joined Rhodes and was soon out to Gregory, making up for lost time in taking his third wicket of the match. Rhodes and, especially, Tate, enjoyed themselves for the next half hour, adding 43 for the eighth wicket. Nothing matched the monumental first-wicket partnership of the day before, nothing could, but England strung together an important series of minor stands, five between 39 and 57. Mailey bowled Larwood with the last ball before lunch to leave England at 430-9, and then it rained hard for an hour.

Emerging from 10 Downing Street where he had been conducting yet more talks on the coal dispute, the Prime Minister spotted a reporter and asked him what he thought of the Test match. 'I think we have a good chance of winning, sir,' said the journalist, 'Oh, I don't mean that,' Baldwin said, 'I meant what did you think of the weather.' It was raining at the time, and he was worried what effect it might have as he was on his way to The Oval. Play could not resume until 3.20pm giving time for Baldwin to meet the teams. A fifth day seemed inevitable. Within four overs Strudwick thick-edged Mailey to point and England's innings ended at 436. Another measure of just how testing conditions had been was that Oldfield conceded 19 byes, an unfeasible number for so adroit a performer, almost twice as many as he had let through in an innings before and only four fewer than he had previously conceded in this entire series.

Australia's target was 415, and since that was 100 more than any side in Test history had made in the fourth innings to win (Australia had won by four wickets at Adelaide in 1902 when Clem Hill, then the best left-handed batsman in the world, made his second ninety of the match) the destiny of the Ashes seemed assured. And yet, and yet ... Had England not made totals of 411 and 363 in the fourth innings in Australia on the previous tour? The timeless nature of the contest still offered Australia a glimpse of the promised land. They were not likely to give it up easily. It was not as if – unlike these days – they had a plane or even a boat to catch. There was still a month of the visit to go. They were bound to give it a shot.

They did no such thing. Larwood, from the Vauxhall End, was once more terrifyingly quick – JM Barrie's WK Thunder of that April luncheon speech come to life. Australia changed their order and their youngest batsmen, the only two still in their twenties, Woodfull and Ponsford, came out to open. Ponsford was almost immediately disconcerted by the speed when he nudged the third ball of the over through the vacant third slip area. It was then that the full benefit of Hobbs' years of experience were felt. He insisted to Chapman that Rhodes should be brought up to gully and Geary moved to third slip, and Chapman listened and acted. Another rapid ball from Larwood, edged by Woodfull in the direction of Geary who held a stinging catch. In came Macartney. Every Australian hope hung on him.

After three overs Rhodes came on for Tate at the Pavilion End. It was a masterstroke by Chapman because the effects of the heavy roller were wearing off, the sun was out, the surface was drying and who better than a veteran Yorkshireman who had bowled almost 160,000 balls in his long career to take advantage? The ball spun straightaway. But before then, Larwood had another victim. Macartney seemed to be settling into his work. A late cut for two off Larwood was followed by a four flicked wide of square-leg. The fifth ball of the over was short and extremely quick, Macartney essayed a cut and again Geary, at third slip, held a catch moving sharply to his right. They knew, the spectators, what this meant. Hats were thrown in the air, handkerchiefs were waved like flags.

Immediately Chapman removed Larwood from the attack, his fearsome work with the new ball done. Rhodes at the other end made capital use of the patch worn on middle and leg by Grimmett's 55 second innings overs. The third ball of his third over turned sharply, Ponsford prodded and Larwood, moved to backward point seconds before precisely for this purpose, sprang forward and took a catch, inches above the ground. Rhodes quickly added a second when Collins, the resolute, immoveable Collins, came out and perhaps realising he would have to bat forever to save this one, was held at slip. It was 31-4. Victory was surely impossible for one side. As Collins departed, he had a quick chat with Chapman, if not yet to offer congratulations, then probably to dispense with the tea interval.

There came for half an hour or so the semblance of resistance. Bardsley pinched some singles and took two fours off Rhodes, Andrews, all but runless all summer, left his crease and drove him twice for four. Chapman brought back Larwood, and that did the trick when Andrews hooked a short ball hard only to find Tate at square-leg leaping high and holding an excellent one-handed catch. England were inspired, the crowd barely able to contain itself. All round the capital and in outposts up north scores were flashed outside shops.

Bardsley and Gregory added 20 before the former skied Rhodes and was caught by Woolley running round from slip and the latter drove Tate to mid-off where Sutcliffe nonchalantly plucked a hard drive from the air. Rhodes bowled Richardson. 87-8. Oldfield held things up a little. After 20 consecutive overs Rhodes was taken off. In all he bowled 45 overs in the match, more than in any Test he had played since Sydney in 1908 when he was merely 30 years old. Stevens, wayward, was punished by the compact, busy Oldfield but then bowled him with a leg-break. Nine down, Mailey came out and to general delight, before taking guard, went to Chapman in the field and shook him vigorously by the hand. Then Chapman did an inspired thing. As if computing that all his bowlers bar one had taken a wicket in this great contest, he stood down Larwood after four overs and summoned Geary. Mailey, in his droll way, blamed himself for not getting the remainder of the 290 runs that Australia required. Instead, at 6.04pm he missed a straight one from Geary. Australia were all out for 125. It was decided at last. England had prevailed by the barely fathomable margin of 289 runs and won the Ashes for the first time since 1912.

Australia had subsided and the chief architects of their downfall were the 48-year-old Rhodes and 21-year-old Larwood who took four and three wickets respectively and were quite magnificent, the older man exploiting the rough patch at one end, the younger again bowling at express pace and unnerving Australia. Everything went right for the home side, everything wrong for the tourists.

Mailey had the presence of mind to grab the ball that bowled him as a souvenir, just ahead of Strudwick, who had to be content with a stump. The players barely made the sanctuary of the pavilion before the ground invasion began. The outpouring of elation was instantaneous, and thousands upon thousands surged onto the outfield at The Oval to cheer their heroes. For 30 minutes they roared their delight and pleaded with the players to emerge onto the balcony. It was the forerunner of so many scenes of English triumph at The Oval (though the reception may have been more muted during some losses). Chapman came out 'to be acclaimed like a very Caesar.' There is some newsreel footage of him in that moment as he gazes out, serene, cherubic but barely able, it seems, to take it all in. If only life could have stopped for him at that moment. How perfect it was, how imperfect it was to become.

The joyous scenes indicated the place that cricket held in people's hearts and minds, but it was also the summation of a nation desperate for something to cheer, as it sought to overcome the bitter legacy of war and the broken promises to improve their lot that followed. Gradually, in answer to the pleas from a crowd which refused to leave until they had feted their heroes, the players appeared on the balcony. Chapman was arm in arm with Collins and they were accompanied by Warner.

Hobbs and Sutcliffe at last emerged and then so did every member of the England team. Collins playfully shook his fist at Hobbs and the crowd loved it. The cheering at last subsided, and the players began drifting away, but even that was not easy. Hobbs had a car waiting for him by the Vauxhall entrance and he, his wife and daughter slipped out quietly – 'away from one of the most magnificent scenes I have ever taken part in, one of the most magnificent scenes in the history of cricket.'

Interviews were conducted with the Press, and even Rhodes was moved to speak, though not much. 'This has been the best day of my life. There's nothing more to say.' Collins was wonderfully magnanimous in defeat – 'the most enjoyable game I have played in in my life, the best team won.' Chapman was characteristically gallant: 'All I have to say is this: my heartfelt thanks, the thanks of us all are due to the courageous batting of Hobbs and Sutcliffe before lunch yesterday and to the brilliant way in which Rhodes used the wicket today.' It summed up how and why England had won quite so handsomely.

Stevens patiently signed endless requests for autographs from anyone who asked. It was well past 8pm when some of the others left, and still there were fans to greet them. Larwood, Geary and Tyldesley had to sprint to a cab, but Tate was surrounded before he would reach them. The old man of the team, Rhodes, made it to a taxi only to be followed in by a female admirer who would not leave until he signed his autograph. Wilf obliged.

Several players from both teams dined at the Carlton that evening, nominally with Chapman as host but his employers picked up the bill. Before dinner they were all made members of the Ancient Order of Froth Blowers, a charitable spoof organisation which had been founded a couple of years earlier and was raising thousands of pounds for deserving causes.

These were delightful scenes by any lights, made the more glorious because Collins and his men were so gracious, prepared to admit that they had been beaten by the better team. That England deserved their victory in the last match was incontrovertible. But the series as a whole –

disappointing as it was because of the weather, the length of the matches and the lack of ambition – also indicated that England were the superior team. England scored 2,076 runs for 41 wickets, an average of 50.63 a wicket, Australia scored 1,833 runs for 55 wickets at 33.33 a wicket. There was, and there was not, a point about there not being sufficient time to achieve a result. In total 9,419 balls were bowled with a run rate of 43.02 by England and 39.93 by Australia.

Compare that with the five-match Ashes series of 2023. Times have changed, of course; the game has moved on. But the approach is clearly different. The series score in 2023 was 2-2 with one match drawn from a total of 9,282 balls. Both sides made vastly more runs, England 3,079 for 85 wickets, Australia 3,010 for 93. A higher price was put on wickets in 1926, but the batsmen then took many fewer risks than the batters of today – unless they were amateurs.

August 18, 1926 was a great day in English life which, if briefly, lifted the spirits of its people. But it could not quite dispel what was happening elsewhere. From The Oval Baldwin had immediately to go to Downing Street and contend with the latest breakdown in talks between the miners and the mine owners. The former wanted to retain the seven-hour day, arguing an increase was unnecessary; they urged that there be a national pay agreement with the industry re-organised and they sought another subsidy from government. The owners refused to discuss any of these points. Four days after the match Baldwin, exhausted, went to seek sanctuary in Aix.

Meanwhile Lord Londonderry, owner of several profitable pits in Co. Durham, wrote an inflammatory letter to *The Times* saying it was wrong to suggest that the miners' families were starving and insisting that welfare support was plentiful. 'The children are looking better and in most cases are better fed than when their fathers were working,' wrote his Lordship from his pile in Wynyard Park. The marquess was considered one of the more moderate owners, but this was hardly a contribution designed to bring an amenable end to the dispute.

In the days and weeks that followed the great victory the players, but especially Chapman, were acclaimed. Wherever he went Chapman was treated as a conquering hero, he and his wife Beet featuring prominently in the society magazines. 'One of the most popular names wherever English is spoken and cricket is played.' Nobody was saying now that the selectors had gone mad. Instead, it had been an inspired choice. How Chapman enjoyed the adulation. He seemed to take it in his winsome stride. There was – but who could tell then? – a foretaste of what was to come a few days after the match when he was involved in a late-night car crash. Travelling home from Folkestone to Hythe in the early hours of Sunday his two-seater collided head-on with a car driven by a London architect. Chapman was lucky to escape with a few minor cuts to his face caused by the smashed windscreen but had to be driven the rest of the journey as his written-off car was towed away. It is easy to surmise that he had been celebrating some more with a drink or two with chums and got carried away.

Chapman played in none of Kent's remaining four Championship matches. Perhaps it would have been a mite too embarrassing to have the England captain led by his county skipper, Captain (later Baron) Stanley Cornwallis. More likely he was content simply to have a gentle outing in the friendly matches, playing for the county against the MCC and the Australians in both of which he was captain when Cornwallis graciously stood aside. And he played for Mackeson's Brewery XI in its annual match against the Kent constabulary and made three and four. When he appeared for the county against the tourists a few days later, Arthur Mailey was perplexed when he was approached by Frederick Simmonds, Chapman's brewery boss, and informed: 'If you can't get him out, I'll send for a policeman.'

As the country at large revelled in the historic victory, an excellent century scored a day later went largely unheralded. There was an air of ironic inevitability about it. Going in at 24-2, Arthur Carr made 138 out of 209 with 22 fours for Notts at Trent Bridge. It was an innings full of resounding drives and saw Carr back to his most effective. Ah, but it was too late. Not that Carr was quite finished yet with the season.

What a time it was to be alive for those few heady days. Nobody minded that great swathes of turf had been cut out of the pitch at The Oval, apparently by the Australians who were intent on transplanting it at home. The Ashes themselves were the subject of speculation, and it was proposed that the bats used by Hobbs and Sutcliffe in their epic partnership and the ball used in the fourth innings should be burned, the remnants placed in an urn and presented to England to form new ashes. Lord Darnley confirmed that the ashes on his mantelpiece related only to the 1883 matches. It came to nothing. The Darnley Ashes were loaned to Lord's for a little of 1926 and later in the year to an exhibition in Oxford Street which was raising funds for the War Seal Foundation.

When Darnley died the following year the urn which had stood on his mantelpiece for 44 years was donated to MCC. The English and Australian players all signed a bat on behalf of the Women's Committee for the Relief of Miners' Wives and Dependents, which was to be sold to the highest bidder. Rhodes wrote across the top: 'Fifth Test Match 1926.' No record exists of whether Lord Londonderry made a bid. Cinemas throughout the country showed the film of the match. 'Come and see how APF Chapman and his Merry Men won back the Ashes,' cooed one. 'The Deluxe Symphonique Orchestra at all performances,' said another, eager to entice customers. Five cameras were used to film the play, and slow motion was employed frequently. All four days were filmed but only comparative fragments still exist.

Somewhat unexpectedly, Rhodes gave a radio talk on the match when he was again playing at The Oval a few days later, for Yorkshire against Surrey, and imparted some secrets of his trade. 'Every time I bowl a ball,' he said, 'I try to impart spin but I do not always know what the ball is going to do. Usually, of course, I pitch the ball on the leg stump and it goes away to the off and but sometimes the ball will do something I don't expect and it is when this happens I very often get a wicket. Good length, plain straight bowling, while having its virtues will not get a good batsman out in a month of Sundays.'

And he revealed a little of his state of mind during the great victory, perhaps more than previously in his entire career. 'I was very proud and pleased when the Selection Committee invited me to play. I can honestly say that I was more anxious during this match than in that first match at Trent Bridge 27 years ago. When the game was over, I was as happy and pleased as any schoolboy for I felt I had not let my friends down. It was a great day for England.'

Like the other professionals, Hobbs went back to play for his county. The five bats he used in the series were given as prizes in a *Weekly Dispatch* competition in which entrants had to forecast the number of runs scored by England in the Oval Test and, as a tie-breaker, predict the total hours of sunshine during the match. The prime bat, the one used in the last match, went to a chap from Birmingham who astonishingly guessed both numbers correctly, 716 runs and 27 hours. He had to wait for his prize, however, as Hobbs wanted to complete the season with the bat in question. And in Surrey's final match against Middlesex at Lord's, he no doubt enhanced its value in every respect by making 316 not out.

It was the highest score of his great career, 40 more than the innings he had played the previous summer when he was a stripling of 42, and also the largest individual score made at Lord's. The first hundred came in three hours, the next 216 in a shade under four, the majority of his 41 fours coming via quite masterful leg-side play. There was a slight note of poignancy about the feat. For 105 years the record for the highest innings at Lord's had been held by William Ward, batting in his top hat to make 278. In 1925 Ward's score was at last overtaken by the Yorkshireman Percy Holmes, a notable opening batsman but like many others destined to live in Hobbs' shadow. But in scoring 315 he would surely have a place in the annals that would last decades. It held for precisely one season.

On the last day of August Lancashire took the Championship title for the first time in 22 years when they defeated Nottinghamshire at Old Trafford by 10 wickets. In the speechifying after the game, Carr, as Notts captain, first congratulated them but then added, as was his wont, a contentious note, reported in the *Manchester Guardian*. 'First of all, about Ernest Tyldesley, I think it was an absolute disgrace that he was not played in the last Test match. He had no business to be left out and if the last Test match had been played in the north of England I think he would have been included.' In the *Daily Mirror* a couple of days later, a report claimed to divulge the secrets of the selection meeting for the final Test. It told how Stevens was almost appointed captain but that Gilligan and Rhodes were adamant that he should not have the job. Warner, who wanted Stevens, proposed dropping Chapman altogether. The report also took shots at the selection committee in general, Warner's appointment in particular and the Board of Control for allowing it.

Warner was furious. He was furious with Carr, and he was furious with what the *Mirror's* 'special correspondent' had written. From Folkestone, where he had ventured for the Festival – the Hon LH Tennyson's XI were playing the Hon FSG Calthorpe's XI – he first sent an angry hand-written letter to Sir Francis Lacey, MCC's secretary, in his final days in the job. His annoyance was such that the note is barely legible. A day later, Warner decided to involve Lord Harris, this time, presumably having calmed down a bit, typing the missive. He says that the *Mirror* report abuses the MCC, the Board of Control, the Selection Committee, and includes 'a leakage of what took place at the Selection Committee meeting,' which tellingly he does not refute. 'The whole thing seems to me scandalous.'

He then turns his ire on Carr for what he calls his recent actions and indicates that Carr's invitation to tour Argentina that winter should be reconsidered 'unless he makes some gesture of repentance and regret shortly.' Warner writes that it would be impossible for both he and Carr to go on the trip. 'Carr, after his recent behaviour, cannot in my humble opinion be allowed to get away with it.' This was the self-absorbed side of Warner coming out, the man who did not take criticism lightly if at all. Lord Harris, now fully recovered, senses what and who he was dealing with. From personal experience, he said in his reply, it was of little use trying to expose Press inaccuracies since editors always supported their reporters. He said that he would not be in the least surprised if Carr denied using the expression which Warner was protesting about. As for the Argentine tour his lordship wrote, with gentle dismissiveness: 'I do not fail to note that – as I read it – you would not go if he was included.' There the matter seems to have ended, though Warner went to the Argentine and Carr, having a convenient appendix operation, did not. All this after England had enjoyed such a triumph.

By the second week in September, with the football season now dominating the sports pages and Burnley making the early running in Division One, there were two mildly significant cricket matches to play. The Australians were finishing the first-class section of their tour against an England XI in Blackpool. It was entirely in keeping with their trip that any chance of a conclusion was prevented by rain.

In a radio interview Herbie Collins reflected on how tough he had found the tour. 'It is no easy task. So long as every member of your team plays up to form and keeps well things will move along fairly smoothly. But such good fortune has eluded us this tour.'

Collins pointed out that Stork Hendry had been laid low almost as soon as they landed: 'In addition, Jack Gregory, our fast bowler, was not always as fit as he would have liked to have been, and this caused me considerable anxiety. In 1921 he could have bowled at his best for hours, but during this present tour a strained leg necessitated his being used very sparingly.' Of course, the selectors had also brought along the 25-year-old fast bowler Sam Everett, billed him as the next big thing and were left in the mire after he proved barely the next small thing.

Another England side, although it was officially The Rest, was in action at The Oval against Lancashire as the champion county. It was like getting the old band together. Rather surprisingly Shrimp Leveson

Gower, in charge of team selection, managed to enlist the eleven players who had won back the Ashes. Not The Rest, then, but England. It was made possible because, perversely, the champion county did not have a representative in the team for the final Test.

There was one major difference to the eleven which only confirms the confusion and double standards prevalent in English cricket. The captain was not Percy Chapman but Jack Hobbs. After losing early wickets – Hobbs and Sutcliffe failed – England were resuscitated by a century from Hendren. Still, a total of 217 suggested they might struggle. When Lancashire's first wicket reached 106, the sheen was wearing off England's glory boys. On the second day, Lancashire imploded as ten wickets went for another 71. England now assumed command. The old firm, Hobbs and Sutcliffe, put on 157 in 95 minutes. Sutcliffe took 20 from one over – 'never has he given a more dazzling display,' said *Wisden*. There was more. Woolley, the great under-performer of the Test series, scored 172 in little more than two hours. His partnership with Hendren produced 243 runs in 95 minutes. Hobbs declared, the Champion County folded again, Stevens toying with their middle order in taking 6-52. It was not perhaps The Oval of a month before, there were few spectators, but this England, put into the field for the second and last time, won by 374 runs. The season was ended. Hobbs, Sutcliffe, Tyldesley and Hendren occupied the first four places in the batting averages published in *Wisden* with Chapman the leading amateur in eighth. Rhodes had to be content with second place in the bowling averages with Tate sixth, Larwood eighth and Geary 12th. The leading bowler by one of those statistical quirks, which make cricket so endearing yet so daft, was one Robert Melsome, who qualified by bowling sufficient overs and took 26 wickets at 14.11, 0.75 runs a wicket better than Rhodes, though his great performances were for the Army against Cambridge and Oxford Universities and the Navy, not at The Oval for England against Australia.

The second display at The Oval by the Boys of 1926 was a marvellous appendix, no more, to their deeds of the previous month. That first victory, in so many eyes, restored national self-esteem and meant that all was well with England after all. It had veterans enjoying an Indian summer and youth rising to the occasion – 'there is a ripeness at the core of a nation which chooses its heroes on the field in that way.' Just briefly, some people were being fooled into thinking that it was after all a land fit for heroes.

THE DEMON BOWLER.

First Miner (*to second ditto*). "DON'T TALK TO ME ABOUT CRICKET. YON'S THE CHAMPION—GOT US ALL OUT FOR NOWT!"

11

THE AFTERMATH

A desperate conflict, conducted at all times with most gallant courtesy, it was an example to cricketers everywhere and always, and a credit to the game and to the race which evolved the game and to all its great servants of the present and the past.
John Marchant in The Greatest Test Match
(published in the autumn of 1926)

The Cabinet was stubborn as well as the owners. They both felt, rightly, that the miners were close to being starved into submission and saw little reason to interfere with this elegant process.
Roy Jenkins in his biography, Baldwin, 1987

By late November the miners were defeated. There was a heatwave in England in the early part of October. But after four or five days the Indian summer ended and was swiftly followed by a bitterly cold period which brought frost and snow. It continued for weeks and was enough finally to break the men, starved into submission. 'FORCED TO PITS BY HUNGER,' said the *Daily Herald,* wearing its heart on its sleeve till the end. More than 100,000 miners drifted back into work in the East Midlands and although the more northerly cohorts held out for a few weeks more they had run out of rope. They went back to work for less pay and longer days, crushed. Not all of them were allowed back.

The last bastion of protest was in the Durham pits. Five months earlier those miners found brief respite in Sunderland for the visit of the Australians. Over two days they packed into the Ashbrooke ground, given concessionary admittance, the stands bedecked with flat caps. Now the Durham Miners' Federation admitted defeat in recommending a deal which brought none of what they sought. 'Force of circumstances are too strong to battle against any longer. Under any circumstances that afforded the slightest ground for hope we would have advised total rejection.' It would be years, decades, before the miners and the Trade Union movement regained their confidence, their will to confront the forces they felt were lined up against them. The Government was already preparing legislation which limited union rights. Baldwin, who for parts of the summer, was a force for moderation and natural justice, appeared less wise and even-handed. The rapprochement that the cricket season had brought, the much-desired England triumph with which it had culminated, was gone. It was a warm memory, but a memory still.

Other matters began to occupy minds at Lord's. MCC despatched teams on two winter tours – to India and to South America. Arthur Gilligan led the team to India and was embroiled in controversy over various matters about dodgy umpiring, poor hotels and snobbishness towards the pros. Warner was captain of the team to Argentina, Chile and Peru – the first excursion to countries outside the Empire it was trilled – and seems to have survived, doubtless helped by Arthur Carr's absence. 'Never did I enjoy a cricket tour more.'

MCC decided to continue to help pay for James Seymour's legal case against the Inland Revenue. It agreed to guarantee 25 per cent of the legal costs (estimated at £2,000) but also, significantly, to fund any shortfall in the funds already raised. It was an unquestionably benevolent gesture without which the case would probably not have proceeded – though it is also true that MCC had reserves of around £115,000 in cash and more than £140,000 in its bank account. The case was heard in the House of Lords the following May and ended with a great victory for all professional cricketers. Four of the five sitting judges overturned the Appeal Court judgement that Seymour, the veteran Kent batsman, should pay income tax on his 1920 benefit. He had bought a fruit farm with the proceeds of £939. Seymour was represented by Sir John Simon, Liberal MP and one of the leading barristers in the country. It was one of his last cases before giving up the bar and turning to politics full time and affected the lot of the cricketer for 80 years. Had the Lords upheld the Appeal Court judgement, Seymour, forced to hand over at least 30 per cent of his proceeds, would have been ruined and the benefits of cricketers at the end of their careers not nearly so generous. There was a certain paradox to Simon's eloquent beseeching on Seymour's behalf: midway through the General Strike 12 months previously he appeared in the House of Commons to denounce the workers' action as illegal. Poor Seymour, whose pioneering determination was so vital for so many of his fellow professionals, hardly had time to enjoy the fruits of victory. He died four years later at the age of 50.

The BBC was duly transposed from Company to Corporation, a not-for-profit organisation that immediately became part of the national fabric. As it had been during the General Strike, when it acquiesced to Government wishes without saying so, it was often to find itself caught between two stools under its founding chairman, John Reith, and nothing much was to change.

As the miners shuffled back, defiance shattered, the newspapers were handed a dream story. Agatha Christie, the best-selling mystery novelist whose latest work published earlier in 1926, *The Murder of Roger Ackroyd*, had revolutionised the genre, disappeared from her Buckinghamshire home. Her car was found abandoned 15 miles away. It was a sensational tale, and the press and the public lapped it up. Nobody, including the police, had a clue what had happened. After a few days the deputy chief constable leading the investigation was convinced that Christie would be found dead. The papers speculated wildly: it was suggested that she could be hiding out in London disguised as a man, and when a search of an isolated Surrey cottage found a bottle labelled 'poison, lead and opium' readers were invited to draw their own conclusions. After 11 days she turned up in a Harrogate spa hotel, her memory of her absence seemingly obliterated. Serialisations of some of Mrs Christie's books were run in many papers, sales of the recent whodunit boomed.

As for the gallant individuals who prevailed at The Oval and the other six who helped to make sure they arrived there all square, their days on the front pages were as good as done. Several books were published on the series in the months afterwards. The team that played together twice in all, only once in a Test match, deserved their moment in the sun. They had answered a nation's prayers. Cricket was only cricket after all, but its capacity to enthral and to unify in a time of division and crisis had been delightfully confirmed. The players' paths diverged widely in the months and years that followed. But it is hard to avoid the conclusion that those few days in Kennington, even for the most illustrious of them, even for the seven who took part in the epic 4-1 Ashes victory in Australia two-and-a-half years later, probably represented the very pinnacle of their careers. Let us see where life took these champions.

Jack Hobbs, despite openly musing that he was done with Test cricket, played for another four years and for Surrey another eight, when his powers, at long last, were dwindling. His place as one of the very best batsmen or batters, whatever they may be called, of all time, is assured.

When *Wisden* conducted a poll among 100 of the great and the good of cricket aficionados to try to determine the cricketers of the 20th century, Hobbs came third behind Donald Bradman and Garfield Sobers. In all future lists of, let us say, the 100 greatest players of all time he should never descend far.

He finished with 199 first-class centuries, 15 of them in Test matches. The former number allied to his record of 61,760 first-class runs will never be overtaken. His place in the game goes well beyond statistics, and his demeanour and bearing made him not only admired but idolised. It took almost 20 years after his retirement from the game for him to be knighted. Then, such honours came much too late, whereas now they come much too soon and too easily. He enjoyed a long life after cricket, serving on the Surrey committee, running the well-established sports shop he had opened with the proceeds of his second benefit and he played lots of golf with Bert Strudwick, his oldest friend in the game. In his later years he nursed his wife Ada, to whom he was devoted. Of Hobbs, more than most, it could be said that he had a life well lived.

His partnership with **Herbert Sutcliffe**, surpassed in quantity after 80 years, though never in quality – as the pair who overtook them, Andrew Strauss and Alastair Cook, would doubtless happily agree – lasted for another four years. They never had a higher average partnership in a series than in 1926 (118.6). In all, the Hobbs-Sutcliffe first wicket partnership in Test matches produced 3,249 runs at an average of 87.81. Sutcliffe brought the tenacity and focus to his life outside the game that he did to his batting. He was meticulous in preparation and execution, and he became a successful businessman, beginning with a Wakefield sports shop, who also served on the Gambling Commission. His bearing and his manner for a lad from Pudsey, orphaned at the age of 10, befuddled the mandarins at Lord's. They were perplexed that someone from so humble a background could so easily have passed off as one of them.

Two winters after the Ashes were regained, Sutcliffe was on his way to South Africa with MCC's touring party when, out of the blue, he was offered the Yorkshire captaincy. To say it was a contentious decision by the county committee, contravening the convention that an amateur should always be the captain whether it be of county or country, was to understate its deviation from the norm. Lord Hawke, hidebound by values he could never properly justify, disagreed with it but at least he kept his counsel in the wake of the vote. If Sutcliffe was at first minded to accept, it quickly became clear that neither Yorkshire nor cricket were ready for this step.

Recognising its potential for division (and probably also sensing that his fellow professional, the vastly more experienced Rhodes, might be none too pleased) he turned it down with a dignity befitting the man. 'It is necessary to approach the question from the point of view whether the game would be better served by my acceptance or my refusal ... I am conscious that there are undercurrents being stirred up that might have done serious damage to the best interests of the county and the game generally. The question is not whether Wilfred Rhodes or Herbert Sutcliffe would make the better captain? Whether the captain should be a professional or an amateur? It is whether we have the interests of the county enough at heart to put our back into the job of getting Yorkshire to the top of the championship table again.'

Sutcliffe showed similar composed integrity four years later when the 1932/33 tour to Australia became embroiled in controversy because of England's bowling strategy, based on pace and designed to undermine the rampant Donald Bradman. As we shall see, Sutcliffe's words of wisdom and support on the voyage home following serious acrimony were testament to his tough and occasionally implacable nature. This was also reflected in a court case in the mid-1930s when he was charged with speeding. Sutcliffe protested to the magistrates about the crude manner in which he had been charged. 'The police officer pulled off a rather dirty cap and substituted a helmet.' The chairman of the bench dismissed the case with the words: 'I think our men have no right pulling people up while wearing private clothes. I do not think it is English.'

Sutcliffe's career lasted until the outbreak of the Second World War – it fitted exactly between the two conflicts apart from one fleeting appearance at Scarborough Festival in 1945 – and by the time he finished he had scored 50,670 runs and 151 centuries. In 1932 he shared with Percy Holmes the world record for a first-wicket partnership of 555, which stood for 45 years. It remains an English record.

If he could comfortably have been at home as an amateur he was proud to be a professional; he stood up for the rights of the professional while recognising the virtues of the amateur. His standards were of his age, but they exuded decency and nobility. Sutcliffe it was who set up a fund in the late 1940s to help his fellow professionals Phil Mead and Len Braund. Mead had gone blind, Braund had had both legs amputated, and Sutcliffe's determined endeavours raised nearly £7,000. He lived to a ripe old age, dying in a nursing home close to where he had lived most of his life. It seems perverse that he was still plain Herbert Sutcliffe, his old partner had been knighted, the cricketers who overtook their England aggregate became Sir Andrew and Sir Alastair in pretty quick time. A century on he would have been Sir Herbert for what he did in 1926 alone.

Frank Woolley played cricket until he was 51 and lived until he was 91. After his retirement he was a frequent, benign presence on Kent grounds and remains the acme of the sublime left-handed batsman. His only son, Richard, died in the Second World War, and Frank spent some of his latter years in the homes of his two daughters. 'I always remember him as a very fair, genuine man who was always immaculately dressed,' recalled his grandson Rob Burnett. 'He had been retired from cricket for 30 years, but I remember when we used to go out for dinner with him there were always people who still recognised him. You could see them tentatively looking and they'd come over to the table and apologise for interrupting and just ask him for a quick word. He was very modest, never propelled himself forward.'

Woolley had been a widower for a decade when on a cruise to South Africa he met a Canadian woman, Martha Wilson. They emigrated to Nova Scotia. 'I think she more or less decided she was marrying him,' recalled Burnett. He still visited Kent in most summers, and the couple appear to have been extremely happy together. She helped him compile the *Early Memoirs of Frank Woolley*, published when he was 89.

Only Hobbs and Woolley ended up scoring more runs than **Patsy Hendren** who defied those who doubted him at the very highest level by continuing to prosper for England in Tests. He was in the 1928/29 winning side when only Wally Hammond, then taking all before him, made more runs. Hendren played on until 1937 and became successively coach to Harrow School – where his influence helped them in 1939 to beat Eton for the first time in 31 years – and then Sussex before rejoining Middlesex as scorer for nine seasons. Cricket continued to be fun till the end.

The Oval match was **Greville Stevens**' second and final home Test. He played seven more times for England, once as captain in South Africa. His only notable success was in Barbados in 1930, the first Test to be played in the Caribbean, when he took five wickets in each innings for match figures of 10-195, which no England bowler has bettered since at Bridgetown. Stevens' appearances for Middlesex became increasingly sporadic, although he managed almost a full season in 1931 and reminded observers of what might have been with an unbeaten 170 at Edgbaston, opening the batting and putting on an unbroken 218 with Hendren. By 1932, still only 31, he was done with the game, the Stock Exchange bell being too insistent for him to get time off. He had little to do with cricket after that, and the feeling persists that the dazzling schoolboy did not quite fulfil his early promise. A curiosity is that he married Mollie Gilligan, who was the first wife of Arthur Gilligan. The couple went to live on the Isle of Bute. Stevens died of cirrhosis of the liver. Does it bespeak of the good life that none of the three amateurs who played for England in the series achieved their three score years and ten?

Having come back at 48, **Wilfred Rhodes** played four more Test matches, against West Indies, at the age of 52 in a winter when MCC embarked on two tours. Although he was not especially successful in the Tests he topped the tour bowling averages. The following summer of 1930 in England was his last and in his final match he took five wickets in an innings against the Australians at Scarborough, his 287th five-wicket haul. Rhodes had Don Bradman dropped at mid-off before he had scored, a pity in so many ways, not least because, had the chance been accepted, Rhodes would have been the only bowler to have dismissed WG Grace and Bradman. He had taken Grace's wicket 30 years before.

After an unhappy period as coach at Harrow School (preceding Hendren in the role) he began gradually to lose his sight. By 1952 he was totally blind. Rhodes continued to attend Test matches, often accompanied by Sydney Barnes, his old England colleague, who was if anything even more taciturn but would provide Rhodes with a running commentary on the play. There is a marvellous photograph taken at the Edgbaston Ashes Test in 1961, of Rhodes, Tiger Smith, the former Warwickshire and England wicketkeeper, Barnes and Frank Woolley sitting together. Rhodes was blind for the last 21 years of his life. He was living with his daughter at her home in Dorset when he died at the age of 95, scorer of 39,802 runs and taker of 4,187 wickets, the latter a record that will stand forever. And his six wickets at The Oval in 1926 might have been the best of all.

Although **Maurice Tate** was never again as effective for England as he had been on the 1924/25 tour, he continued to be one of the first names on the team sheet until the start of the 1930s. On the next Australian tour, together with Larwood and Geary, he was as usual utterly dependable. England won a great victory. He went on the 1932/33 Ashes tour but only after a long stand-off with the selection committee and played in none of the Test matches.

For such a genial man, one who always had time for all, the slow decline towards the end was sad to watch. He fell out with MCC, he fell out with Sussex. Tate did some schoolboy coaching later on and also became a well-known pub landlord around Sussex. He ran three pubs in all, and there was no doubt he was drinking more than was good for him. He was only 60 when he died of a heart attack. Arthur Gilligan, his former captain and opening bowling partner, said of him: 'Tate, I must say at once, was the greatest bowler our country has ever produced.' There were some other contenders before and there have been a few since but not so many that Gilligan did not have a reasonable point.

Like Tate, like Larwood, **George Geary** had some Test cricket left in him, not least in the overwhelming English triumph Down Under in 1928/29. If he was usually a member of the supporting cast, he always knew his lines and his timing was impeccable. In common with so many of the others who form the 1926 sides, Geary's cricket career was long, starting in 1912 and ending in 1938. Not entirely unsung, he should, as it were, have been more sung.

He became coach to Charterhouse School after retirement, and there nurtured the young Peter May, later to be England captain. Geary lived until he was 86. His last years were blighted by dementia. Like so many distinguished sportsmen of bygone eras he was not one to dwell on, or bask in, his achievements. His analysis of 10-18 against Glamorgan at Pontypridd, were the best figures in the game for only three years, overtaken by Hedley Verity's 10-10 for Yorkshire in 1932. When he arrived home from Wales, Geary told his wife, who never watched him play, that he had enjoyed quite a good match, taking 10 for 18 in an innings. 'Oh, yes,' she said, without turning round, 'well I've left the grate for you to blacklead.'

Harold Larwood lived up to his promise and emerged as one of the greatest of all fast bowlers. As the chief exponent of fast leg-theory bowling aimed at the body – Bodyline to give it its most evocative tag – he was also the most infamous. Larwood played an important role along with several others in making sure that England retained the Ashes in 1928/29 but like everyone else found himself overwhelmed by the staggering dominance of Don Bradman in the home series of 1930. To counter the Bradman threat, Douglas Jardine, England's captain for the 1932/33 series, turned leg theory, which had been used for years in small doses, into a full-blown weapon of war. His major combatants were Larwood and his county colleague Bill Voce. It worked, Larwood took 33 wickets, Voce 15, England won back the Ashes. Along the way, there was almost a diplomatic breakdown between the countries, so aggrieved were Australia, and the pusillanimous approach of England's tour manager Plum Warner helped nobody. On the return voyage, however, Sutcliffe gave voice to the players' opinions in a formal presentation to Jardine: 'Our games in Australia were by no means as pleasant as they might have been. Nevertheless, we had the satisfaction of knowing we were playing under a great skipper, a great fighter and a man under who we all felt it was a great privilege to serve.' Larwood's international career was ended. Not until the year after the series did Bodyline's full implications become clear and the establishment had no trouble blaming Larwood for all the trouble, especially after he gave a series of incendiary newspaper interviews. Sutcliffe, of all people, again had a word or two to say on the matter. Speaking at a dinner in Scunthorpe, of all places, after it was clear Larwood was *persona non grata*, he said the rest of the England team had been surprised Larwood and Voce had been deprived of their Test places. 'I say emphatically that no England side can be complete without Larwood and Voce. They are a little too fast for our leading batsmen.' Larwood's excommunication after Bodyline still stands as a woeful indictment of the cricket establishment. After running a sweet shop in Blackpool he emigrated to Australia in 1950, lived more than half his life there and finally, finally, was awarded an MBE in 1990, as if he were forgiven at last. As if there were anything to forgive.

Bert Strudwick played one more season for Surrey, his 22nd excluding the years of the war, and promptly became the county scorer which he did for another 32. It is fair to say that he was probably more adept as a wicketkeeper, whose aggregate of victims was a record for three decades and still stands third on the all-time list, than as a notcher. But his friendly demeanour, a trait of the boys of 1926, placed him as one of the game's most popular figures.

Roy Kilner was the man who had to give way to Rhodes in the eleven for the final Test. He was unlucky but the selectors, led by Warner, were convinced that he was not spinning the ball enough. But Kilner was 35, he still had plenty of cricket left in him; a recall to Tests was not out of the question. Even as England were regaining the Ashes he was taking nine Worcestershire wickets in a Yorkshire innings victory that kept the Championship alive.

At the end of the 1927 season he accepted an invitation from the Maharajah of Patiala to coach for the winter in India. He had been several times before and enjoyed the cricket and the country. Although some suggested later that he was not his normal cheery self he seemed in good spirits when he sent a cable in November to his local sports paper in Sheffield. 'Red Hot, Red Sea, Don't forget to send Green 'Un to Patiala state. Buck up United and Wednesday.' Towards the end of the trip Kilner began to feel distinctly unwell and was extremely keen to get home to Yorkshire. By the time he reached Marseilles on the homeward journey he had taken a turn for the worse and on arriving in Southampton he was severely ill. Kilner was suffering from enteric fever. He insisted on being conveyed to Wombwell to be with his wife and was immediately despatched to the Barnsley fever hospital. The illness was too far advanced to treat, and a few days later he died. Wombwell was then a town of 20,000 inhabitants. More than 100,000 squeezed into the place for Kilner's funeral. The doors of the church had to be locked. 'A Yorkshire wicket has fallen and one of Yorkshire's best men is out,' said Canon SFJ Smith.

If Kilner was desperately unlucky to be overlooked for the Oval Test, **Fred Root** must have felt robbed. Virtually promised a place he was dropped despite being the bowler with the lowest average and economy rate. He never played another Test, the selectors deciding that his version of leg theory (i.e. not express pace) was not going to be effective against batsmen of high quality and certainly not on a southern pitch. He ploughed his furrow effectively in county cricket for a few more years, both coached and umpired a little, but established himself as an engaging sports reporter with forthright views. His memoir *A Cricket Pro's Lot* has been equalled a time or two but not improved on.

George Macaulay should have played more than eight Test matches. The timing of his best years perhaps did not help, but there was always the suspicion that his volatile temperament told against him. Although his form dipped a little in the late 1920s, he recovered it gloriously as Yorkshire again dominated the Championship in the early 1930s. Life soured after he retired from cricket in 1935, businesses failed, he fell out with Yorkshire, he was drinking too much. But each year he still managed to take a team to Barnard Castle, where he went to school, to play both the School and town sides. Macaulay died while serving with the RAF in Scotland in 1940.

Like all the other professional batsmen in the 1926 team, **Ernest Tyldesley** played until well into his forties. He never quite matched his breathtaking form of 1926 – ten hundreds, 12 fifties, ten successive innings above 50 – but was a considerable performer until he finally withdrew from the fray in 1936 at the age of 47, perhaps slighted, justifiably, at being overlooked for the Lancashire captaincy. He is one of the 25 players to have scored 100 hundreds at first-class level, five of whom played in the 1926 series. After retiring as a cricketer, he became the first former professional to serve on the Lancashire committee. He sold light bulbs for a living, and it is said his biggest order was for the Blackpool Illuminations.

Jack Hearne did not bat, bowl or field in the series, but the first match nevertheless remains the last of his 24 Test caps. Perhaps he did not have the international career his talents as a stylish batsman and leg-break bowler suggested he ought to have done, but career totals of 37,252 runs and 1,839 wickets were testament to his ability. He played until he was 45 and was Middlesex coach for 14 years.

And that leaves two: the men who captained England in 1926 (excepting Hobbs' brief stewardship at Manchester). **Arthur Carr** continued to lead Nottinghamshire, taking them to the Championship in 1929 and thus breaking, or at least interrupting, the long monopoly of Lancashire and Yorkshire. In that year he was surprisingly recalled as England captain for two Test matches. He continued to be a controversial figure, but his care for his players was unquestioned and he never wavered in his support for his protégé Larwood, whose devotion was reciprocated. Eventually, almost inevitably, Carr fell out with Nottinghamshire as well and was sacked as captain in 1935. He had little to do with the county or with cricket afterwards. He and his wife separated, and their son Angus was killed in action during the Second World War. Arthur and his second wife went to live in the village of West Witton in Wensleydale, North Yorkshire. Carr seems to have spent most of his days at racing stables in nearby Middleham. He was shovelling snow in front of his semi-detached bungalow in 1961 when he collapsed and died from a heart attack. Perhaps he was content, perhaps not, but it seemed a world away from *The Loom of Youth* and Rempstone Hall.

For a few years **Percy Chapman** was touched by the gods. He looked the part – tall with a mass of curls and cherubic countenance. And he was able to play it perfectly – a batsman of natural gifts which he was happy to unleash, ever personable.

His astonishing elevation to the captaincy for the final Test of 1926 seemed afterwards to be an appointment of genius. He was feted wherever he went, usually with a glass in his hand. His leadership of the team in Australia in 1928/29 cemented his reputation. True, he had at his disposal an exceptional team, but he let them give full vent to their talents.

In 1930 he scored his only Test century, a defiant 121 from 165 balls in the second match to delay Australia's inevitable victory. It made him the only player to score hundreds at Lord's in the Varsity match, in the Gentlemen v Players match and in a Test match, and it is safe to say that it will never be equalled.

The trouble was that Percy was already drinking too much and was not far off from becoming a hopeless drunk. With the Ashes on the line in the final Test of 1930, as they had been in 1926, he himself was dropped to national uproar in favour of Bob Wyatt. This time England lost, this time Australia had Bradman and he scored 232. Chapman had already been selected to lead England to South Africa that winter, but he never played another Test afterwards.

He was made captain of Kent in 1931, lasted until 1936 and helped them to three top three finishes in the Championship. But his own contribution during the period was marked more by an expanding waist line and a podgy face than runs for the county, of which there were 3,247 at an average which crept just above 20. Rumours swirled that he was leaving the field for a drink. He remained kind and welcoming. 'You cannot catch Chapman in a temper or even in a downcast mood,' wrote a reporter after Kent had had a taxing day in the field at Headingley in 1934 as a 17-year-old batsman named Len Hutton kept them at bay for four hours in making 70 and ensuring Yorkshire held out for a draw. Chapman willingly sang Hutton's praises as one with a great future in the game.

But the game was losing its appeal. He no longer moved fluently, and as the seasons went by, he was reluctant to bat. His job as a brewery representative demanded that he socialise and he was ready to oblige. The days of glory were behind him but he could never leave them.

'The gods have been good to you,' it was said of Oscar Wilde's character Dorian Gray, 'but what the gods give they quickly take away. You have only a few years in which to live really, perfectly, and fully. When your youth goes, your beauty will go with it and then you will suddenly discover that there are no triumphs left for you.' It could have been Percy Chapman.

By the late 1930s his marriage to Beet was in trouble, in 1942 they divorced, in 1946 she returned to live in New Zealand. Chapman's weight ballooned; he was bloated and ruddy in complexion; at some point a fondness for a drink tipped over into alcoholism. Those who were once his friends avoided him, there were embarrassing incidents at cricket functions. He lived for 14 years in the home of the steward of West Hill Golf Club in Alton, Hampshire. He died after a fall at home a few days after his 61st birthday.

Those who saw him from time to time testified to his continuing *bonhomie*, his easy charm. He never grew up. Not really. For Percy life was never better than on that day in 1926 when he bestrode an Oval balcony and exhibited that beatific smile. That is his true legacy. His team had only won a cricket match. But more than that, they united a troubled country.

THE GREAT RECOVERY.

JOHN BULL. "WELL, SO MUCH FOR THE ASHES; NOW FOR THE COAL."

FIRST TEST

Trent Bridge, Nottingham   **12, 14, 15 June 1926**

Close of play on day 1: England 32/0 (Hobbs 19, Sutcliffe 13)
No play on days 2 & 3

ENGLAND – First Innings

			balls	mins	4s	6s
J.B. Hobbs	*not out*		19	57	46	1	-
H. Sutcliffe	*not out*		13	49	46	2	-
F.E. Woolley							
J.W. Hearne							
E.H. Hendren							
A.P.F. Chapman							
R. Kilner							
A.W. Carr *							
M.W. Tate							
C.F. Root							
H. Strudwick +							
Extras							
(for 0 wkts)		**32**					

Runs per over: 1.85   Overs per hour: 22.61

AUSTRALIA BOWLING

Gregory	8	1	18	0
Macartney	8.2	2	14	0
Richardson	1	1	0	0

Match drawn

Toss won by England
Umpires: R.D. Burrows, F. Chester

AUSTRALIA

H.L. Collins *
W. Bardsley
C.G. Macartney
J.M. Taylor
T.J.E. Andrews
W.M. Woodfull
J. Ryder
J.M. Gregory
A.J. Richardson
W.A.S. Oldfield +
A.A. Mailey

SECOND TEST

Lord's, London   **26, 28, 29 June 1926**

Close of play on day 1: Australia 1st inns 338/8 (Bardsley 173)
Close of play on day 2: England 1st inns 297/2 (Woolley 50, Hendren 42)

AUSTRALIA – First Innings

			balls	mins	4s	6s	out at
H.L. Collins *	b Root	1	12	8	-	-	1/11
W. Bardsley	*not out*	193	448	398	14	-	
C.G. Macartney	c Sutcliffe b Larwood	39	94	70	4	-	2/84
W.M. Woodfull	c Strudwick b Root	13	60	50	-	-	3/127
T.J.E. Andrews	c & b Kilner	10	35	30	1	-	4/158
J.M. Gregory	b Larwood	7	21	20	1	-	5/187
J.M. Taylor	c Carr b Tate	9	15	15	2	-	6/208
A.J. Richardson	b Kilner	35	105	85	6	-	7/282
J. Ryder	c Strudwick b Tate	28	83	65	3	-	8/338
W.A.S. Oldfield +	c Sutcliffe b Kilner	19	52	40	2	-	9/379
A.A. Mailey	lbw b Kilner	1	4	6	-	-	10/383
Extras	*b 12, lb 16*	28					
		383					

Runs per over: 2.47   Overs per hour: 23.3

AUSTRALIA – Second Innings

			balls	mins	4s	6s	out at
H.L. Collins *	c Sutcliffe b Larwood	24	197	155	1	-	2/125
J.M. Gregory	c Sutcliffe b Root	0	15	15	-	-	1/2
C.G. Macartney	*not out*	133	243	205	13	-	
T.J.E. Andrews	b Root	9	29	25	-	-	3/163
W.A.S. Oldfield +	c Sutcliffe b Tate	11	31	25	2	-	4/187
W.M. Woodfull	c Root b Woolley	0	10	10	-	-	5/194
J. Ryder	*not out*	0	3	6	-	-	
W. Bardsley							
J.M. Taylor							
A.J. Richardson							
A.A. Mailey							
Extras	*b 5, lb 12*	17					
	(for 5 wkts)	**194**					

Runs per over: 2.20   Overs per hour: 26.4

ENGLAND BOWLING

Tate	50	12	111	2	25	11	38	1
Root	36	11	70	2	19	9	40	2
Kilner	34.5	11	70	4	22	2	49	0
Larwood	32	2	99	2	15	3	37	1
Woolley	2	0	5	0	7	1	13	1

Match drawn

Toss won by Australia
Umpires: L.C. Braund, A.E. Street

ENGLAND – First Innings			*balls*	*mins*	*4s*	*6s*	*out at*
J.B. Hobbs	c Richardson b Macartney	119	297	249	10	-	2/219
H. Sutcliffe	b Richardson	82	224	199	11	-	1/182
F.E. Woolley	lbw b Ryder	87	169	161	13	-	3/359
E.H. Hendren	*not out*	127	243	208	18	-	
A.P.F. Chapman	*not out*	50	76	96	5	-	
A.W. Carr *							
R. Kilner							
M.W. Tate							
H. Larwood							
C.F. Root							
H. Strudwick +							
Extras	*b 4, lb 4, w 1, nb 1*	10					
(for 3 wkts, declared)		**475**					

Runs per over: 2.83   Overs per hour: 22.0

AUSTRALIA BOWLING

Gregory	30	3	125	0
Macartney	33	8	90	1
Mailey	30	6	96	0
Richardson	48	18	73	1
Ryder	25	3	70	1
Collins	2	0	11	0

THIRD TEST

Headingley, Leeds   **10, 12, 13 July 1926**

Close of play on day 1: Australia 1st inns 366/3 (Woodfull 134, Richardson 70)
Close of play on day 2: England 1st inns 203/8 (Geary 6, Macaulay 18)

AUSTRALIA – First Innings

			balls	mins	4s	6s	out at
W. Bardsley *	c Sutcliffe b Tate	0	1	1	-	-	1/0
W.M. Woodfull	b Tate	141	336	295	12	-	4/378
C.G. Macartney	c Hendren b Macaulay	151	206	170	21	-	2/235
T.J.E. Andrews	lbw b Kilner	4	16	12	-	-	3/249
A.J. Richardson	run out	100	234	186	10	-	7/452
J.M. Taylor	c Strudwick b Geary	4	12	16	-	-	5/385
J.M. Gregory	c Geary b Kilner	26	37	31	3	-	6/423
J. Ryder	b Tate	42	75	65	6	-	8/485
W.A.S. Oldfield +	lbw b Tate	14	57	45	1	-	9/492
C.V. Grimmett	c Sutcliffe b Geary	1	19	12	-	-	10/494
A.A. Mailey	*not out*	1	1	2	-	-	
Extras	*b 2, lb 4, nb 4*	10					
		494					

Runs per over: 2.99   Overs per hour: 23.3

ENGLAND BOWLING

Tate	51	13	99	4
Macaulay	32	8	123	1
Kilner	37	6	106	2
Geary	41	5	130	2
Woolley	4	0	26	0

Match drawn

Toss won by England
Umpires: H.R. Butt, W. Reeves

ENGLAND – First Innings

			balls	mins	4s	6s	out at
J.B. Hobbs	c Andrews b Mailey	49	131	110	3	-	2/104
H. Sutcliffe	c & b Grimmett	26	93	77	2	-	1/59
F.E. Woolley	run out	27	53	45	2	-	4/110
E.H. Hendren	c Andrews b Mailey	0	4	6	-	-	3/108
A.W. Carr *	lbw b Macartney	13	56	47	2	-	6/140
A.P.F. Chapman	b Macartney	15	23	24	2	-	5/131
R. Kilner	c Ryder b Grimmett	36	63	57	7	-	8/182
M.W. Tate	st Oldfield b Grimmett	5	16	16	-	-	7/175
G. Geary	*not out*	35	171	155	3	-	
G.G. Macaulay	c & b Grimmett	76	155	123	10	-	9/290
H. Strudwick +	c Gregory b Grimmett	1	4	1	-	-	10/294
Extras	*b 4, lb 6, nb 1*	11					
		294					

Runs per over: 2.30   Overs per hour: 22.4

ENGLAND – Second Innings

			balls	mins	4s	6s	out at
J.B. Hobbs	b Grimmett	88	158	152	8	-	1/156
H. Sutcliffe	b Richardson	94	250	209	11	-	3/210
F.E. Woolley	c Macartney b Grimmett	20	55	49	3	-	2/208
E.H. Hendren	*not out*	4	21	27	-	-	
A.P.F. Chapman	*not out*	42	32	24	6	1	
A.W. Carr *							
R. Kilner							
M.W. Tate							
G. Geary							
G.G. Macaulay							
H. Strudwick +							
Extras	*b 5, lb 1*	6					
	(for 3 wkts)	**254**					

Runs per over: 2.95   Overs per hour: 21.7

AUSTRALIA BOWLING

Gregory	17	5	37	0		6	2	12	0
Macartney	31	13	51	2	(3)	4	1	13	0
Grimmett	39	11	88	5	(2)	29	10	59	2
Richardson	20	5	44	0		16	7	22	1
Mailey	21	4	63	2		18	2	80	0
Ryder						9	2	26	0
Andrews						4	0	36	0

FOURTH TEST

Old Trafford, Manchester   24, 26, 27 July 1926

Close of play on day 1: Australia 1st inns 6/0 (Woodfull 6, Bardsley 0)
Close of play on day 2: Australia 1st inns 322/8 (Oldfield 2, Grimmett 4)

AUSTRALIA – First Innings

			balls	mins	4s	6s	out at
W.M. Woodfull	c Hendren b Root	117	331	259	6	-	3/252
W. Bardsley *	c Tyldesley b Stevens	15	59	52	2	-	1/29
C.G. Macartney	b Root	109	218	178	14	-	2/221
T.J.E. Andrews	c sub (Chapman) b Stevens	8	37	33	1	-	4/256
W.H. Ponsford	c & b Kilner	23	63	65	-	-	7/300
A.J. Richardson	c Woolley b Stevens	0	4	5	-	-	5/257
J. Ryder	c Strudwick b Root	3	27	15	-	-	6/266
J.M. Gregory	c Kilner b Root	34	73	57	6	-	8/317
W.A.S. Oldfield +	*not out*	12	61	50	2	-	
C.V. Grimmett	c Stevens b Tate	6	25	18	-	-	9/329
A.A. Mailey	b Tate	1	7	7	-	-	10/335
Extras	*b 2, lb 1, w 1, nb 3*	7					
		335					

Runs per over: 2.29   Overs per hour: 24.1

ENGLAND BOWLING

Tate	36.2	7	88	2
Root	52	27	84	4
Kilner	28	12	51	1
Stevens	32	3	86	3
Woolley	2	0	19	0

Match drawn

Toss won by Australia
Umpires: H. Chidgey, H.I. Young

ENGLAND – First Innings

			balls	mins	4s	6s	out at
J.B. Hobbs	c Ryder b Grimmett	74	183	160	7	-	2/135
H. Sutcliffe	c Oldfield b Mailey	20	86	74	1	-	1/58
G.E. Tyldesley	c Oldfield b Macartney	81	218	160	7	-	3/225
F.E. Woolley	c Ryder b Mailey	58	92	93	5	2	4/243
E.H. Hendren	*not out*	32	91	78	5	-	
G.T.S. Stevens	c Bardsley b Mailey	24	31	20	4	-	5/272
R. Kilner	*not out*	9	50	36	2	-	
A.W. Carr *							
M.W. Tate							
C.F. Root							
H. Strudwick +							
Extras	*b 4, lb 3*	7					
	(for 5 wkts)	**305**					

Runs per over: 2.44   Overs per hour: 23.8

AUSTRALIA BOWLING

Gregory	11	4	17	0
Grimmett	38	9	85	1
Mailey	27	4	87	3
Ryder	15	3	46	0
Richardson	17	3	43	0
Macartney	8	5	7	1
Andrews	9	5	13	0

FIFTH TEST

The Oval, London   **14, 16, 17, 18 August 1926**

Close of play on day 1: Australia 1st inns 60/4 (Woodfull 22, Collins 1)
Close of play on day 2: England 2nd inns 49/0 (Hobbs 28, Sutcliffe 20))
Close of play on day 3: England 2nd inns 375/6 (Rhodes 0)

ENGLAND – First Innings

		balls	mins	4s	6s	out at
J.B. Hobbs	b Mailey	37	62	58	3	-	1/53
H. Sutcliffe	b Mailey	76	252	215	6	-	6/214
F.E. Woolley	b Mailey	18	57	37	3	-	2/91
E.H. Hendren	b Gregory	8	15	18	-	-	3/108
A.P.F. Chapman *	st Oldfield b Mailey	49	84	77	5	-	4/189
G.T.S. Stevens	c Andrews b Mailey	17	16	12	2	1	5/213
W. Rhodes	c Oldfield b Mailey	28	48	48	1	-	10/280
G. Geary	run out	9	15	8	1	-	7/231
M.W. Tate	b Grimmett	23	16	16	2	1	8/266
H. Larwood	c Andrews b Grimmett	0	3	1	-	-	9/266
H. Strudwick +	*not out*	4	7	7	1	-	
Extras	*b 6, lb 5*	11					
	280						

Runs per over: 2.92   Overs per hour: 22.5

ENGLAND – Second Innings

		balls	mins	4s	6s	out at
J.B. Hobbs	b Gregory	100	271	227	10	-	1/172
H. Sutcliffe	b Mailey	161	477	439	16	-	6/375
F.E. Woolley	lbw b Richardson	27	41	45	3	-	2/220
E.H. Hendren	c Oldfield b Grimmett	15	47	47	1	-	3/277
A.P.F. Chapman *	b Richardson	19	40	49	3	-	4/316
G.T.S. Stevens	c Mailey b Grimmett	22	67	54	4	-	5/373
W. Rhodes	lbw b Grimmett	14	73	57	2	-	8/425
G. Geary	c Oldfield b Gregory	1	12	15	-	-	7/382
M.W. Tate	*not out*	33	46	60	3	-	
H. Larwood	b Mailey	5	10	3	1	-	9/430
H. Strudwick+	c Andrews b Mailey	2	14	25	-	-	10/436
Extras	*b 19, lb 18*	37					
	436						

Runs per over: 2.38   Overs per hour: 21.7

AUSTRALIA BOWLING

Gregory	15	4	31	1	18	1	58	2
Grimmett	33	12	74	2	55	17	108	3
Mailey	33.5	3	138	6	42.5	6	128	3
Macartney	7	4	16	0	26	16	24	0
Richardson	7	2	10	0	41	21	81	2

England won by 289 runs

Toss won by England
Umpires: F. Chester, H.I. Young

AUSTRALIA – First Innings

			balls	mins	4s	6s	out at
W.M. Woodfull	b Rhodes	35	159	154	1	-	5/90
W. Bardsley	c Strudwick b Larwood	2	17	26	-	-	1/9
C.G. Macartney	b Stevens	25	35	29	2	-	2/44
W.H. Ponsford	run out	2	16	12	-	-	3/51
T.J.E. Andrews	b Larwood	3	10	10	-	-	4/59
H.L. Collins *	c Stevens b Larwood	61	286	227	2	-	8/231
A.J. Richardson	c Geary b Rhodes	16	56	35	1	-	6/122
J.M. Gregory	c Stevens b Tate	73	120	106	10	-	7/229
W.A.S. Oldfield +	*not out*	33	113	96	1	-	
C.V. Grimmett	b Tate	35	89	78	3	-	9/298
A.A. Mailey	c Strudwick b Tate	0	12	9	-	-	10/302
Extras	*b 5, lb 12*	17					
		302					

Runs per over: 1.98   Overs per hour: 23.4

AUSTRALIA – Second Innings

			balls	mins	4s	6s	out at
W.H. Ponsford	c Larwood b Rhodes	12	38	36	1	-	3/31
W.M. Woodfull	c Geary b Larwood	0	6	7	-	-	1/1
C.G. Macartney	c Geary b Larwood	16	23	23	1	-	2/31
W. Bardsley	c Woolley b Rhodes	21	72	71	2	-	6/83
H.L. Collins *	c Woolley b Rhodes	4	11	11	-	-	4/35
T.J.E. Andrews	c Tate b Larwood	15	39	29	2	-	5/63
J.M. Gregory	c Sutcliffe b Tate	9	28	26	1	-	7/83
A.J. Richardson	b Rhodes	4	3	7	1	-	8/87
W.A.S. Oldfield +	b Stevens	23	47	33	2	-	9/114
C.V. Grimmett	*not out*	8	36	37	1	-	
A.A. Mailey	b Geary	6	12	8	1	-	10/125
Extras	*lb 7*	7					
		125					

Runs per over: 2.38   Overs per hour: 20.7

ENGLAND BOWLING

Tate	37.1	17	40	3	(2)	9	4	12	1
Larwood	34	11	82	3	(1)	14	3	34	3
Geary	27	8	43	0	(4)	6.3	2	15	1
Stevens	29	3	85	1	(5)	3	1	13	1
Rhodes	25	15	35	2	(3)	20	9	44	4

TEST MATCH AVERAGES

ENGLAND

BATTING	M	I	NO	Runs	HS	Ave	100s	Balls
J.B. Hobbs	5	7	1	486	119	81.00	2	1159
H. Sutcliffe	5	7	1	472	161	78.67	1	1431
E.H. Hendren	5	6	3	186	127*	62.00	1	421
A.P.F. Chapman	4	5	2	175	50*	58.33	-	255
F.E. Woolley	5	6	-	237	87	39.50	-	467
M.W. Tate	5	3	1	61	33*	30.50	-	78
G. Geary	2	3	1	45	35*	22.50	-	198
G.T.S. Stevens	2	3	-	63	24	21.00	-	114
H. Strudwick	5	3	1	7	4*	3.50	-	25

Also batted:

	M	I	NO	Runs	HS	Ave	100s	Balls
G.E. Tyldesley	1	1	-	81	81	81.00	-	218
G.G. Macaulay	2	1	-	76	76	76.00	-	155
R. Kilner	3	2	1	45	36	45.00	-	113
W. Rhodes	1	2	-	42	28	21.00	-	121
A.W. Carr	4	1	-	13	13	13.00	-	56
H. Larwood	2	2	-	5	5	2.50	-	13

C.F. Root (3 Tests) & J.W. Hearne (1 Test) did not bat

BOWLING	Overs	Mdns	Runs	Wkts	Best	Ave	5wi
W. Rhodes	45	24	79	6	4-44	13.17	-
C.F. Root	107	47	194	8	4-84	24.25	-
H. Larwood	95	19	252	9	3-34	28.00	-
M.W. Tate	208.3	64	388	13	4-99	29.85	-
G.T.S. Stevens	64	7	184	5	3-86	36.80	-
R. Kilner	121.5	31	276	7	4-70	39.43	-
G. Geary	74.3	15	188	3	2-130	62.67	-
F.E. Woolley	15	1	63	1	1-13	63.00	-
G.G. Macaulay	32	8	123	1	1-123	123.00	-

FIELDING

8   H. Sutcliffe
6   H. Strudwick
4   G. Geary
3   R. Kilner, G.T.S. Stevens, F.E. Woolley
2   E.H. Hendren
1   A.W. Carr, H. Larwood, C.F. Root, M.W. Tate, G.E. Tyldesley

A.P.F. Chapman took one catch as a substitute fielder

AUSTRALIA

BATTING	M	I	NO	Runs	HS	Ave	100s	Balls
C.G. Macartney	5	6	1	473	151	94.60	3	819
W. Bardsley	5	5	1	231	193*	57.75	1	597
W.M. Woodfull	5	6	-	306	141	51.00	2	902
A.J. Richardson	5	5	-	155	100	31.00	1	402
W.A.S. Oldfield	5	6	2	112	33*	28.00	-	361
J.M. Gregory	5	6	-	149	73	24.83	-	294
J. Ryder	4	4	1	73	42	24.33	-	188
H.L. Collins	3	4	-	90	61	22.50	-	506
C.V. Grimmett	3	4	1	50	35	16.67	-	169
W.H. Ponsford	2	3	-	37	23	12.33	-	117
T.J.E. Andrews	5	6	-	49	15	8.17	-	166
A.A. Mailey	5	5	1	9	6	2.25	-	36

Also batted:

	M	I	NO	Runs	HS	Ave	100s	Balls
J.M. Taylor	3	2	-	13	9	6.50	-	27

BOWLING	Overs	Mdns	Runs	Wkts	Best	Ave	5wi
C.V. Grimmett	194	59	414	13	5-88	31.85	1
A.A. Mailey	172.4	25	592	14	6-138	42.29	1
C.G. Macartney	117.2	49	215	4	2-51	53.75	-
A.J. Richardson	150	57	273	4	2-81	68.25	-
J.M. Gregory	105	20	298	3	2-58	99.33	-
J. Ryder	49	8	142	1	1-70	142.00	-

Also bowled:

	Overs	Mdns	Runs	Wkts	Best	Ave	5wi
T.J. Andrews	13	5	49	-	-	-	-
H.L. Collins	2	-	11	-	-	-	-

FIELDING

7   W.A.S. Oldfield *(5 ct, 2 st)*
5   T.J.E. Andrews
3   J. Ryder
2   C.V. Grimmett
1   W. Bardsley, J.M. Gregory, C.G. Macartney, A.A. Mailey, A.J. Richardson

STATISTICAL EXTRAS

In addition to the excitement engendered, there were some singular aspects to the series.

The combined ages of both teams in the First Test at Trent Bridge, 790 years, average 35 years and 324 days, remains greater than in any other Test.

Discarding the winter of 1929/30 when two England teams went on tour at the same time, their team in the Fourth Test at Old Trafford was the oldest in a Test match with an average age of 36 years 57 days.

Australia's teams at Lord's (35 years 341 days), Trent Bridge (35 years 327 days), Headingley (35 years 225 days), The Oval (35 years 144 days) and Old Trafford (35 years 72 days) were respectively their five oldest teams to play in Test matches.

Only England at Lord's fielded a team with an average age below 35 (34 years 247 days).

The only players to appear for England in the series still in their twenties were Larwood, Stevens, Chapman and Macaulay. Australia had only two: Woodfull and Ponsford.

Much printers' ink was spent on fulminating about the Test matches being much too short to produce a winner. While there is some merit in the argument that three days was insufficient, the lack of adventure was also a factor. At Lord's, for instance, a total of 1,052 runs were scored in 411 overs – a rate of 2.55 runs an over or 42.6 per 100 balls using the modern method to delineate scoring rates – for 18 wickets. There have never been fewer wickets taken in an Ashes Test at Lord's since 1926. This was probably a combination of unadventurous batting, non-penetrative bowling, and docile pitches. Nor did it change much for decades. In 1953, the next time that England won the Ashes at home, the Lord's Test produced 1,368 runs in 526 overs, 2.6 runs an over or 43.3, for 37 wickets – and was also a draw.

Still, of the 18 Tests played at Lord's between England and Australia from 1930 to 2023, 10 have produced a winner. At Headingley, there have been 13 Tests since 1926 containing fewer balls and only the 1975 contest, abandoned on the final day after vandals poured oil on the pitch overnight, ended in a draw.

England averaged 50.63 a wicket during the series, a figure they have not approached in the 25 home Ashes rubbers since. Their scoring rate of 43.09 per 100 balls seems fairly dismal, but it was lower still in eight of the ten series that followed until 1975. Rates gradually increased, and in 2023 England changed the way they approached batting in Test matches and scored at a rate of almost 80.

Second Test, Lord's

Australia took 1,008 balls to dismiss three England batsmen, 336 balls a wicket. Only at Brisbane in 2010/11 have Australia's bowlers been less successful when England scored 517-1 from 912 balls.

Warren Bardsley's score of 193* remains the highest percentage of team runs (50.93) by an Australia batsman at Lord's. It is also the highest by a player over 40 in the Ashes.

When he reached 83 in England's only innings, Jack Hobbs became the first player to reach an aggregate of 4,000 runs in Test cricket.

Until Andrew Strauss and Alistair Cook (196) overtook it in 2009, the stand of 182 by Jack Hobbs and Herbert Sutcliffe remained the highest for England's first wicket in an Ashes match at Lord's.

England's innings remains a record total in England for the loss of only three wickets.

Third Test, Headingley

Bardsley was the first Australia batsman to be dismissed by the first ball of a Test.

Macartney was the second player, after Victor Trumper at Old Trafford in 1902, to score a hundred before lunch. His 112 runs remain the highest before the break.

The partnership of 235 between Macartney and Woodfull was the highest by either side for any wicket in England, though it has since been surpassed on 16 occasions.

This was the first occasion that three England bowlers conceded more than 100 runs in an innings in England. It has happened 22 times subsequently in Ashes Tests to 2023. Once, in 2009 at Cardiff, five bowlers brought up three figures, though some may claim that was in Wales.

In England's second innings, Hobbs overtook Clem Hill's record of 2,660 runs in Ashes Tests.

Fourth Test, Old Trafford

Macartney was the first player to score three hundreds in a series in England.

Hobbs, who took over from the ill Carr on the second day, was the first professional to captain England since Arthur Shrewsbury in 1886/87.

Fifth Test, The Oval

The partnership of 172 between Hobbs and Sutcliffe in England's second innings is one of only seven century first-wicket stands for England at The Oval in Ashes Tests. The feat has not been achieved since 1934.

Wilfred Rhodes became the first player to bowl in 50 Tests.

Frank Woolley played his 52nd successive Test for England, which was a record until overtaken by Tony Greig in the Centenary Test at Melbourne in March 1977.

Full Career Records
Test & First-Class Cricket

ENGLAND

Jack Hobbs

Died: 21.12.1963, aged 81

Tests	Last	Runs	HS	Ave	Wkts	BB	Ave	ct
61	1930	5,410	211	56.94	1	1-19	165.00	17
F/C	Last	Runs	HS	Ave	Wkts	BB	Ave	ct
834	1934	61,760	316*	50.70	108	7-56	25.04	340

Herbert Sutcliffe

Died: 22.1.1978, aged 83

Tests	Last	Runs	HS	Ave	Wkts	BB	Ave	ct
54	1935	4,555	194	60.73	-	-	-	23
F/C	Last	Runs	HS	Ave	Wkts	BB	Ave	ct
754	1945	50,670	313	52.02	14	3-15	40.21	473

Frank Woolley

Died: 18.10.1978, aged 91

Tests	Last	Runs	HS	Ave	Wkts	BB	Ave	ct
64	1934	3,283	154	36.07	83	7-76	33.91	64
F/C	Last	Runs	HS	Ave	Wkts	BB	Ave	ct
978	1938	58,959	305*	40.77	2,066	8-22	19.87	1,018

Patsy Hendren

Died: 4.10.1962, aged 73

Tests	Last	Runs	HS	Ave	Wkts	BB	Ave	ct
51	1934/5	3,525	205*	47.63	1	1-27	31.00	33
F/C	Last	Runs	HS	Ave	Wkts	BB	Ave	ct
833	1938	57,611	301*	50.80	47	5-43	54.76	754

Percy Chapman

Died: 16.9.1961, aged 61

Tests	Last	Runs	HS	Ave	Wkts	BB	Ave	ct
26	1930/1	925	121	28.90	-	-	-	32
F/C	Last	Runs	HS	Ave	Wkts	BB	Ave	ct
394	1939	16,309	260	31.97	22	5-40	41.86	356

Greville Stevens

Died: 19.9.1970, aged 69

Tests	Last	Runs	HS	Ave	Wkts	BB	Ave	ct
10	1929/30	263	69	15.47	20	5-90	32.40	9
F/C	Last	Runs	HS	Ave	Wkts	BB	Ave	ct
243	1933	10,376	182	29.56	684	8-38	26.84	213

Wilfred Rhodes

Died: 8.7.1973, aged 95

Tests	Last	Runs	HS	Ave	Wkts	BB	Ave	ct
58	1929/30	2,325	179	30.19	127	8-68	26.96	60
F/C	Last	Runs	HS	Ave	Wkts	BB	Ave	ct
1,110	1930	39,969	267*	30.81	4,204	9-24	16.72	765

Maurice Tate

Died: 18.5.1956, aged 60

Tests	Last	Runs	HS	Ave	Wkts	BB	Ave	ct
39	1935	1,198	100*	25.48	155	6-42	26.16	11
F/C	Last	Runs	HS	Ave	Wkts	BB	Ave	ct
679	1937	21,717	203	25.04	2,784	9-71	18.16	284

George Geary

Died: 6.3.1981, aged 87

Tests	Last	Runs	HS	Ave	Wkts	BB	Ave	ct
14	1934	249	66	15.56	46	7-70	29.41	13
F/C	Last	Runs	HS	Ave	Wkts	BB	Ave	ct
549	1938	13,504	122	19.80	2,063	10-18	20.03	451

Harold Larwood

Died: 22.7.1995, aged 90

Tests	Last	Runs	HS	Ave	Wkts	BB	Ave	ct
21	1932/3	485	98	19.40	78	6-32	28.35	15
F/C	Last	Runs	HS	Ave	Wkts	BB	Ave	ct
361	1938	7,289	102*	19.91	1,427	9-41	17.51	234

Bert Strudwick

Died: 14.2.1970, aged 90

Tests	Last	Runs	HS	Ave	Wkts	BB	Ave	ct/st
28	1926	230	24	7.93	-	-	-	60/12
F/C	Last	Runs	HS	Ave	Wkts	BB	Ave	ct/st
674	1927	6,445	93	10.88	1	1-9	102.00	1242/254

Arthur Carr

Died: 7.2.1963, aged 69

Tests	Last	Runs	HS	Ave	Wkts	BB	Ave	ct
11	1929	237	63	19.75	-	-	-	3

F/C	Last	Runs	HS	Ave	Wkts	BB	Ave	ct/st
468	1935	21,051	206	31.56	31	3-14	37.09	393/1

Roy Kilner

Died: 5.4.1928, aged 37

Tests	Last	Runs	HS	Ave	Wkts	BB	Ave	ct
9	1926	233	74	33.28	24	4-51	30.58	6

F/C	Last	Runs	HS	Ave	Wkts	BB	Ave	ct
416	1927	14,707	206*	30.01	1,003	8-26	18.46	266

Fred Root

Died: 20.1.1954, aged 63

Tests	Last	Runs	HS	Ave	Wkts	BB	Ave	ct
3	1926	-	-	-	8	4-84	24.25	1

F/C	Last	Runs	HS	Ave	Wkts	BB	Ave	ct
365	1933	7,911	107	14.78	1,512	9-23	21.11	244

Ernest Tyldesley

Died: 5.5.1962, aged 73

Tests	Last	Runs	HS	Ave	Wkts	BB	Ave	ct
14	1928/9	990	122	55.00	-	-	-	2

F/C	Last	Runs	HS	Ave	Wkts	BB	Ave	ct
648	1936	38,874	256*	45.46	6	3-33	57.66	293

George Macaulay

Died: 13.12.1940, aged 43

Tests	Last	Runs	HS	Ave	Wkts	BB	Ave	ct
8	1933	112	76	18.66	24	5-64	27.58	5

F/C	Last	Runs	HS	Ave	Wkts	BB	Ave	ct
468	1935	6,056	125*	18.07	1,837	8-21	17.65	373

Jack Hearne

Died: 14.9.1965, aged 74

Tests	Last	Runs	HS	Ave	Wkts	BB	Ave	ct
24	1926	806	114	26.00	30	5-49	48.73	13

F/C	Last	Runs	HS	Ave	Wkts	BB	Ave	ct
647	1936	37,252	285*	40.98	1,839	9-61	24.42	348

AUSTRALIA

Herbie Collins

Died: 28.5.1959, aged 70

Tests	Last	Runs	HS	Ave	Wkts	BB	Ave	ct
19	1926	1,352	203	45.06	4	2-47	63.00	13
F/C	*Last*	*Runs*	*HS*	*Ave*	*Wkts*	*BB*	*Ave*	*ct*
168	1926	9,924	282	40.01	181	8-31	21.38	115

Warren Bardsley

Died: 20.1.1954, aged 71

Tests	Last	Runs	HS	Ave	Wkts	BB	Ave	ct
41	1926	2,469	193*	40.47	-	-	-	12
F/C	*Last*	*Runs*	*HS*	*Ave*	*Wkts*	*BB*	*Ave*	*ct*
250	1926/7	17,025	264	49.92	-	-	-	113

Bill Woodfull

Died: 11.8.1965, aged 67

Tests	Last	Runs	HS	Ave	Wkts	BB	Ave	ct
35	1934	2,300	161	46.00	-	-	-	7
F/C	*Last*	*Runs*	*HS*	*Ave*	*Wkts*	*BB*	*Ave*	*ct*
174	1934/5	13,388	284	64.99	1	1-12	24.00	78

Charlie Macartney

Died: 9.9.1958, aged 72

Tests	Last	Runs	HS	Ave	Wkts	BB	Ave	ct
35	1926	2,131	170	41.78	45	7-58	27.55	17
F/C	*Last*	*Runs*	*HS*	*Ave*	*Wkts*	*BB*	*Ave*	*ct*
249	1926/7	15,019	345	45.78	419	7-58	20.95	102

Bill Ponsford

Died: 6.4.1991, aged 90

Tests	Last	Runs	HS	Ave	Wkts	BB	Ave	ct
29	1934	2,122	266	48.22	-	-	-	21
F/C	*Last*	*Runs*	*HS*	*Ave*	*Wkts*	*BB*	*Ave*	*ct*
162	1934/5	13,819	437	65.18	-	-	-	71

Tommy Andrews

Died: 28.1.1970, aged 79

Tests	Last	Runs	HS	Ave	Wkts	BB	Ave	ct
16	1926	592	94	26.90	1	1-23	116.00	12
F/C	*Last*	*Runs*	*HS*	*Ave*	*Wkts*	*BB*	*Ave*	*ct*
151	1928/9	8,095	247*	39.48	95	6-109	32.10	85

Arthur Richardson

Died: 23.12.1973, aged 85

Tests	Last	Runs	HS	Ave	Wkts	BB	Ave	ct
9	1926	403	100	31.00	12	2-20	43.41	1
F/C	Last	Runs	HS	Ave	Wkts	BB	Ave	ct
86	1933	5,238	280	41.57	209	6-28	31.36	34

Jack Gregory

Died: 7.8.1973, aged 77

Tests	Last	Runs	HS	Ave	Wkts	BB	Ave	ct
24	1928/9	1,146	119	36.96	85	7-69	31.15	37
F/C	Last	Runs	HS	Ave	Wkts	BB	Ave	ct
129	1928/9	5,659	152	36.50	504	9-32	20.99	195

Bert Oldfield

Died: 10.8.1976, aged 81

Tests	Last	Runs	HS	Ave	Wkts	BB	Ave	ct/st
54	1936/7	1,427	65*	22.65	-	-	-	78/52
F/C	Last	Runs	HS	Ave	Wkts	BB	Ave	ct/st
245	1937/8	6,135	137	23.77	-	-	-	400/262

Clarrie Grimmett

Died: 2.5.1980, aged 88

Tests	Last	Runs	HS	Ave	Wkts	BB	Ave	ct
37	1935/6	557	50	13.92	216	7-40	24.21	17
F/C	Last	Runs	HS	Ave	Wkts	BB	Ave	ct
248	1940/1	4,720	71*	17.67	1,424	10-37	22.28	139

Arthur Mailey

Died: 31.12.1967, aged 81

Tests	Last	Runs	HS	Ave	Wkts	BB	Ave	ct
21	1926	222	46*	11.10	99	9-121	33.91	14
F/C	Last	Runs	HS	Ave	Wkts	BB	Ave	ct
158	1930/1	1,530	66	12.33	779	10-66	24.09	157

Jack Ryder

Died: 3.4.1977, aged 87

Tests	Last	Runs	HS	Ave	Wkts	BB	Ave	ct
20	1928/9	1,394	201*	51.67	17	2-20	43.70	17
F/C	Last	Runs	HS	Ave	Wkts	BB	Ave	ct
177	1931/2	10,501	295	44.30	238	7-53	29.68	133

Johnny Taylor

Died: 12.5.1971, aged 75

Tests	Last	Runs	HS	Ave	Wkts	BB	Ave	ct
20	1926	997	108	35.60	1	1-25	45.00	11
F/C	Last	Runs	HS	Ave	Wkts	BB	Ave	ct
135	1926/7	6,274	180	33.37	1	1-25	53.00	68

BIBLIOGRAPHY

In writing this book, I have drawn on many written sources, all of them invaluable: books, newspapers, magazines, websites and not least the archives of MCC.

Newspapers:

Daily Herald, Westminster Gazette, Daily News, Daily Mail, Daily Express, Daily Mirror, Weekly Dispatch, Reynolds's Newspaper, Sunday Pictorial, Manchester Guardian, The Times, Daily Chronicle, Daily Telegraph, Morning Post and many local newspapers available from the British Newspaper Archive

Magazines:

The Cricketer, Bioscope, Kinematograph Weekly, The Sphere, Illustrated London News, Punch, Athletics Weekly, Sporting Chronicle, The Sketch, The Bystander, The Tatler

Reference books:

Hansard
Lancashire CCC Yearbook 2004
Wisden Cricketers' Almanack
Philip Bailey, Philip Thorn & Peter Wynne Thomas, *Who's Who of Cricketers* (Hamlyn, 1993)
Bill Frindall, *The Wisden Book of Test Cricket* (Macdonald and Jane's 1979)
EW Swanton, John Woodcock & George Plumptree, *Barclays World of Cricket* (Collins, 1986)
Simon Wilde, *Wisden Cricketers of the Year* (John Wisden, 2013)

Other books:

David Rayvern Allen, *Cricket On The Air* (BBC, 1985)
David Rayvern Allen (ed), *A Breathless Hush In The Close* (Methuen, 2004)
John Arlott, *Maurice Tate* (Phoenix House, 1951)
John Arlott, *Jack Hobbs* (John Murray, 1981)
John Arlott (ed), *The Great All Rounders* (Pelham, 1969)
Warwick Armstrong, *The Art of Cricket* (Methuen, 1922)
Norman Barrett (ed), *The Daily Telegraph Chronicle of Cricket* (Guinness, 1994)
Derek Birley, *The Willow Wand* (Wisden, 1979)
Derek Birley, *A Social History of English Cricket* (Aurum, 1999)
Max Bonnell, *Lucky* (cricketbooks.com.au, 2015)
Donald Bradman, *The Bradman Archives* (Lansdowne, 1987)
Gerald Brodribb, *Maurice Tate* (London Magazine, 1976)
Handaysyde Buchanan (ed), *Great Cricket Matches* (Eyre & Spottiswoode, 1962)
Neville Cardus, *Cardus On The Ashes* (Souvenir, 1989)
Dudley Carew, *England Over* (Martin Secker, 1927)
AW Carr, *Cricket With The Lid Off* (Hutchinson, 1935)

Adam Chadwick, *A Portrait of Lord's* (MCC, 2013)

Stephen Chalke, *The Way It Was* (Fairfield, 2008)

Stephen Chalke, *Summer's Crown* (Fairfield, 2015)

Agatha Christie, *The Murder of Roger Ackroyd* (Collins, 1926)

Max Davidson, *We'll Get Them In Sequins* (Wisden Sports Writers, 2012)

Patrick Eagar, *Caught In The Frame* (Collins Willow, 1992)

Roderick Easdale, *England's One-Test Wonders* (Parapress, 1999)

David Foot, *Fragments of Idolatry* (Fairfield, 2001)

David Foot, *Wally Hammond, The Reasons Why* (Robson, 1996)

David Foot, *Beyond Bat and Ball* (Good Books, 1993)

David Foot, *Cricket's Unholy Trinity* (Stanley Paul, 1985)

AER Gilligan, *Collins's Men* (Arrowsmith, 1926)

Home Gordon, *Background of Cricket (*Arthur Barker, 1939)

Duncan Hamilton, *Harold Larwood* (Quercus, 2009)

Charles Harvey (ed), *Almanack of Sport* (Samson Low, 1966)

JB Hobbs, *Playing For England* (Camelot, 1931)

JB Hobbs, *My Cricket Memories* (Heinemann, 1924)

JB Hobbs, *My Life Story* (The Star, 1935)

Nick Hoult (ed), *The Daily Telegraph Book of Cricket* (Aurum, 2009)

David Jeater, *PA Perrin* (ACS, 2006)

Roy Jenkins, *Baldwin* (Collins, 1987)

Thomas Jones, *Whitehall Diaries* (ed Keith Middlemass, OUP, 1969)

Dennis Lambert, *George Geary* (ACS, 2000)

Pat Landsberg, *Jack Hobbs, Gentleman and Player* (Todd, 1953)

Harold Larwood, *Bodyline? (*Elkin, Matthews & Marrot 1933)

David Lemmon, *Percy Chapman* (Queen Anne Press, 1985)

Jerry Lodge, *Jack Hobbs Innings by Innings* (ACS 2001)

John Lucas, *The Awkward Squad* (Shoestring, 2015)

CG Macartney, *My Cricketing Days* (Heinemann, 1930)

Leo McKinstry, *Jack Hobbs* (Yellow Jersey, 2011)

Arthur Mailey, *10-66 And All That* (Phoenix, 1958)

John Marchant, *The Greatest Test Match* (Faber & Gwyer, 1926)

Christopher Martin-Jenkins, *The Complete Who's Who of Test Cricket* (Orbis, 1980)

Christopher Martin-Jenkins, *The Top 100 Cricketers Of All Time* (Corinthian, 2009)

Ronald Mason, *Jack Hobbs* (Hollis & Carter, 1960)

Lawrence Meynell, *Plum Warner (*Phoenix House, 1951)

AA Milne, *Winnie-the-Pooh* (Methuen, 1926)

Howard Milton, *Frank Woolley* (ACS, 1986)

Margaret Morris, *The General Strike* (Penguin, 1926)

Patrick Murphy, *The Centurions* (Fairfield, 2009)

MA Noble, *Those Ashes* (Cassell, 1927)

WA Oldfield, *The Rattle of the Stumps* (Newnes, 1954)

Justin Parkinson, *Then Came Massacre* (Pitch, 2003)

Ian Peebles, *Woolley, The Pride of Kent* (Hutchinson, 1969)

Ian Peebles, *Patsy Hendren* (Macmillan, 1969)

Anne Perkins, *A Very British Strike* (Macmillan, 2006)

Anne Perkins, *Baldwin* (Haus, 2006)

Mick Pope, *The Laughing Cricketer of Wombwell* (Dart, 1990)

Jonathan Rice, *The Presidents of MCC* (Methuen, 2006)

Sidney Rogerson, *Wilfred Rhodes* (Hollis & Carter, 1960)

Fred Root, *A Cricket Pro's Lot* (Arnold, 1935)

Rachelle Pope Saltzman, *A Lark for the Sake of their Country*
          (Manchester University Press, 2012)

Herbert Strudwick, *25 Years Behind The Stumps* (Hutchinson, 1925)

Herbert Sutcliffe, *For England and Yorkshire* (Arnold, 1935)

Herbert Sutcliffe, *Batting* (Blackie, 1937)

Maurice Tate, *My Cricketing Reminiscences* (Stanley Paul, 1933)

Kevin Telfer, *Peter Pan's First XI* (Sceptre, 2010)

AA Thomson, *Hirst and Rhodes* (Epworth Press, 1959)

Oliver Warner, *Frank Woolley* (Phoenix House, 1952)

PF Warner, *How We Recovered The Ashes* (Methuen, 2003 centenary edition)

PF Warner, *The Fight for The Ashes in 1926* (Geo. Harrap, 1926)

PF Warner, *Cricket Between Two Wars* (Chatto & Windus, 1942)

PF Warner, *Long Innings* (Geo. Harrap, 1951)

Alec Waugh, *The Loom of Youth* (Bloomsbury, 2003 first published 1917)

Richard Whitehead (ed), *The Times On The Ashes* (History Press, 2015)

Geoffrey Wilde, *Ernest Tyldesley* (ACS, 2011)

Charles Williams, *Gentlemen & Players* (Weidenfeld & Nicolson, 2013)

Frank Woolley & Martha Wilson Woolley, *Early Memoirs* (The Cricketer, 1976)

Peter Wynne-Thomas, *England On Tour* (Hamlyn, 1982)

Peter Wynne-Thomas, *Arthur Carr* (Chequered Flag, 2017)

ACKNOWLEDGEMENTS

The help received in writing this book has been boundless, essential and incomparable. It never ceased to amaze how willing people were to answer the daftest queries without raising an eyebrow.

From the outset, MCC was remarkable. Its archives and its library are of course excellent and without its readiness to assist, much of what is covered in the book would have been impossible to find elsewhere. Neil Robinson, its excellent curator, opened the door and Alan Rees, one of his able lieutenants, could not have been more diligent and willing in tracking down important nuggets of information once I had passed through it. MCC is an organisation transformed in the past 25 years, one that bears no comparison to how it was in 1926, and I am probably not alone in hoping that one day, somehow, it can find room at Lord's for the sort of glorious museum and library our great game deserves.

Tim Wigmore and Richard Whitehead, both of whom had books of their own to write, still found time to send me pertinent material they had come across in their own researches. It is unlikely I would have found it myself.

Chris Jackson of *Railway Gazette* used his expertise to nail down 1926 rail fares. Cricketers in 1926 travelled by train, some more luxuriously than others.

The eminent Australian statistician Charles Davis has done great work on Test match scorecards and that was instrumental, along with contemporary reports, in piecing together the matches as they unfolded. Ric Finlay's website *Tastats* has kept me company for more than 20 years and was again hugely helpful.

Many of the 1926 team did not have children and so the line ended with them. But Rob Burnett and his sister Rosalie Uwakaneme, grandchildren of Frank Woolley, offered not only their fascinating personal memories of the great cricketer but treasured memorabilia.

At Fairfield Books, Matt Thacker decided there and then that this book was something right up his street. Without him the epic story of 1926 might not have been told. I am extremely grateful.

My friends Colin Bateman and David Lloyd, with whom I shared many happy hours in cricket press boxes and post-match restaurants, willingly read the manuscript time and again and not only pointed out silly mistakes but lapses in tone. When they thought their work was done, I asked them to go through it yet again and they did so. I cannot thank them enough and I promise not to ask them again until the next time.

Similarly, David Llewellyn offered a scrupulous eye and Paul Coupar-Hennessy a scholarly, enthusiastic younger perspective, both of which were important. And to Pat Murphy, BBC legend and author of scores of cricket books, some of which rank among the very best, my deep appreciation. Murph's knowledge of cricket history kept me in check.

And finally, most significantly, to Stephen Chalke who has embraced and nurtured this chronicle of a cricket series which was so much more than that. He has been involved at every turn, at every spit and comma, if you like, and has been constantly encouraging. He was the person I first mentioned it to, the idea that the book should not simply be about the cricket but the country in which it was played, and he understood straightaway. He has read and re-read, designed and re-designed, edited and re-edited, all in an unfussy, understated fashion which is his hallmark. He is always someone you would want on your side in writing a book.

There may be others who have helped who are not mentioned here, and I apologise for their omission in advance. In an enterprise such as this, much guidance from others is both welcome and necessary. Without it the book would have been more liable to error and much less enjoyable to write. If there are mistakes after all that, they are mine and mine alone.

Stephen Brenkley
Barnard Castle
August 2024

INDEX